Italian Verb Workbook

Marcel Danesi, Ph.D.
University of Toronto

BARRON'S

Barron's Educational Series, Inc.

All inquiries should be addressed to:
Barron's Educational Series, Inc.
250 Wireless Boulevard
Hauppauge, New York 11788
http://www.barronseduc.com

ISBN-13: 978-0-7641-3024-3
ISBN-10: 0-7641-3024-2

Library of Congress Catalog Card No. 2004049774

Library of Congress Cataloging-in-Publication Data

Danesi, Marcel, 1946–
    Italian Verb Workbook / by Marcel Danesi.
        p. cm.
    Includes index.
    ISBN 0-7641-3024-2
    1. Italian language—Verb.   I. Title.

    PC1271.D36 2005
    458.2'421—dc22

                                                    2004049774

Printed in the United States of America
9 8 7

Contents

Part Four
The Subjunctive Tenses   *203*

Part Five
Other Tenses   *241*

Introduction

Mastering verb forms is for many the most challenging aspect of learning a new language. But this book is designed to make the task effortless and enjoyable. It is an in-depth and comprehensive manual on how to conjugate and use Italian verbs. Its simple method will help you learn the basics of Italian verbs in a straightforward way. All you need is this book, no matter at what stage of learning you find yourself. It can thus be used profitably by

- those who know some Italian, but who wish to improve their knowledge of Italian verbs in a comprehensive and intensive, but user-friendly, way;

- students enrolled in an Italian language course in a high school, college, or university who feel that they need more practice with Italian verbs;

- students enrolled in continuing education classes;

- people anticipating a business or pleasure trip to Italy;

- beginners of the language.

If you are a true beginner, you will find that this book makes no assumptions. You will learn about the other aspects of Italian grammar as you work your way through it. If you are someone who already possesses some knowledge of Italian, you will find this book particularly helpful, because it also reviews other aspects of grammar, connecting them to the Italian verb system.

Thus, whether you are just beginning your study of Italian or have had some training in the language, this book is for you. Previous knowledge has not been taken for granted in these pages; definitions and explanations are concise and clear, and examples use and reuse a core of basic vocabulary.

You should not skip any chapter, especially if you are a beginner. The book is designed to be sequential and coherent. It builds on notions and vocabulary introduced in previous chapters. By the end, you will be in a position to grasp the fundamentals of the Italian verb system. You can also use this book as a reference manual, consulting the table of contents to guide you to the areas of Italian verb conjugation and use for information or practice.

An introductory *Pronunciation Guide*, which explains the basics of Italian pronunciation and spelling, is also provided in Appendix A at the back for beginners.

Buon divertimento! (*Have fun!*)

How to Use This Book

This book is divided into five main parts, each consisting of a number of chapters. Part 1 covers the present indicative and progressive indicative tenses, Part 2 the past tenses, Part 3 the future and conditional tenses, Part 4 the subjunctive tenses, and Part 5 the imperative and other tenses.

Overview Units

Before starting to do the exercises and activities in the chapters of a specific part, read the overview unit at the beginning, especially if you are unsure about grammatical terms or concepts. This unit explains the relevant technical terms used in the part in a nontechnical and easy-to-follow way—what is a *conjugation*, what is a verb *tense*, what is the *subjunctive*, and so on.

Conjugation Information at the Beginning of a Chapter

Each of the chapters is organized around a specific tense or a problematic verb (or verbs). There are several recurring sections and features in each chapter.

In the introductory section, you are given all the information you will need on how to conjugate verbs in a specific tense and mood. This is followed by exercises that, although they may appear mechanical, are nevertheless necessary. These are akin to the scales and arpeggios of musical practice. A student will never become a good pianist or violinist without mastery over them. So too, you will need to do these exercises consistently and faithfully so as to gain mastery over Italian verbs. You cannot use verbs that you do not know how to conjugate!

Illustrative Dialogue

Each chapter has one illustrative dialogue (and in a few cases more than one). This is designed to show you how the tense being learned is used in common conversations. English translations are provided throughout for your convenience. Read the dialogue out loud several times. If you have forgotten what some word means from a previous chapter, consult the glossaries at the back of the book. At times you might have to review previous chapters in order to understand some new structure more clearly. Content questions that focus on verb usage follow. Always do these, because they literally allow you to "kill two birds with one stone"—to practice the verbs and to gain understanding of how they are to be used.

The dialogue is preceded by a vocabulary box (if necessary) that summarizes the vocabulary introduced in the dialogue. If needed, the dialogue is followed by a grammar box that goes over the relevant items of grammar, other than verbs, that the dialogue contains.

Uses and Features

This section contains a summary of how the verb or verb tense is to be used and what its features are. Exercises focusing on usage follow. Many of these involve translating from English to Italian. In this area of grammar, there is no better way to grasp differences in usage than by comparing how the two languages express certain things (especially if you are a self-learner).

Prospettiva personale

In most chapters, you will find one or more sections that involve a "personalized touch," so to speak. These allow you to use the verb tense in relation to your own personal situation. No answers are provided for this part because of its highly personalized nature. They will, however, be self-evident.

Crossword Puzzle

Each chapter ends with a crossword puzzle that is designed to provide an entertaining format for reinforcing what you have learned in the chapter. There is no easier or more enjoyable way to learn! The clues provided will vary in nature and in level of difficulty. This puzzle section will keep you on your mental toes throughout!

Tips, Notes, ...

Throughout a chapter, tips on how to use a verb, notes on aspects of grammar that are relevant to the chapter, charts introducing new vocabulary, and the like are interspersed. This feature will allow you to stay within the confines of this single book. You will not need to resort to other materials. Nothing has been taken for granted!

Back Matter

At the back of the book, you will find summaries of certain aspects of verbs (verbs conjugated with **essere** / *to be* in compound tenses, irregular gerunds, and irregular past participles), but not the usual verb charts. The reason is obvious—the book is intended itself to give you skill at verbs, rendering such charts superfluous!

If you are a beginner and need information on how to pronounce and spell Italian words, you will find a pronunciation guide at the back as well.

Finally, you will find the answers to the exercises of all chapters and the glossaries of all the words that have been used in the book.

As you can see, the ***Italian Verb Workbook*** is an easy-to-use book, designed according to a self-teaching system that lets you learn effortlessly.

Part One

The Present Indicative and Progressive

The Present: An Overview

What Are Verbs?

Verbs are words that indicate the action performed by the subject of a sentence. For this reason, they agree with the *person* (first, second, third) and *number* (singular or plural) of the subject:

Lei	**canta**	She sings
↑	↑	
3rd person singular subject pronoun	3rd person singular form of verb **cantare** / *to sing*	

Gli amici	**cantano**	The friends sing
↑	↑	
3rd person plural subject pronoun	3rd person plural form of verb **cantare**	

Infinitives and Conjugations

The *infinitive* is the form of a verb not inflected (modified) for person or number. In English, it is commonly preceded by *to*—*to sing, to eat,* and so on. In a dictionary, verbs are listed in their infinitive form.

Italian verbs are divided into three conjugations according to their infinitive endings. A *conjugation* is the systematic arrangement of the verb forms according to tense and mood. The infinitive endings in Italian are **-are** (first conjugation), **-ere** (second conjugation), and **-ire** (third conjugation).

TIP

The infinitive endings allow you to determine which person and number endings a verb must take when you conjugate it. Learn these now!

parlare / to speak	**mettere** / to put	**dormire** / to sleep
↑	↑	↑
first conjugation	second conjugation	third conjugation

Tense

A verb *tense* indicates the time an action occurred—now (present tense), before (past tense), after (future tense):

La mangio adesso. / *I'm eating it now.* ⟶ *present tense*

L'ho mangiata ieri. / *I ate it yesterday.* ⟶ *past tense*

La mangerò domani. / *I will eat it tomorrow.* ⟶ *future tense*

Mood

Not only do verbs allow you to express the time an action took place, but they also allow you to convey manner of thinking, point of view, etc. This aspect of verbs is known as *mood:*

Maria legge quel romanzo.
  / *Mary is reading that novel.* ⟶ *indicative mood = statement*

Maria, leggi, quel romanzo!
  / *Mary, read that novel!* ⟶ *imperative mood = command*

**È probabile che Maria stia
  leggendo quel romanzo.**
  / *It's probable that Mary is
  reading that novel.* ⟶ *subjunctive mood = probability*

Regular and Irregular Verbs

A *regular verb* is one that is conjugated according to a recurring pattern. A verb that is not so conjugated is known as *irregular*.

The Present Indicative

The present indicative, called the **presente dell'indicativo** in Italian, allows you to express, indicate, or refer to actions that are ongoing, permanent, or imply the present time in some way. It is the most commonly used tense in everyday conversation. For this reason, it is the focus of the first eight chapters of this book.

The Present Progressive

The second main present tense is the present progressive, called the **presente progressivo** in Italian. It is an alternative to the present indicative, allowing you to zero in on an ongoing action. It will be dealt with in Chapter 7.

Subject Pronouns

Pronoun function

To conjugate verbs, you will need to know (or review) the subject pronouns, called the **pronomi in funzione di soggetto** in Italian (fam. = familiar, pol. = polite):

Subject

	Singular		Plural
1st person	**io** / *I*	1st person	**noi** / *we*
2nd person	**tu** / *you* (fam.)	2nd person	**voi** / *you* (fam. and in general)
3rd person	**lui** / *he* **lei** / *she* **Lei** / *you* (pol.)	3rd person	**loro** / *they* **Loro** / *you* (pol.)

Notice that **io** is not capitalized (unless it is the first word of a sentence). Subject pronouns are generally optional because it is easy to tell from the verb ending which person and number are involved.

USAGE NOTE

As you can see, there are both familiar and polite forms of address in Italian. These are not to be used alternatively! If you address someone incorrectly, it might be taken as rudeness! So, be careful.

Simply put, the familiar forms are used to address people with whom you are on familiar terms: members of the family, friends, etc. If you call someone by a first name, then you are obviously on familiar terms. Otherwise, you must use polite forms.

In writing, the polite forms (**Lei, Loro**) are often capitalized in order to distinguish them from **lei** (*she*) and **loro** (*they*); but this is not obligatory.

In the plural, there is a strong tendency in current Italian to use **voi** as the plural of both **tu** and **Lei**. **Loro** is restricted to very formal situations (e.g., when addressing an audience).

What Are Sentences?

A *sentence* is an organized sequence of words that allows you to make a statement, ask a question, express a thought, offer an opinion, etc. In writing, a sentence is easily identified because it starts with a capitalized word and ends with either a period, a question mark, or an exclamation mark:

Lui è italiano. / *He is Italian.* ⟶ *affirmative sentence*

Chi è quell'uomo? / *Who is that man?* ⟶ *interrogative sentence*

Vengo anch'io! / *I'm coming too!* ⟶ *emphatic sentence*

Sentences have two basic parts: a *subject* and a *predicate*. A subject is "who" or "what" the sentence is about. It is often the first element in a simple sentence:

Maria *parla italiano.* / *Mary speaks Italian.*

Lei *è italiana.* / *She is Italian.*

But be careful! The subject is not necessarily always the first word:

Sì, anche **Maria** *parla italiano.* / *Yes, Mary also speaks Italian.*

No, forse **Lei** *non è italiana.* / *No, maybe she is not Italian.*

A *predicate* is the remaining part of the sentence. It provides information about the subject. In many simple sentences, you will find it after the subject.

Alessandro parla **italiano**. / *Alexander speaks Italian.*

Lui è **italiano**. / *He is Italian.*

go over — do ri passo

1
Present Indicative of Regular Verbs

First-Conjugation Verbs

As you learned in the preceding overview unit, the infinitives of regular Italian verbs end in **-are, -ere,** or **-ire.** Those ending in **-are** are first-conjugation verbs. To form the present indicative of such verbs, called the **presente dell'indicativo** in Italian, do the following:

1. Drop the infinitive ending, **-are.** This produces the "verb stem," as it is called:

    parlare / *to speak* →   **parl-**

2. Add the following endings to the stem:

(io)	**-o**
(tu)	**-i**
(lui/lei/Lei)	**-a**
(noi)	**-iamo**
(voi)	**-ate**
(loro)	**-ano**

Voi sapete?
do you know?

3. Here's the result:

(io)	**parlo**	I speak, I am speaking, I do speak
(tu)	**parli**	you (fam.) speak, you are speaking, you do speak
(lui/lei/Lei)	**parla**	he, she, you (pol.) speak(s), he, she, you is/are speaking, he, she, you does/do speak
(noi)	**parliamo**	we speak, we are speaking, we do speak
(voi)	**parlate**	you speak, you are speaking, you do speak
(loro)	**parlano**	they speak, they are speaking, they do speak

sing form formal

TIP

Be careful when you pronounce the third person plural form! The accent is not *placed on the ending, but on a syllable before the ending:*

    parlano / *they speak*
    |
    stress

To make any sentence negative in Italian, just put **non** before the predicate (**no** / *no*, **sì** / *yes*):

Affirmative	Negative
Sì, Maria parla italiano. Yes, Mary speaks Italian.	**No, Maria non parla italiano.** No, Mary does not speak Italian.
Sì, loro arrivano domani. Yes, they are arriving tomorrow.	**No, loro non arrivano domani.** No, they are not arriving tomorrow.

TIP

*Notice that the **presente dell'indicativo** is rendered by three English verb forms:*

$$\text{parlo} \quad = \quad \begin{bmatrix} \textit{I speak} \\ \textit{I am speaking} \\ \textit{I do speak} \end{bmatrix}$$

Below are some common regular first-conjugation verbs that will come in handy for basic communication. They are used in the exercise set below:

abitare	to live	entrare	to enter
amare	to love	guardare	to look at, to watch
arrivare	to arrive	lavorare	to work
ascoltare	to listen to	parlare	to speak
aspettare	to wait for	portare	to wear, to carry
ballare	to dance	preparare	to prepare
cantare	to sing	sperare	to hope
comprare	to buy	suonare	to play an instrument

Prospettiva personale

Vero ("true") **o falso** ("false")? Indicate which of the following statements is true ("V") or false ("F") from your personal perspective. Note that the pronoun "**io** / *I*" refers to *you*, the user of this manual.

_F_ 1. **Io parlo italiano molto bene.**

_V_ 2. **Io parlo inglese molto bene.**

_V_ 3. **Io amo la lingua italiana** (the Italian language).

_F_ 4. **Io canto molto bene** (very well).

_F_ 5. **Io ballo molto bene.**

_V_ 6. **Io lavoro troppo** (too much).

_F_ 7. **Mia moglie** (My wife) **suona la chitarra** (guitar).

_V_ 8. **Mia figlia** (My daughter) **lavora troppo.**

_V_ 9. **Mia moglie non balla molto bene.**

Illustrative Dialogue

(m. = masculine, f. = feminine)

a	at	la figlia	daughter
a che ora	at what time	la moglie (f.)	wife
anche	also, too	lo (m.)	it
arrivare	to arrive	ma	but
bene	well	molto	very, much, a lot
e	and	parlare	to speak
gentile	kind	prego	you're welcome
grazie	thank you	qualche	a few, some
invece	instead	scusi	excuse me (pol.)
il minuto	minute	tra qualche minuto	in a few minutes
l'autobus (m.)	bus	tra	in, within
l'inglese (m.)	English	un po'	a bit
l'italiano	Italian	vero	true

Turista inglese: (English Tourist)	**Scusi, Lei *parla* inglese?**	Excuse me, do you speak English?
Donna : (Woman)	**No, non *parlo* inglese. Ma Lei *parla* italiano, no?**	No, I do not speak English. But you speak Italian, don't you?
Turista:	**Un po'. Mia moglie e mia figlia invece *parlano* italiano molto bene.**	A bit. My wife and my daughter instead speak Italian very well.
Donna:	**Ma anche Lei lo *parla* molto bene!**	But you speak it very well too!
Turista:	**No, non è vero. Lei è molto gentile. A che ora *arriva* l'autobus?**	No, it's not true. You're very kind. At what time is the bus arriving?
Donna:	***Arriva* tra qualche minuto.**	It's arriving in a few minutes.
Turista:	**Grazie.**	Thank you.
Donna:	**Prego.**	You're welcome.

Grammar Notes

Italian nouns are either masculine or feminine. You can generally identify the noun's gender by the ending. If it ends in -**o**, the noun is (generally) masculine; if it ends in -**a** it is (generally) feminine. If the noun ends in -**e** then it can be either:

Masculine	Feminine
italiano	**figlia**
inglese	**moglie**

Note the forms of the definite article ("the") introduced above:

l' = before any singular noun beginning with a vowel:
l'italiano, l'inglese

il = before any singular masculine noun beginning with any
consonant (except **z**, **s** plus a consonant, **gn**, and **ps**):
il minuto

la = before any singular feminine noun beginning with any
consonant:
la moglie

Note, finally, the feminine singular form **mia** of the possessive adjective "my" introduced above: **mia moglie** / *my wife*, **mia figlia** / *my daughter*.

EXERCISE Set 1–1

A. Supply the missing Italian verb ending and then give the English equivalent.

EXAMPLE: lui parl_   =   _____
           lui parla   =   he speaks, he is speaking, he does speak

1. io suon__   =   _io suono_____

2. tu sper__   =   _tu speri_____

3. noi prepar__   =   _noi prepariamo_____

4. loro port__   =   _portano_____

5. voi lavor__   =   _lavorate_____

6. Lei entr__   =   _entra_____

7. lei guard__   =   _guardi_____

8. Loro am__   =   _amano_____

9. loro arriv__   =   _arrivano_____

10. io ascolt__   =   _ascolto_____

11. tu aspett__   =   _aspetti_____

12. noi ball__   =   _balliamo_____

13. lei cant__   =   _canta_____

14. noi compr__   =   _compriamo_____

15. loro parl__   =   _parlano_____

B. How do you say the following things in Italian (sing. = singular, pl. = plural)?

la chitarra	guitar	**sempre**	always
la giacca	jacket	**la televisione**	television
la lingua	language	**troppo**	too much
nuovo	new	**una giacca nuova**	a new jacket
il piano(forte)	piano	**vicino**	near, nearby
la radio	radio	**il violoncello**	cello

1. Excuse me, do you speak English? *mi Scusi, lei parla l'inglese?*

2. Yes, I speak English very well. *Sì, parlo l'inglese molto bene!*

3. They do not speak Italian very well. *Loro non parlano italiano bene, molto*

4. We speak Italian a little bit. *Noi parliamo italiano un po.*

5. Maria, you also speak Italian, don't you? (fam.) *Maria, anche tu parli italiano, è vero non*

6. I instead do not speak Italian, but my daughter does speak it very well. *Io invece non parlo italiano, ma mia figlia parla molto bene.*

7. No, it's not true, the bus is not arriving in a few minutes. *No, Non è vero*

8. Thank you, you are very kind. I love the Italian language.
   Grazie, lei è molto simpatico. Io amo la lingua italiana

9. Alessandro plays the cello very well, and Sarah plays the piano and dances very well.
   Alessandro suona il violocello molto bene, e Sarah suona la pianoforte e balla molto bene

10. She listens to the radio too much. *Lei senta la radio troppo*

11. We watch TV a lot. *Noi guadiamo troppo.*

12. They play the piano well. *Loro suonano il pianoforte bene*

13. You (fam., sing.) are always watching TV. *Tu guadi il televisione sempre.*

14. You (pol., sing.) are wearing a new jacket, aren't you? *Lei porta una giacca nuova, no è vero?*

15. You (fam., pl.) are waiting for Maria, aren't you? She lives nearby.
    Lei aspettare per maria, non è vera abita vicino.

Second-Conjugation Verbs

Infinitives ending in **-ere** are classified as second-conjugation verbs. To form the present indicative of these verbs, do exactly the same things you did above with first-conjugation verbs:

1. Drop the infinitive ending **-ere**:

    scrivere / *to write*   →   **scriv-**

2. Add the following endings to the stem:

(io)	**-o**	*scrivo*
(tu)	**-i**	*scrivi*
(lui/lei/Lei)	**-e**	*scrive*
(noi)	**-iamo**	*scriviamo*
(voi)	**-ete**	*scrivete*
(loro)	**-ono**	*scrivano*

3. Here's the result:

(io)	**scrivo**	I write, I am writing, I do write
(tu)	**scrivi**	you write (fam.), you are writing, you do write
(lui/lei/Lei)	**scrive**	he, she, you (pol.) write(s), he, she, you is/are writing, he, she, you does/do write
(noi)	**scriviamo**	we write, we are writing, we do write
(voi)	**scrivete**	you write, you are writing, you do write
(loro)	**scrivono**	they write, they are writing, they do write

---

TIP

Be careful again when you pronounce the third person plural forms! The accent is not placed on the ending, but on a syllable before the ending:

scrivono / *they write*
|
stress

Below are some common regular second-conjugation verbs that will come in handy for basic communication. They are used in the exercise set below:

chiudere	to close		**ridere**	to laugh
comprendere	to comprehend		**rompere**	to break
correre	to run		**scrivere**	to write
credere	to believe		**temere**	to fear
godere	to enjoy		**vedere**	to see
leggere	to read		**vendere**	to sell
mettere	to put		**vivere**	to live
prendere	to take			

Prospettiva personale

Vero o falso? Indicate which of the following statements is true ("V") or false ("F") from your personal perspective.

_V_ 1. **Io comprendo la lingua italiana.**

_F_ 2. **Il mio amico** (my friend) **crede sempre a tutto** (everything).

_V_ 3. **La mia amica corre sempre.**

_V_ 4. **Io godo la vita** (life).

_F_ 5. **Mia moglie legge l'italiano molto bene.**

_F_ 6. **Anche mia figlia legge l'italiano molto bene.**

_V_ 7. **Io scrivo molto bene in italiano.**

_V_ 8. **Il mio amico ride sempre.**

Illustrative Dialogue

a più tardi	later	**fra**	within (equivalent to tra)
allora	then, therefore, thus	**francese**	French
l'amica	female friend	**in**	in

l'amico	male friend		leggere	to read
arrivederci	good-bye (fam.)		perché	because
che	what		scrivere	to write
chiamare	to call		scusa	excuse me (fam.)
ciao	bye, hi (fam.)		ti	you
			venti	twenty

Amico:	**Scusa, Claudia, che *scrivi*?**	Excuse me, Claudia, what are you writing?
Amica:	***Scrivo* un' e-mail a una mia amica francese.**	I am writing an e-mail to my French friend.
Amico:	**In italiano?**	In Italian?
Amica:	**Sì, perché la mia amica *legge* la lingua italiana molto bene.**	Yes, because my friend reads the Italian language very well.
Amico:	**Allora, arrivederci a più tardi.**	Then, good-bye till later.
Amica:	**Ciao. Ti chiamo fra venti minuti.**	Bye. I'll call you in twenty minutes.

Grammar Notes

Note the forms of the indefinite article ("a/an") introduced above:

un = before any singular masculine noun beginning with a vowel or consonant, except z, s plus a consonant, **gn**, and **ps**:
un amico, un minuto

un' = before any singular feminine noun beginning with a vowel:
un'amica

una = before any singular feminine noun beginning with a consonant:
una lingua

Note the use of the definite article before a possessive adjective: **la mia amica.** The article is dropped if the possessive modifies a singular kinship noun, as you saw above: **mia moglie.**

The corresponding masculine singular form is **il mio: il mio amico**.

EXERCISE Set 1–2

A. Supply the missing Italian verb ending and then give the English equivalent.

EXAMPLE:	lui scriv_	=	
	lui scrive	=	he writes, he is writing, he does write

1. **io scriv__** = o _____

2. **tu comprend__** = i _____

3. **noi cred__** = iamo _____

4. **loro mett__** = ono _____

5. **voi god__** = _iete_ _____

6. **Lei legg__** = _e_ _____

7. **la mia amica mett__** = _mette_ _____

8. **Loro rid__** = _ono._ _____

9. **loro romp__** = _ono_ _____

10. **io tem__** = _o_ _____

11. **tu ved__** = _i_ _____

12. **noi vend__** = _iamo_ _____

13. **lui chiud__** = _e_ _____

14. **noi mett__** = _iamo_ _____

15. **loro prend__** = _ono_ _____

B. How do you say the following things in Italian? Review the illustrative dialogue and the chart of common verbs before you start.

il figlio	son	**qualcosa**	something
il fratello	brother	**la sorella**	sister
la macchina	car	**tutto**	everything
la nonna	grandmother	**va bene**	OK
il nonno	grandfather	**la vita**	life

1. Hi, Maria and Claudia, what are you reading? _____ _legate_ _____

2. I'm not reading. I'm writing an e-mail to a French friend (f.). _____

3. Excuse me (fam.), but are you (sing., fam.) writing the e-mail in Italian? _____

4. Yes, because my friend (f., sing.) speaks, reads, and writes the Italian language very well.

   _____

5. Good-bye, till later. Do you comprehend (fam., pl.)? _____ _Comprendete_

6. I'll write you (fam., sing.) an e-mail in twenty minutes. OK? _____

7. No, it's not true, my friend (f., sing.) is not selling the car. _____

8. My grandmother enjoys life! She comprehends everything! _____

9. My son and my daughter believe you (**ti** before the verb). _____

10. My grandfather always fears everything! _____

11. My brother is also selling the car. _____

12. My sister always breaks something. _____

13. My French friend (f., sing.) always laughs. _____

14. My Italian friend (m., sing.) always runs. _____

15. We enjoy life, because we live in Italy! _____

Third-Conjugation Verbs

Infinitives ending in **-ire** are called third-conjugation verbs. In this case there are two types of conjugations in present indicative.

Type 1

To form the present indicative of the first type, do the same things you have been doing so far:

1. Drop the infinitive ending, **-ire**:

  dormire / *to sleep*   →   **dorm-**

2. Add the following endings to the stem:

(io)	**-o**
(tu)	**-i**
(lui/lei/Lei)	**-e**
(noi)	**-iamo**
(voi)	**-ite**
(loro)	**-ono**

3. Here's the result:

(io)	**dormo**	I sleep, I am sleeping, I do sleep
(tu)	**dormi**	you (fam.) sleep, you are sleeping, you do sleep
(lui/lei/Lei)	**dorme**	he, she, you (pol.) sleep(s), he, she, you is/are sleeping, he, she, you does/do sleep
(noi)	**dormiamo**	we sleep, we are sleeping, we do sleep
(voi)	**dormite**	you sleep, you are sleeping, you do sleep
(loro)	**dormono**	they sleep, they are sleeping, they do sleep

Below are some common Type 1 verbs that will come in handy for basic communication:

aprire	to open		**scoprire**	to discover
coprire	to cover		**sentire**	to feel, to hear
dormire	to sleep		**soffrire**	to suffer
partire	to leave, to depart			

Type 2

To form the present indicative of the second type of third-conjugation verb, do exactly the same things, but instead of the endings above, add on the following ones:

1. Drop the infinitive ending, **-ire,** to produce the verb stem:

  finire / *to finish*   →   **fin-**

2. Add the following endings:

(io)	**-isco**
(tu)	**-isci**
(lui/lei/Lei)	**-isce**
(noi)	**-iamo**
(voi)	**-ite**
(loro)	**-iscono**

3. Here's the result:

(io)	**finisco**	I finish, I am finishing, I do finish
(tu)	**finisci**	you (fam.) finish, you are finishing, you do finish
(lui/lei/Lei)	**finisce**	he, she, you (pol.) finish(es), he, she, you is/are finishing, he, she, you does/do finish
(noi)	**finiamo**	we finish, we are finishing, we do finish
(voi)	**finite**	you finish, you are finishing, you do finish
(loro)	**finiscono**	they finish, they are finishing, they do finish

---

TIP

Be careful once again when you pronounce the third person plural forms of both types! The accent is not placed on the ending, but on a preceding syllable:

dormono / *they sleep*   **finiscono** / *they finish*

| |

stress   stress

There is no way to predict to which type of conjugation an **-ire** belongs. A good dictionary will provide this kind of information. However, as a rule of thumb, if you see two consonants before the **-ire** ending (**aprire** / to open, **partire** / to leave) the conjugation is usually Type 1; if there is a vowel (**capire** / to understand, **pulire** / to clean), the conjugation is usually Type 2. This is only a rule of thumb, but it works very often.

Below are some common Type 2 verbs that will come in handy for basic communication:

capire	to understand	pulire	to clean
finire	to finish	punire	to punish
garantire	to guarantee	spedire	to send, to mail
preferire	to prefer	unire	to unite

Prospettiva personale

Vero o falso? Indicate which of the following statements is true ("V") or false ("F") from your personal perspective.

_V_ 1. **I negozi aprono alle sette e mezzo** (at 7:30).

_F_ 2. **I miei amici dormono fino a tardi** (till late).

_F_ 3. **Io parto per l'Italia tra poco** (in a little while).

_V_ 4. **Io capisco l'italiano.**

_F_ 5. **I miei amici** (my friends) **preferiscono il francese.**

_F_ 6. **Io pulisco sempre la casa** (house).

_V_ 7. **Preferisco parlare inglese.**

_F_ 8. **Mio fratello parte domani** (tomorrow) **per l'Italia.**

_V_ 9. **Mia moglie non capisce il francese.**

Illustrative Dialogue

aprire	to open	mezzo	half
arrivederLa	good-bye (pol.)	il negozio	store
buongiorno	good day, good morning	non c'è di che	don't mention it
capire	to understand	oggi	today

| desiderare | to want, to help out | qui | here |
| interessante | interesting | sette | seven |

Donna:	**Buongiorno, Lei *capisce* l'italiano?**	Good day, do you understand Italian?
Uomo (Man):	**Sì, *desidera*?**	Yes, may I help you?
Donna:	**A che ora *aprono* i negozi qui?**	At what time do stores open up here?
Uomo:	**Alle sette e mezzo e chiudono alle venti. Perché?**	They open at 7.30 AM and they close at 8 PM. Why?
Donna:	**Io e le mie amiche desideriamo comprare qualcosa oggi.**	My friends and I wish to buy something today.
Uomo:	**Interessante, anche io e i miei amici!**	Interesting, so do my friends and I!
Donna:	***Capisco*. Grazie e arrivederLa.**	I understand. Thank you and good-bye.
Uomo:	**Non c'è di che!**	Don't mention it!

Grammar Notes

Masculine nouns are made plural (in general) by changing their final vowel to **-i:**

Singular	Plural
amico / friend	**amici** / friends
inglese / English person	**inglesi** / English persons

Feminine nouns are made plural (in general) by changing the final **-a** to **-e** or the final **-e** to **-i:**

Singular	Plural
lingua / language	**lingue** / languages
moglie / wife	**mogli** / wives

Note the plural forms of the definite article ("the"):

Masculine

Singular	Plural
il	**i**
l'	**gli**
il fratello / the brother	**i fratelli** / the brothers
l'inglese / English person	**gli inglesi** / English persons

Feminine

Singular	Plural
la	**le**
l'	**le**
la lingua / language	**le lingue** / languages
l'amica / friend (f.)	**le amiche** / friends (f.)

Note the plural forms of "my":

Singular	Plural
il mio amico / my friend	**i miei amici** / my friends
la mia macchina / my car	**le mie macchine** / my cars

EXERCISE Set 1–3

A. Supply the missing Italian verb ending and then give the English equivalent.

EXAMPLE: **lui cap_**   =   _____
           lui capisce =   he understands, he does understand

1. **io un__**   = _____
2. **tu sped__**   = _____
3. **noi pun__**   = _____
4. **loro pul__**   = _____
5. **voi prefer__**   = _____
6. **Lei soffr__**   = _____
7. **lei fin__**   = _____
8. **Loro cap__**   = _____
9. **i negozi apr__** = _____
10. **io copr__**   = _____
11. **tu dorm__**   = _____
12. **noi part__**   = _____
13. **lei scopr__**   = _____
14. **noi sent__**   = _____
15. **loro garant__** = _____

B. Which of the following two options, **a** or **b**, is the correct one?

americana	American (f.)	**italiana**	Italian (f.)
americano	American (m.)	**italiano**	Italian (m.)
il caffè	coffee	**il marito**	husband
casa	house	**niente**	nothing
di	of	**la pasta**	pasta, pastry
domani	tomorrow	**per**	for
fino a	until	**tardi**	late
l'Italia	Italy	**tra poco**	in a little while

1. **A che ora aprono i negozi qui?**
   a. **Alle sette e mezzo.**
   b. **Non c'è di che!**

2. **Interessante, anche io e mio marito . . .**
   a. **chiudiamo alle venti.**
   b. **dormiamo sempre fino a tardi.**

3. **Buongiorno, Lei . . . l'italiano?**
   a. **capisci**
   b. **capisce**

4. **Desidera qualcosa?**
   a. **Sì, io e le mie amiche dormiamo fino a tardi.**
   b. **No, niente, grazie.**

5. **A che ora . . . gli amici di Alessandro?**
   a. **finisce**
   b. **finiscono**

6. **Anche tu . . . sempre la casa?**
   a. **pulisce**
   b. **pulisci**

7. **Molti americani . . . la lingua italiana.**
   a. **preferite**
   b. **preferiscono**

8. **Le mie amiche americane . . . per l'Italia domani.**
   a. **partono**
   b. **partiamo**

9. **I miei amici italiani non . . . la lingua inglese.**
   a. **capiscono**
   b. **capisce**

10. **Le mie amiche italiane non . . . molto.**
    a. **dormono**
    b. **uniscono**

11. **Che sente Lei?**
    a. **Non sente niente.**
    b. **Non sento niente.**

12. **Anche tu dormi fino a tardi?**
    a. **Sì, anch'io dormo fino a tardi.**
    b. **Sì, anche noi dormiamo fino a tardi.**

13. **Anche Lei pulisce sempre la casa?**
    a. **Sì, anch'io pulisco sempre la casa.**
    b. **Sì, anche lei pulisce sempre la casa.**

14. **Sì, anch'io . . . il caffè espresso.**
    a. **preferisco**
    b. **preferisci**

15. **Sarah sempre . . . le paste!**
    a. **finisce**
    b. **finisci**

Uses and Features

The **presente dell'indicativo** is used in everyday conversation to refer to actions, events, and ideas that imply the present situation or some permanent or habitual situation. Specifically, it is used as follows:

1. To indicate an action or a state of being that is taking place at the present time:

> *Parlo* **a Claudia in questo momento.** / I am speaking to Claudia at this moment.
>
> *Guardo* **la TV adesso.** / I am watching TV now.

2. To indicate an action or a state of being that is permanent or continuous:

> *Parlo* **italiano anch'io.** / I too speak Italian.
>
> **Lei** *capisce* **sempre tutto.** / She always understands everything.

3. To emphasize something at the present time:

> **Sì,** *capisco*! / Yes, I do understand!
>
> **No, non** *sento* **niente!** / No, I do not hear anything!

4. To indicate a habitual action:

> *Suono* **la chitarra ogni giorno.** / I play the guitar every day.
>
> **Il lunedì** *puliamo* **la casa.** / On Mondays, we clean the house.

5. To convey a general truth:

> I negozi *aprono* alle sette e mezzo. / Stores open at 7.30 AM.
>
> Gli italiani *lavorano* molto. / Italians work a lot.

6. To express an action that may occur in the near future:

> Lui *arriva* domani. / He's arriving tomorrow.
>
> Tra poco *scrivo* un' e-mail. / In a little while I'm going to write an e-mail.

VOCABULARY TIP

The present indicative is often used with words and expressions such as

a quest'ora	at this hour
adesso / ora	now
domani	tomorrow
in questo momento	in / at this moment
oggi come oggi	nowadays, these days
oggi	today
ogni giorno	every day

Asking Questions

Verbs can be used to ask questions. In writing, an interrogative sentence always has a question mark at the end. The two most common methods of turning an affirmative sentence into an interrogative one are

1. Simply put a question mark at the end in writing. In speaking, raise your tone of voice, as in English:

> Maria parla italiano? / *Mary speaks Italian?*

2. Put the subject at the end of the sentence, adding a question mark in writing or raising your tone of voice when speaking:

> Parla italiano, Maria? / *Does Mary speak Italian?*

Interrogative sentences can also be formed with interrogative adjectives or pronouns when certain information is required.

> Chi *parla italiano qui?* / *Who speaks Italian here?*
>
> Dove *abita Marco?* / *Where does Marco live?*

VOCABULARY NOTE

Chi? / *Who?*

Che? / *What?*   also: Cosa? / Che cosa?

Come? / *How?*

Dove? / *Where?*

Perché? / *Why?*

Quale? / *Which?*

Quando? / *When?*

Quanto? / *How much?*

Note that **quale** and **quanto** agree with any noun they modify. This means their endings must agree in gender (masculine or feminine) and number (singular and plural) with the noun:

Masculine Singular	Masculine Plural
Quale fratello arriva? Which brother is arriving?	**Quali fratelli arrivano?** Which brothers are arriving?
Quanto caffè desideri? How much coffee do you want?	**Quanti caffè desideri?** How many coffees do you want?

Feminine Singular	Feminine Plural
Quale sorella arriva? Which sister is arriving?	**Quali sorelle arrivano?** Which sisters are arriving?
Quanta pasta desideri? How much pasta do you want?	**Quante paste desideri?** How many pastries do you want?

Use either **no?**, **vero?**, or **non è vero?** to seek approval, consent, agreement, etc. when asking a "rhetorical" question:

> **Maria parla italiano, *no*?** / *Mary speaks Italian, doesn't she?*
>
> **Lei parla molto bene, *non è vero*?** / *She speaks very well, doesn't she?*
>
> **Alessandro arriva ora, *vero*?** / *Alexander is arriving now, isn't he?*

Familiar and Polite Forms of Address

Remember that, in the singular, the **tu** forms are used for familiar address and the **Lei** forms for polite address:

> **Cosa *preferisci*, tu?** / *What do you (fam.) prefer?*
>
> **Cosa *preferisce*, Lei?** / *What do you (pol.) prefer?*

Second person plural forms are used commonly to address anyone in general:

> **Cosa *scrivete*, voi?** / *What are you (fam./pol.) writing?*
>
> **Cosa *preferite*, voi?** / *What do you (fam./pol.) prefer?*

Third person plural forms are used to address people politely in very limited ways—mainly in very formal situations:

> **Cosa *scrivono*, Loro?** / *What are you (very formal) writing?*
>
> **Cosa *preferiscono*, Loro?** / *What do you (very formal) prefer?*

Odds and Ends

Recall from the previous overview unit that subject pronouns are optional. Note that the subject pronoun "it" (plural "they") is not normally expressed:

> ***Apre*** **alle sette e mezzo.** / *It opens at 7:30 AM.*
>
> ***Chiudono*** **alle sei.** / *They close at six.*

The English genitive form "Sarah's friends," "my brother's cello," etc. is rendered in Italian with the preposition **di**:

> **Le amiche *di* Sarah preferiscono il caffè.** / *Sarah's friends prefer coffee.*
>
> **Vedi il violoncello *di* mio fratello?** / *Do you see my brother's cello?*

Prospettiva personale

Vero o falso? Indicate which of the following statements is true ("V") or false ("F") from your personal perspective.

_____ 1. **Oggi come oggi gli americani lavorano troppo.**

_____ 2. **Ogni giorno io e mio marito / mia moglie guardiamo la TV.**

_____ 3. **La mia amica / il mio amico balla molto bene.**

_____ 4. **Mio fratello / mia sorella gode la vita molto.**

_____ 5. **Mio marito / mia moglie legge l'italiano molto bene.**

_____ 6. **In questo momento mio figlio / mia figlia ascolta la radio.**

_____ 7. **Ogni giorno io pulisco la casa.**

_____ 8. **Adesso preferisco il caffè espresso.**

EXERCISE Set 1–4

A. Missing from each of the following sentences is the verb. The missing verbs are given to you in their infinitive forms. Put each verb, in its correct form, in each sentence according to the sense.

Verbs: **guardare, amare, ascoltare, pulire, capire, chiudere, vivere, arrivare, suonare**

1. **Mia sorella _____ il pianoforte molto bene.**

2. **I miei amici _____ l'Italia.**

3. **Adesso noi _____ in Italia perché desideriamo parlare la lingua italiana bene.**

4. **In questo momento loro _____ la TV.**

5. **A che ora _____ gli amici di Paolo?**

6. **Ogni giorno io e mia moglie _____ la casa.**

7. **Anch'io _____ un po' di francese.**

8. **Quando _____ quel (that) negozio?**

9. **A quest'ora mio fratello _____ sempre la radio.**

B. Choose the appropriate answer to each question.

1. **Dove abiti?**
   a. **Abito negli Stati Uniti** (in the U.S.).
   b. **Non abito.**

2. **Aspettate Marco?**
   a. **Sì, aspettate Marco.**
   b. **Sì, aspettiamo Marco.**

3. **Alessandro parla italiano?**
   a. **Sì, e anche lo legge e lo scrive.**
   b. **Sì, parliamo, leggiamo e scriviamo italiano.**

4. **Lavora in quel** (that) **negozio, Sarah?**
   a. **No, non lavoriamo in quel negozio.**
   b. **No, non lavora in quel negozio.**

5. **Che cosa legge Marco?**
   a. **Legge un romanzo** (a novel).
   b. **Leggo un romanzo.**

6. **Come prende il caffè, Claudia?**
   a. **Non prende il caffè.**
   b. **Non prendiamo il caffè.**

7. **Quando arrivano?**
   a. **Tra poco.**
   b. **Oggi come oggi.**

8. **Perché ridete?**
   a. **Non ridiamo.**
   b. **Non ridono.**

9. **Quali paste comprate e quante paste comprate?**
   a. **Compriamo sette paste alla crema (with cream).**
   b. **Comprano sette paste alla crema (with cream).**

Crossword Puzzle 1

Orizzontali (Across)

  7. we comprehend

10. you are putting (fam., pl.)

12. we unite

13. I am selling

14. he does break

Verticali (Down)

  1. they are sending

  2. you believe (fam., sing.)

  3. he punishes

  4. I run

  5. I guarantee

  6. we enjoy

  8. they are preparing

  9. I hope

11. you fear (pol., sing.)

2
Essere & Avere

Conjugation of *Essere*

The verb **essere** / *to be* is an irregular verb. Unlike the verbs that you learned to conjugate in the previous chapter, you cannot predict its forms on the basis of the infinitive. You will simply have to memorize them:

(io)	sono	I am
(tu)	sei	you (fam.) are
(lui/lei/Lei)	è	he, she, you (pol.) is/are
(noi)	siamo	we are
(voi)	siete	you are
(loro)	sono	they are

Telling Time

One of the more practical uses of this verb is for telling time. In order to do so, however, you will first need to know (or review) the numbers from one to sixty:

1	uno	21	ventuno	41	quarantuno
2	due	22	ventidue	42	quarantadue
3	tre	23	ventitré	43	quarantatré
4	quattro	24	ventiquattro	44	quarantaquattro
5	cinque	25	venticinque	45	quarantacinque
6	sei	26	ventisei	46	quarantasei
7	sette	27	ventisette	47	quarantasette
8	otto	28	ventotto	48	quarantotto
9	nove	29	ventinove	49	quarantanove
10	dieci	30	trenta	50	cinquanta
11	undici	31	trentuno	51	cinquantuno
12	dodici	32	trentadue	52	cinquantadue
13	tredici	33	trentatré	53	cinquantatré
14	quattordici	34	trentaquattro	54	cinquantaquattro
15	quindici	35	trentacinque	55	cinquantacinque
16	sedici	36	trentasei	56	cinquantasei
17	diciassette	37	trentasette	57	cinquantasette
18	diciotto	38	trentotto	58	cinquantotto
19	diciannove	39	trentanove	59	cinquantanove
20	venti	40	quaranta	60	sessanta

The hours are feminine in gender. Therefore, they are preceded by the feminine forms of the definite article:

> **È l'una.** / *It's one o'clock* (= the only singular form).
> **Sono le due.** / *It's two o'clock.*
> **Sono le tre.** / *It's three o'clock.*
> **Sono le quattro.** / *It's four o'clock.*
>
> . . .
>
> **Sono le ventiquattro.** / *It's midnight.*

Officially, telling time in Italy is on the basis of the 24-hour clock. However, in common conversations, you can employ the same system used in the U.S.:

> **Sono le quattordici = Sono le due.** / *It's two PM.*
> **Sono le venti = Sono le otto.** / *It's eight PM.*

To indicate minutes, simply add them to the hour with the conjunction **e** / *and.*

> **Sono le tre *e* venti.** / *It's three-twenty.*
> **Sono le quattro *e* dieci.** / *It's ten after four.*
> **È l'una *e* quaranta.** / *It's one-forty.*
> **Sono le sedici *e* cinquanta.** / *It's 4:50 PM.*
> **Sono le ventidue *e* cinque.** / *It's 10:05 PM.*

A. Supply the missing form of the verb **essere**, giving the English equivalent.

EXERCISE Set 2–1

EXAMPLE: lui _____   =   _____
             lui è   =   he is

1. io _____   =   _____   6. il mio amico _____   =   _____

2. tu _____   =   _____   7. le mie amiche _____   =   _____

3. noi _____   =   _____   8. io e tu _____   =   _____

4. voi _____   =   _____   9. tu e lui _____   =   _____

5. Lei _____   =   _____

B. Give the indicated times in Italian. Use the 24-hour clock system.

EXAMPLES: 2:45 AM
              Sono le due e quarantacinque.

              2:45 PM
              Sono le quattordici e quarantacinque.

Che ora è?

1. 1:33 AM   _____

2. 1:33 PM   _____

3. 5:12 AM   _____

4. 5:12 PM   _____

5. 8:55 AM   _____

6. 8:55 PM   _____

7. 11:18 AM   _____

8. 11:18 PM   _____

Illustrative Dialogue

certo	certainly, of course	meno	less, minus
ci vediamo	see you later	preciso (-a)	exactly, precisely
essere	to be	proprio	really
la lezione	class, lesson	sicuro (-a)	sure

Paolo:	**Teresa, che ore *sono*?** (equivalent of **che ora è**)	Teresa, what time is it?
Teresa:	***Sono* le undici meno dieci.**	It's 10:50 (11:00 minus 10).
Paolo:	**A che ora *è* la lezione d'italiano?**	At what time is the Italian class?
Teresa:	***È* all'una precisa.**	It's at exactly one o'clock.
Paolo:	***Sei* proprio sicura?**	Are you really sure?
Teresa:	**Certo. Ci vediamo.**	Of course. I'll see you.
Paolo:	**Ciao!**	Bye!

Grammar Notes

Adjectives agree in number and gender with the nouns they modify. Notice that they generally follow the noun:

Masculine Singular	Masculine Plural
il violoncello nuovo the new cello	**i violoncelli nuovi** the new cellos

Feminine Singular	Feminine Plural
la chitarra nuova the new guitar	**le chitarre nuove** the new guitars

Note the following contractions:

a + l'   =   **all'una** / at one o'clock

a + le   =   **alle due** / at two o'clock

Finally, notice that as the next hour approaches, an alternative way of expressing the minutes is as follows: the next hour minus (**meno**) the number of minutes left to go.

8:58   =   **le otto e cinquantotto** or **le nove meno due**

EXERCISE Set 2–2

A. Choose the appropriate answer, **a** or **b,** to each question.

1. **Dov'è la chitarra?**
   a. **È in casa.**
   b. **È l'una precisa.**

2. **Che ore sono?**
   a. **Sono le ventiquattro meno cinque.**
   b. **È una radio.**

3. **Perché sei qui?**
   a. **Perché abito qui.**
   b. **Perché siete italiani.**

4. **Com'è la pasta?**
   a. **È molto buona** *(very good).*
   b. **È in casa.**

5. **Siete italiani?**
   a. **Sì, siamo italiani.**
   b. **Sì, sono italiani.**

6. **Sono americani?**
   a. **Sì, sono americano.**
   b. **Sì, sono americani.**

7. **Lei è italiano?**
   a. **Sì, sei italiano.**
   b. **Sì, sono italiano.**

8. **Quando è la lezione?**
   a. **Sono le quattro precise.**
   b. **È alle quattro precise.**

9. **Chi siete voi?**
   a. **Sono italiano.**
   b. **Siamo italiani.**

B. How do you say the following things in Italian?

buono	good	molto	very
in punto	on the dot	o	or
la mezzanotte	midnight	quarto	quarter
mezzo	half	secondo	second
il mezzogiorno	noon	il/la turista (m./f.)	tourist

1. Paul, what time is it? _____

2. It's twenty minutes to four. I'll see you soon. _____

3. The Italian class is at a quarter past seven. _____

4. Is it midnight or noon? _____

5. The pastries are very good. _____

6. Maria, are you sure? _____

7. Yes, it's really true, the class is at exactly one o'clock. _____

8. It's half past nine. No, it's ten on the dot. _____

9. Are you (pl., fam.) American (f.)? _____

10. They are American tourists (**turisti**). _____

Uses and Features

Among the many uses of **essere** (in addition to telling time), here are some of the more practical ones.

1. Indicating and referring to dates

> **È il quindici settembre.** / *It's September 15.*
>
> **È sabato.** / *It's Saturday.*

Note that the cardinal numbers are used for dates. The exception is the first day of every month, for which the ordinal number primo is used:

> **È il *primo* ottobre.** / *It's October 1.*
>
> **È il *primo* giugno.** / *It's June 1.*

Days of the Week		Months of the Year	
il giorno	day	**il mese**	month
la settimana	week	**l'anno**	year
lunedì	Monday	**gennaio**	January
martedì	Tuesday	**febbraio**	February
mercoledì	Wednesday	**marzo**	March
giovedì	Thursday	**aprile**	April
venerdì	Friday	**maggio**	May
sabato	Saturday	**giugno**	June
domenica	Sunday	**luglio**	July
		agosto	August
		settembre	September
		ottobre	October
		novembre	November
		dicembre	December

Notice also that the definite article is used with dates:

> **Il 1492 è un anno importante.** / *1492 is an important year.*
>
> **Oggi è *il* ventun settembre.** / *Today is September 21st.*

The formula *on Mondays, on Tuesdays*, etc. is rendered with the definite article:

> **il martedì** / *on Mondays*
>
> **la domenica** / *on Sundays*

(The days are masculine, except for **domenica**, which is feminine.)

2. To indicate origin or nationality

> **Di dove è Lei?** / *Where are you from?*
>
> ***Sono* di Milano.** / *I am from Milan.*
>
> **Noi *siamo* italiani.** / *We are Italian.*

A Few Nationalities			
africano	African	**italiano**	Italian
americano	American	**messicano**	Mexican
australiano	Australian	**olandese**	Dutch
canadese	Canadian	**spagnolo**	Spanish
cinese	Chinese	**svedese**	Swedish
francese	French	**svizzero**	Swiss
giapponese	Japanese	**tedesco**	German
inglese	English		

3. To describe something or someone

> **Mio fratello _è_ alto.** / _My brother is tall._
> **Mia sorella _è_ intelligente.** / _My sister is intelligent._

A Few Traits			
alto	_tall_	**intelligente**	_intelligent_
basso	_short_	**magro**	_skinny_
bello	_beautiful, handsome_	**piccolo**	_small_
buono	_good_	**povero**	_poor_
cattivo	_bad_	**ricco**	_rich_
giovane	_young_	**simpatico**	_nice, pleasant_
grande	_big_	**vecchio**	_old_
grasso	_fat_		

4. To indicate a job or a profession

> **Io sono un _avvocato_.** / _I am a lawyer._
> **Tu sei un _medico_, vero?** / _You're a doctor, aren't you?_

A Few Jobs and Professions			
l'avvocato	lawyer	**il (la) meccanico (-a)**	mechanic
il/la dentista (m./f.)	dentist	**il medico**	doctor
l'ingegnere (m./f.)	engineer	**il professore**	professor (m.)
l'insegnante (m./f.)	teacher	**la professoressa**	professor (f.)

Also useful for everyday conversation is the verb form **esserci** / *to be there*. It is used to acknowledge that something or someone is somewhere. It thus has only two forms:

Singular	Plural
C'è l'insegnante? Is the teacher here/there?	*Ci sono* gli insegnanti? Are the teachers here/there?

The form **ecco** is used instead to actually point out something or someone:

Singular	Plural
Ecco l'insegnante! Here / there is the teacher!	*Ecco* gli insegnanti! Here / there are the teachers!

Thus, you must be careful with the following confusingly similar structures!

Singular	Plural
Essere	
Che cosa *è*? What is it?	Che cosa *sono*? What are they?
È una macchina nuova. It's a new car.	*Sono* due macchine nuove. They are two new cars.
Esserci	
C'è Alessandro? Is Alexander there?	*Ci sono* Alessandro e Sarah? Are Alexander and Sarah there?
Sì, *c'è*. Yes, he is (there).	Sì, *ci sono*. Yes, they are (there).
Ecco	
Dov'è Alessandro? Where is Alexander?	Dove *sono* Alessandro e Sarah? Where are Alexander and Sarah?
Ecco Alessandro! Here's Alexander!	*Eccoli!* Here they are!

Prospettiva personale

Vero o falso? Indicate which of the following statements is true ("V") or false ("F") from your personal perspective.

_____ 1. **Il mio giorno preferito (preferred) è venerdì.**

_____ 2. **Il mio mese preferito è febbraio.**

_____ 3. **Io sono americano (-a).**

_____ 4. **Io sono alto (-a).**

_____ 5. **Io sono giovane.**

_____ 6. **Io sono ricco (-a).**

_____ 7. **Io sono un medico.**

_____ 8. **Io sono un ingegnere.**

_____ 9. **Mio fratello è vecchio.**

_____ 10. **Mia moglie è simpatica. / Mio marito è simpatico.**

_____ 11. **Il mio amico è piccolo.**

_____ 12. **La mia amica è grande.**

_____ 13. **Io non sono grasso (-a).**

_____ 14. **Il mio dentista è americano./La mia dentista è americana.**

_____ 15. **Il mio medico vive negli Stati Uniti.**

EXERCISE Set 2–3

A. Answer each question with the appropriate form of **essere**, **esserci**, or **ecco**.

EXAMPLE: **Dov'è Paolo?**
_____ (There is Paul!)
Ecco Paolo!

Stano-
they are here?

1. **C'è Paolo?** _no, non c'è Paolo_

2. **Dov'è Paolo?** _ecco Paolo_

3. **Siete italiani, vero?** _Noi siamo italiani_

4. **Ci sono Marco e Mario?** _Sì Marco e Mario sono qui_

5. **Dove sono Marco e Maria?** _Eccoli_

6. **Sei ricco (-a), non è vero?** _non sono ricca_

7. **È martedì oggi?** _no oggi è mercoledì_

8. **Dov'è Maria?** _Maria è in casa_

9. **C'è Maria?** _eccola_

10. **Loro sono australiani, non è vero?** _no, sono americani_

B. Can you guess what each one is?

EXAMPLE: **È il giorno dopo** (after) **lunedì.**
Il giorno dopo lunedì è martedì.

l'autunno	autumn, fall	**prima di**	before
come	like, as	**la primavera**	spring
come va?	how's it going?	**signora**	Mrs., Ms.
dopo	after	**signore**	Mr., Sir
l'estate (f.)	summer	**signorina**	Ms., Miss
importante	important	**gli Stati Uniti**	the United States
l'inverno	winter	**ultimo**	last

1. **È il giorno dopo mercoledì.** _Il giorno dopo mercoledì è giovedì_

2. **Sono gli ultimi due giorni della settimana.** _Gli ultimi giorni della settimana sono sabato e Domenica_

3. **È il giorno prima di sabato.** _Il giorno prima di sabato è venerdì_

4. **È il mese dopo gennaio.** _Il mese dopo gennaio è febbraio._

5. Sono i mesi della primavera negli Stati Uniti. _I mesi della primavera negli USA sono Marzo Aprile e maggio_

6. Sono i mesi dell'inverno negli Stati Uniti. _Dicembre, gennaio è febraio_

7. Sono i mesi dell'autunno negli Stati Uniti. _Setembre, ottobre, novembre_

8. Sono i mesi dell'estate negli Stati Uniti. _giugno luglio agosto_

Grammar Notes

Here are some more contractions summarized for you:

in + il = nel	in + i = nei
in + la = nella	in + le = nelle
in + l' = nell'	in + gli = negli
di + il = del	di + i = dei
di + la = della	di + le = delle
di + l' = dell'	di + gli = degli

With titles you use the article, unless you are talking directly to the person (drop the -e of **signore** before a name):

Ecco il signor Smith. /
Here's Mr. Smith.

C'è la signora Dini? /
Is Mrs. Dini here?

Buongiorno, signor Smith. /
Good day, Mr. Smith.

Come va, signora Dini? /
How's it going, Mrs. Dini?

C. How do you say the following things in Italian?

1. 1492 is an important year. _____

2. It's March 1. _____

3. It's December 4. _____

4. It's May 3. _____

5. On Wednesdays there's always Italian class. _____

6. Are there Italian classes on Sundays? _____

7. I am from Firenze, like my teacher (*m.*). _____

8. Where are you from, Mr. Sosa? Are you French, Spanish, or Canadian?

_____

9. Where's Mrs. Dini? _____

10. Are you African, Miss Hariri? And you're an engineer, aren't you?

_____

11. Marco and Maria, are you from Milan? _____

12. Maria is very intelligent. And she is not a bad professor. _____

13. I am also very skinny, like my dentist (*f.*) and my doctor (*m.*). _____

14. My sister is very beautiful. And she is not fat, like my lawyer (*m.*) or my mechanic (*m.*).

_____

15. My friends are tall and big, but poor. _____

16. He is German and she is Swiss. _____

17. My two friends (*f.*) are Dutch. _____

18. No, my husband is not Mexican; he's English. _____

19. My two friends (*m.*) are Japanese, not Chinese. _____

Conjugation of *Avere*

Like **essere**, **avere** / *to have* is an important irregular verb that you should learn to use thoroughly:

(io)	ho	I have
(tu)	hai	you (fam.) have
(lui/lei/Lei)	ha	he, she, you (pol.) has/have
(noi)	abbiamo	we have
(voi)	avete	you have
(loro)	hanno	they have

Note that the "h" is not pronounced. It is only written and can be compared to the "silent h" of English *hour*.

Useful Idiomatic Expressions

avere bisogno (di)	to need
avere caldo	to be hot
avere fame	to be hungry
avere freddo	to be cold
avere fretta	to be in a hurry
avere paura	to be afraid
avere pazienza	to be patient, to have patience
avere ragione	to be right
avere sete	to be thirsty
avere sonno	to be sleepy
avere torto	to be wrong
avere vergogna	to be ashamed
avere voglia (di)	to feel like

TIP

When using **molto** / *much, a lot or* **poco** / *little with such expressions make sure you treat them as adjectives. They must agree with the gender of the noun:*

Ho *molta* **fame.** / I am very hungry (**la fame** = feminine).

Ha *molto* **sonno.** / He/she is very sleepy (**il sonno** = masculine).

Abbiamo *poca* **voglia di uscire.** / We have *little* desire to go out (**la voglia** = feminine).

Prospettiva personale

Vero o falso? Indicate which of the following statements is true ("V") or false ("F") from your personal perspective.

_____ 1. **Io ho poca pazienza.**

_____ 2. **Mia moglie / Mio marito ha sempre molto caldo.**

_____ 3. **Io non ho sempre ragione.**

_____ 4. **Io ho sempre sonno.**

_____ 5. **Il mio amico/la mia amica ha sempre molta fretta.**

_____ 6. **Io non ho vergogna di niente.**

_____ 7. **Mio fratello / mia sorella ha sempre freddo.**

_____ 8. **Io non ho paura di niente.**

_____ 9. **Io ho bisogno di una nuova macchina.**

EXERCISE Set 2–4

A. Supply the missing form of the verb **avere**, giving the English equivalent.

EXAMPLE:	lui ____	=	_____
	lui ha	=	_he has_

1. **io** ____	=	_____	
2. **tu** ____	=	_____	
3. **io e Maria** ____	=	_____	
4. **tu e Marco** ____	=	_____	
5. **Lei** ____	=	_____	
6. **il signor Smith** ____	=	_____	
7. **le mie amiche** ____	=	_____	
8. **noi** ____	=	_____	
9. **voi** ____	=	_____	

B. Put the appropriate form of **avere** in the blanks.

la cognata	sister-in-law	il/la nipote (m./f.)	nephew, grandchild
il cognato	brother-in-law	il padre	father
il cugino/la cugina	cousin	lo psicologo	psychologist
la famiglia	family	lo studente	student
lo gnocco	dumpling	tutti/e	everyone
la madre	mother	la zia/lo zio	aunt, uncle

1. **Anch'io** _____ **bisogno di una nuova macchina.**

2. **Mia sorella e mia madre** _____ **sempre voglia di guardare la televisione.**

3. **Mia cognata** _____ **sempre molto caldo.**

4. **I miei cugini non** _____ **vergogna di niente.**

5. **Loro** _____ **molta fame. Preferiscono gli gnocchi.**

6. **Lo zio di mia moglie** _____ **molta pazienza.**

7. **Mia zia e mio padre** _____ **sempre ragione.**

8. **Gli studenti** _____ **paura del professor Marchi!**

9. **Nella mia famiglia, tutti _____ sempre molta fretta.**

10. **Io _____ fame e mio cognato _____ sete.**

11. **Mio nipote _____ sempre ragione. È un avvocato.**

12. **_____ torto anche voi, non è vero?**

13. **Oggi noi _____ molto caldo.**

14. **Maria, perché _____ sempre fretta?**

15. **Anche tu _____ sonno?**

Grammar Note

The form of the definite article before a masculine noun beginning with **z**, **s** plus a consonant, **gn**, or **ps** is **lo** (plural **gli**). The corresponding indefinite article form is **uno**:

lo zio / *the uncle*	*uno* zio / *an uncle*
lo studente / *the student*	*uno* studente / *a student*
lo psicologo / *the psychologist*	*uno* psicologo / *a psychologist*
gli zii / *the uncles*	*gli* gnocchi / *the dumplings*
gli studenti / *the students*	*gli* psicologi / *the psychologists*

Uses and Features

In addition to the idiomatic expressions you have learned so far, two other common uses of **avere** are as follows:

1. To indicate age

Quanti anni *hai*? / *How old are you?* (literally: *How many years do you have?*)
***Ho* trentasei anni.** / *I am 36 years old.* (literally: *I have 36 years.*)

Note that the verb *to be* is used in English, whereas **avere** is used in Italian. Thus, when asking someone's age in Italian, you will literally be asking him or her "how many years he or she has."

2. To indicate possession

***Ho* molti amici.** / *I have many friends.*
Anche tu *hai* una nuova FIAT, vero? / *You also have a new FIAT, don't you?*

Prospettiva personale

Answer the questions on page 34 about yourself and your family in Italian.

EXAMPLE: **Quanti anni hai?**
                        Ho venticinque/trentasei . . . anni.

Grammar Note

Note the forms of the possessive "your" (fam., sing.):

Masculine Singular	Masculine Plural
il tuo amico your friend (m.)	**i tuoi amici** your friends (m.)

Feminine Singular	Feminine Plural
la tua amica your friend (f.)	**le tue amiche** your friends (f.)

Again, do not forget to drop the article in front of a singular, unmodified kinship noun:

tuo cugino / *your cousin*   **tua zia** / *your aunt*

1. **Quanti anni hai?** _____

2. **Che macchina hai?** (*What car do you have?*) _____

3. **Quanti anni hanno tuo padre e tua madre?** _____

4. **Quanti anni hanno i tuoi cugini?** _____

5. **Quanti anni hanno i tuoi zii?** _____

6. **Tu hai molta pazienza?** _____

7. **Chi ha sempre ragione nella tua famiglia?** _____

EXERCISE Set 2–5

Grammar Note

Note that adjectives ending in **-e**, such as **intelligente**, have only one form in the singular (**-e**) and one in the plural (**-i**), no matter what the gender of the noun is:

Singular	Plural
l'amico intelligente **l'amica intelligente**	**gli amici intelligenti** **le amiche intelligenti**

A. Missing from each of the following sentences is **essere**, **esserci**, or **avere**. Put each verb, in its correct form, in each sentence.

1. **Mio zio** _____ **molti anni.**

2. **Mio zio** _____ **molto simpatico.**

3. _____ **anche mio zio a casa tua, vero?**

4. _____ **le nove e mezzo.**

5. **Noi** _____ **di Firenze.**

6. **Anche voi** _____ **molto alti.**

7. **Ma voi non** _____ **molta pazienza.**

8. **Mia zia** _____ **un medico.**

9. _____ **un medico qui?**

10. **Domani** _____ **il quindici settembre, vero?**

11. **Signor Marchi, perché** _____ **paura?**

12. **Marco e Maria, quanti amici** _____ **?**

B. Write an e-mail in Italian! Here's what to say in it.

ambizioso	ambitious	occupato	busy
ancora	yet, still	purtroppo	unfortunately
caro	dear	telefonare	to phone
forse	maybe	il tempo	time

strong feeling
sfortunatamente

Dear Maria:

How's it going? How old are you now? And how old are your brother and your sister? I am now a doctor. Are you a psychologist yet? What car do you now have? Are you still very nice? You are certainly intelligent!

I feel like phoning. Unfortunately, I have always little time. I am always very busy. Maybe, one day!

You are right, I am too ambitious and I have little time for my friends.

Bye!

grazie per le tue complimenti

Francesca

Cara amica

dò ho

Tutto va bene qui. hai settanuno anni
Il mio fratello é sessanta tre anni
Il mio fratello più grande sfortunatamente è morto.
Sono un'infermiera e pensione.
Forse domani io telefonare a te.
Ho una machina, bella si ciama Montego.
Purtroppo, neanche io ho troppo tempo ancora.
Hai ragione e io sono troppo occupata per le
amica mia

Vorrei - Do you want. Telefono

Tu hai ragione. Io sono troppo
ambigiosa e ho poco tempo per
miei amici

Crossword Puzzle 2

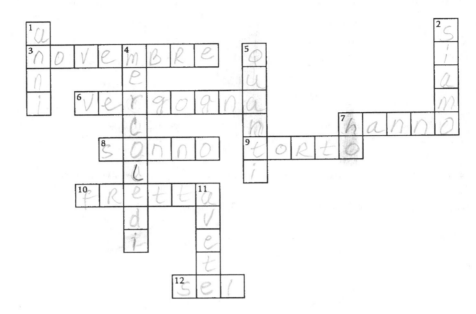

Orizzontali

3. È il mese prima di dicembre.
6. Lui non ha . . . di niente. *vergogna*
7. I tuoi amici non . . . paura. *hanno*
8. Marco, hai . . . ? *sonno*
9. Voi avete sempre ragione o . . . ? *torto (wrong)*
10. Perché hai sempre . . . ? *fretta (in a hurry)*
12. Maria, . . . molto simpatica! *sei*

Verticali

1. Quanti . . . hai, Teresa? *anni*
2. Anche noi . . . americani. *siamo*
4. È il giorno dopo martedì. *Mercoledi*
5. . . . anni ha, signora Smith?
11. Anche voi . . . molta pazienza. *avete*

3
Sapere & Conoscere

Conjugation of *Sapere* and *Conoscere*

The verb **sapere** / *to know* is an important and often-used irregular verb in the present indicative. It is conjugated as follows:

(io)	**so**	I know, I do know
(tu)	**sai**	you (fam.) know, you do know
(lui/lei/Lei)	**sa**	he, she, you (pol.) knows/know, he, she, you does/do know
(noi)	**sappiamo**	we know, we do know
(voi)	**sapete**	you know, you do know
(loro)	**sanno**	they know, they do know

There is another verb in Italian meaning *to know*: **conoscere**. It is a regular second-conjugation verb:

(io)	**conosco**	I know, I do know, I am familiar with
(tu)	**conosci**	you (fam.) know, you do know, you are familiar with
(lui/lei/Lei)	**conosce**	he, she, you (pol.) knows/know, he, she, you does/do know, he, she, you is/are familiar with
(noi)	**conosciamo**	we know, we do know, we are familiar with
(voi)	**conoscete**	you know, you do know, you are familiar with
(loro)	**conoscono**	they know, they do know, they are familiar with

The main differences between **sapere** and **conoscere** can be summarized, for now, as follows:

1. **sapere** means essentially *to know something* (information, ideas, etc.) or *how to do something* (to speak Italian, to swim, etc.):

   ***So** tante cose anch'io.* / *I also know many things.*

   *Gina, **sai** parlare lo spagnolo?* / *Gina, do you know how to speak Spanish?*

2. **conoscere** means, instead, *to know someone* or *to be familiar with something*:

   ***Conosco** Gina molto bene.* / *I know Gina quite well.*

   *Non **conosciamo** questo ristorante.* / *We are not familiar with this restaurant.*

Prospettiva personale

Vero o falso? Indicate which of the following statements is true ("V") or false ("F") from your personal perspective.

   F 1. **Io so parlare l'italiano molto bene.**

   F 2. **Mio fratello/mia sorella sa parlare l'italiano meglio di me** (better than I/me).

   V 3. **Io conosco molte persone** (persons).

   V 4. **Io conosco molti ristoranti italiani buoni.**

_F___ 5. **Nella mia famiglia tutti sanno parlare l'italiano.**

_V___ 6. **La mia famiglia conosce tanta gente** (people).

_V___ 7. **Io so suonare il pianoforte.**

_V___ 8. **Io conosco un bravo** (good) **insegnante d'italiano.**

EXERCISE Set 3–1

A. Supply the missing present indicative form of the verb **sapere**, giving the English equivalent. Finally, make up any sentence freely with each form.

EXAMPLE: **lui _____**   =   _____
              lui sa   =   he knows
              Lui sa tante cose./Lui sa parlare italiano./...

bene	well	**nessuno**	no one, nobody
bravo	good	**il numero**	number
la città	city	**la persona**	person
la cosa	thing	**il ristorante**	restaurant
di me	than I/me	**tanto**	much, a lot
la gente	people	**il telefono**	phone
l'indirizzo	address	**la via**	street
meglio	better		

1. **noi** _Sapiamo_ = _we know nessuno_
   _____

2. **voi** _Sapete_ = _you know tanto_
   _____

3. **io** _So_ = _I know_
   _____

4. **tu** _Sai_ = _____
   _____

5. **Lei** _Sa_ = _____
   _____

6. **mio zio** _Sa_ = _My uncle knows the city_
   _____

7. **i tuoi cugini** ____ = _Sanno_
   _____

8. **io e tu** _Sappiamo_ = _____ _you and I_
   _____

9. **tu e lui** _Sapete_ = _____ _you and he_
   _____

Now, supply the missing present indicative form of the verb **conoscere**, giving the English equivalent. Like above, make up any sentence freely with each form.

EXAMPLE: **lui** ____   =   _____
            lui conosce   he knows, he is familiar with
            Lui conosce molta gente./Lui conosce un ristorante italiano./...

10. **io** _Conosco_ = _____

_____

11. **tu** _Conosci_ = _____

_____

12. **noi** _Conosciamo_ ___=___ _____

_____

13. **voi** _Conoscete_ =____ _____

_____

14. **Lei** _Conosce_ = _____

_____

15. **tuo cognato** _conosce_ ____ = _____

_____

16. **le tue sorelle** ____ _Conoscono_ = _____

_____

17. **tu e lei** ____ _Conoscete_ = _____

_____

18. **tu e io** ____ _Conosciamo_ = _____

_____

B. Choose the appropriate verb form, **a** or **b**, according to the sense.

1. **Mio cugino ... parlare spagnolo molto bene.**
    a. **sa**
    b. **conosce**

2. **Io non ... tanta gente in questa città** (this city).
    a. **so**
    b. **conosco**

3. **Signor Marchi, Lei ... dov'è via Nazionale** (National Street)**?**
    a. **sa**
    b. **conosce**

4. **Noi ... un buon ristorante in via Nazionale** (a good restaurant on National Street).
    a. **sappiamo**
    b. **conosciamo**

5. **Loro non ... il mio indirizzo di casa** (house address).
    a. **sanno**
    b. **conoscono**

6. **Voi ... il mio numero di telefono** (phone number)**?**
    a. **sapete**
    b. **conoscete**

7. **Tu ... mio fratello?**
    a. **sai**
    b. **conosci**

8. **Chi ... la città di Firenze?**
    a. **sa**
    b. **conosce**

9. **Io non ... nessuno in questa città** (in this city).
    a. **so**
    b. **conosco**

Illustrative Dialogue

l'appuntamento	appointment, date	**il ragazzo**	young male, boy
con	with	**la ragazza**	young female, girl
il divertimento	enjoyment, fun	**vicino a**	near
il lavoro	work		

Sorella:	**Bruno, tu *conosci* un buon ristorante in questa città? Ho un appuntamento importante con un ragazzo.**	Bruno, do you know a good restaurant in this city? I have an important date with a young man.
Fratello:	**Sì, c'è un buon ristorante vicino in via Garibaldi. *Sai* dov'è, no?**	Yes, there's a good restaurant near Garibaldi Street. You know where it is, don't you?
Sorella:	**Sì, grazie.**	Yes, thanks.
Fratello:	**Con chi hai un appuntamento?**	With whom do you have a date?
Sorella:	***Conosci* Claudio?**	Do you know Claudio?
Fratello:	**No, chi è?**	No, who is he?
Sorella:	**È un amico di lavoro. Lui *conosce* tutti i miei amici. Ciao!**	He's a friend from work. He knows all my friends. Bye!
Fratello:	**Buon divertimento!**	Have fun!

Grammar Notes

Note the forms of the possessive adjective quesfo:

Masculine Singular	Masculine Plural
questo ragazzo this boy	questi ragazzi these boys

Feminine Singular	Feminine Plural
questa ragazza this girl	queste ragazze these girls

The form **quest'** is often used before words beginning with a vowel:

quest'amico	quest'amica
this friend (m.)	this friend (f.)

The adjective **buono** can be used before or after the noun it modifies. If it is put after, then its endings change in the usual fashion. If it is put before, then its singular forms undergo the same kinds of changes that the indefinite article does:

Masculine Singular	Masculine Plural
un buon lavoro a good job	**buoni lavori** good jobs
un buon amico a good friend	**buoni amici** good friends
un buono zio a good uncle	**buoni zii** good uncles

Feminine Singular	Feminine Plural
una buona pasta a good pastry	**buone paste** good pastries
una buon'amica a good friend	**buone amiche** good friends

EXERCISE Set 3–2

How do you say the following things in Italian?

1. Giovanni, do you know a good restaurant in this city?

_____

2. Mr. Smith, do you know my address and phone number?

_____

3. They know a lot of things and they also know a lot of people.

_____

4. Your sister knows how to speak Italian better than me.

_____

5. My Italian teacher is very good. She also knows how to speak English very well.

_____

6. Maria is a good friend. Does your brother know Maria?

_____

7. We don't know the restaurant. But we know where it is. It is near Nazionale Street.

_____

8. My brother knows how to play the cello very well.

_____

9. All my friends know your sister. She knows many things.

_____

Uses and Features

The main uses and features of the verbs **sapere** and **conoscere** can be summarized as follows.

Sapere is used

1. to indicate that you or others *know something:*
   Marco *sa* il tuo indirizzo. / *Marco knows your address.*
   Io non *so* il tuo nome. / *I don't know your name.*
   Noi non *sappiamo* perché tu sei triste. / *We don't know why you are sad.*

2. to indicate that you or others *know that…*
   ***So* che lui è felice.** / *I know that he is happy.*
   Loro non *sanno* che io sono qui. / *They do not know that I am here.*

3. to indicate that you or others *know how to do something* (which means that **sapere** is followed by the infinitive):
   Alessandro *sa* suonare il pianoforte. / *Alexander knows how to play the piano.*
   Io non *so* scrivere in italiano. / *I do not know how to write in Italian.*

Conoscere is used

1. to indicate that you or others *know someone:*
   Claudia, *conosci* un buon medico? / *Claudia, do you know a good doctor?*
   Noi non *conosciamo* questa persona. / *We do not know this person.*

2. to indicate that you or others are *familiar with something (such as a place):*
   ***Conosci* Roma?** / *Are you familiar with Rome?*
   ***Conosco* un ristorante qui vicino.** / *I know a restaurant near here.*

TIP
As a rule of thumb, use **conoscere** *when referring to people and* **sapere** *to things, unless* familiarity *is implied.*

EXERCISE Set 3–3

certamente	certainly	**il/la parente**	relative
che	that, which	**la parola**	word
felice	happy	**quanto**	how
il genitore	parent	**solo**	only
nome	name	**triste**	sad

A. Missing from each of the following sentences is **sapere** or **conoscere**. Put each verb, in its correct form, in each sentence according to the sense.

1. Io non _____ la città di Pisa.

2. I miei parenti _____ solo qualche parola in italiano.

3. Nessuno _____ che io parlo francese molto bene.

4. Anche voi _____ suonare la chitarra, non è vero?

5. I tuoi genitori non _____ il mio nome.

6. Maria, io non _____ perché tu sei sempre triste.

7. È vero che tu _____ Paolo?

8. Chi _____ via Nazionale?

9. Chi _____ dov'è via Nazionale?

B. Each question is given to you in a familiar form (singular or plural). Change each one to its corresponding polite form.

EXAMPLE: **Tu sai di dove sono io?**
             Lei sa di dove sono io?

1.   **Tu sai il nome di quella** *(that)* **persona?**

     _____

2.   **Voi conoscete un buon ristorante in questa città?**

     _____

3.   **Anche tu sai suonare il pianoforte, vero?**

     _____

4.   **Conoscete i genitori di quella persona?**

     _____

5.   **Sai il mio indirizzo?**

     _____

6.   **Conosci l'insegnante d'italiano?**

     _____

7.   **Sapete chi sono io?**

     _____

Crossword Puzzle 3

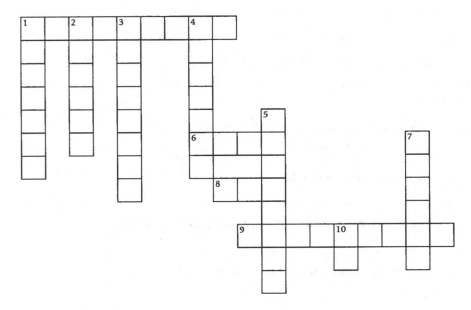

Orizzontali

1. **Loro non … questa città molto bene.**

6. **Non so il tuo ….**

8. **Alessandro, … dov'è un buon ristorante?**

9. **Voi … i miei amici, no?**

Verticali

1. **Claudia, tu … la mia amica?**

2. **Forse lui non sa il … di telefono.**

3. **Noi … che loro arrivano domani.**

4. **… sa che io vivo qui.**

5. **I miei … sanno tante cose.**

7. **Anche voi … suonare il pianoforte, vero?**

10. **Lei … tutto!**

4
Piacere

Conjugation of *Piacere*

The verb **piacere** / *to be pleasing to, to like* is another important and very common irregular verb. Its present indicative forms are given below:

(io)	**piaccio (a)**	I am pleasing to
(tu)	**piaci (a)**	you (fam.) are pleasing to
(lui/lei/Lei)	**piace (a)**	he, she, you (pol.) is/are pleasing to
(noi)	**piacciamo (a)**	we are pleasing to
(voi)	**piacete (a)**	you are pleasing to
(loro)	**piacciono (a)**	they are pleasing to

This verb allows you to express what you *like* in Italian. But it is a tricky verb because it really means *to be pleasing to*:

1. In order to use it appropriately, you will first need to know the indirect object pronouns *to me, to you,* etc.:

Singular		Plural	
1st person	**mi** / *to me*	1st person	**ci** / *to us*
2nd person	**ti**/ *to you* (fam.)	2nd person	**vi** / *to you* (fam. and in general)
3rd person	**gli** / *to him* **le** / *to her* **Le** / *to you* (pol.)	3rd person	**gli** / *to them*

2. The best initial learning strategy is to rephrase the English expression in your mind as shown below. Notice that object pronouns precede the verb:

English Expression	Rephrase to	Italian Expression
↓	↓	↓
I like that book	"To me is pleasing that book"	**Mi piace quel libro**
We like those books	"To us are pleasing those books"	**Ci piacciono quei libri**

3. If the object is not a pronoun, use the preposition **a** before it:

English Expression	Rephrase to	Italian Expression
↓	↓	↓
John likes Mary	"Mary is pleasing to John"	**Maria piace a Giovanni**
My friends like your teacher	"Your teacher is pleasing to my friends"	**Il tuo/La tua insegnante piace ai miei amici**
Mary likes me	"I am pleasing to Mary"	**Io piaccio a Maria**

Grammar Note

The forms of **quello** / *that* are like those of the definite article. Here they are:

Masculine Forms

Singular   Plural

Before z, s plus consonant, gn, and ps:

quello   **quegli**
quello zio / *that uncle*   **quegli zii** / *those uncles*
quello spagnolo / *that Spaniard*   **quegli spagnoli** / *those Spaniards*

Before all other consonants:

quel   **quei**
quel medico / *that doctor*   **quei medici** / *those doctors*
quel libro / *that book*   **quei libri** / *those books*

Before any vowel:

quell'   **quegli**
quell'amico / *that friend*   **quegli amici** / *those friends*

Feminine Forms

Singular   Plural

Before all consonants:

quella   **quelle**
quella ragazza / *that girl*   **quelle ragazze** / *those girls*
quella zia / *that aunt*   **quelle zie** / *those aunts*

Before any vowel:

quell'   **quelle**
quell'amica / *that friend*   **quelle amiche** / *those friends*

EXERCISE Set 4-1

A. Rephrase each sentence as shown, and then give its Italian equivalent.

EXAMPLE: I like the book.
                "The book is pleasing to me" → *Il libro mi piace./Mi piace il libro.*

il cinema	cinema	**la moda**	fashion
il film (i film)	movie, film (movies)	**la musica**	music
il formaggio	cheese	**la rivista**	magazine
la frutta	fruit	**la verdura**	vegetables, greens
il giornale	newspaper	**gli spaghetti**	spaghetti
il libro	book		

1. I like Maria.

   _____

2. Maria likes me.

   _____

3. You *(fam., sing.)* like those books.

   _____

4. Those girls like you *(fam., sing.)*.

   _____

5. She likes that boy.

   _____

6. That boy likes her.

   _____

7. My parents like that restaurant.

   _____

8. We like cheese.

   _____

9. They like us.

   _____

10. He likes fruit.

    _____

11. She likes him.

    _____

12. You *(pl.)* like that newspaper.

    _____

13. My parents like you *(pl.)*.

    _____

14. They like those magazines.

    _____

15. I like them.

    _____

B. Do the following: (1) give the missing form of **piacere**, (2) translate the sentence into English, and (3) provide an alternative form of the sentence in Italian.

EXAMPLE: **Io ... a lei.**

(1) *piaccio*
(2) She likes me ("I am pleasing to her").
(3) *Io le piaccio.*

Grammar Note

Note the following pronoun equivalents:

	Unstressed Forms (above)	**Stressed Forms**
to me	**mi**	**a me**
to you (fam., sing.)	**ti**	**a te**
to him	**gli**	**a lui**
to her	**le**	**a lei**
to you (pol., sing.)	**Le**	**a Lei**
to us	**ci**	**a noi**
to you (pl.)	**vi**	**a voi**
to them	**gli**	**a loro**

1. **Tu ... a me.**

    (1) _____

    (2) _____

    (3) _____

2. **Io ... a te.**

    (1) _____

    (2) _____

    (3) _____

3. **Lei ... a noi.**

    (1) _____

    (2) _____

    (3) _____

4. **Noi ... a lei.**

    (1) _____

    (2) _____

    (3) _____

5. **Lei ... a noi.**

    (1) _____

    (2) _____

    (3) _____

6. **Voi ... a lui.**

    (1) _____

    (2) _____

    (3) _____

7. **Lui ... a voi.**

    (1) _____

    (2) _____

    (3) _____

8. **Loro ... a me.**

    (1) _____

    (2) _____

    (3) _____

9. **Io ... a loro.**

    (1) _____

    (2) _____

    (3) _____

Prospettiva personale

Vero o falso? Indicate whether the following things are true ("V") or false ("F") from your personal perspective.

A me...

____ 1. **mi piace il cinema.**

____ 2. **mi piacciono i film di Spielberg.**

____ 3. **mi piace suonare il pianoforte.**

____ 4. **mi piacciono gli gnocchi.**

A tua sorella/A tuo fratello...

____ 5. **le/gli piace la televisione.**

____ 6. **le/gli piacciono gli spaghetti.**

____ 7. **le/gli piace la musica di Beethoven.**

____ 8. **le/gli piacciono le riviste di moda.**

Ai tuoi genitori...

____ 9. **gli piace il film *Cinema paradiso*.**

___ 10. **gli piacciono i film italiani.**

___ 11. **gli piace la musica italiana.**

___ 12. **gli piacciono i formaggi italiani.**

Rule of Thumb

As you can see, **piacere** can be very confusing for anyone accustomed to the English verb *to like*. The following rule of thumb might help you use this important verb more readily.

Since the verb is often used with indirect object pronouns, just think of the pronouns as subjects; then make the verb agree with the predicate.

Mi   piace   quella   rivista.
↓   ↓   ↓   ↓
I   like   that   magazine.
("That magazine is pleasing to me.")

Ti   piacciono   quelle   riviste.
↓   ↓   ↓   ↓
You   like   those   magazines.
("Those magazines are pleasing to you.")

Gli   piace   quella   rivista.
↓   ↓   ↓   ↓
He   likes   that   magazine.
("That magazine is pleasing to him.")

Le   piacciono   quelle   riviste.
↓   ↓   ↓   ↓
She   likes   those   magazines.
("Those magazines are pleasing to her.")

Ci   piace   la   frutta.
↓   ↓   ↓   ↓
We   like   (the)   fruit.
("Fruit is pleasing to us.")

Vi   piacciono   i   formaggi italiani.
↓   ↓   ↓   ↓
You   like   (the)   Italian cheeses.
("Italian cheeses are pleasing to you.")

Gli   piace   la   verdura.
↓   ↓   ↓   ↓
They   like   (the)   vegetables.
("Vegetables are pleasing to them.")

Remember that this is merely a rule of thumb. If you are unsure, you must go through the process described above.

EXERCISE Set 4–2

Say the following things in Italian, as indicated.

EXAMPLES: I like that book.
Mi piace quel libro.

They like those books.
Gli piacciono quei libri.

I like…

1. Beethoven's music

   _____

2. spaghetti

   _____

You (fam., sing.) like…

3. that movie

   _____

4. those magazines

   _____

You (pol., sing.) like…

5. my friend (m.)

   _____

6. my friends (m.)

   _____

He likes…

7. your car

   _____

   8. those cars

   _____

She likes…

   9. that book

   _____

   10. those books

   _____

We like…

   11. that newspaper

   _____

   12. those persons

   _____

You (pl.) like…

   13. my friend (f.)

   _____

   14. my friends (f.)

   _____

They like…

   15. that new magazine

   _____

   16. those new magazines

   _____

Illustrative Dialogue

Claudia:	**Franco, ti *piace* il nuovo film di Giuseppe Tornatore?**	Franco, do you like the new film by Giuseppe Tornatore?
Franco:	**Sì, mi *piace* molto. E a te?**	Yes, I like it a lot. And you?
Claudia:	**A me *non* mi *piace* affatto!**	I don't like it at all!
Franco:	***Mi dispiace!* Perché non ti *piace*?**	Sorry to hear it. Why don't you like it?
Claudia:	**Non lo so, ma non *piace* neanche alle mie amiche.**	I don't know, but my friends also do not like it.
Franco:	**Quali film nuovi ti *piacciono*?**	Which new movies do you like?
Claudia:	**In questo momento *non* mi *piace* nessun film nuovo!**	Right now (at this moment) I do not like any new movie!
Franco:	**Capisco!**	I understand!

Grammar Note

Note the following negatives:

non...mai / *never*
non...nessuno / *no one*
non...niente, nulla / *nothing*
non...più / *no more, no longer*
non...neanche, nemmeno, neppure / *not even*
non...né...né / *neither...nor*
non...mica / *not really, quite*

EXERCISE Set 4-3

Say the following things in Italian.

1. I never like to play the piano.

   _____

2. They like no one in this city.

   _____

3. I don't like that movie at all.

   _____

4. I am sorry. But I know that she is not sorry.

   _____

5. Right now, I don't like any new movie.

   _____

6. We're sorry.

   _____

7. We don't like cheese any longer.

   _____

8. You (fam., sing.) don't really like that new book, do you?

   _____

9. I like neither that new book nor that new movie.

   _____

10. She doesn't even like my new car.

    _____

Summary

As mentioned above, in order to use the verb **piacere** correctly, you must always think of what it really means:

I like that movie

Mi	**piace**	**quel film.**
↓	↓	↓
To me	*is pleasing*	*that film.*

I like those movies

Mi	**piacciono**	**quei film.**
↓	↓	↓
To me	*are pleasing*	*those films.*

If you think this way, you will always be correct. Notice the preferred word order:

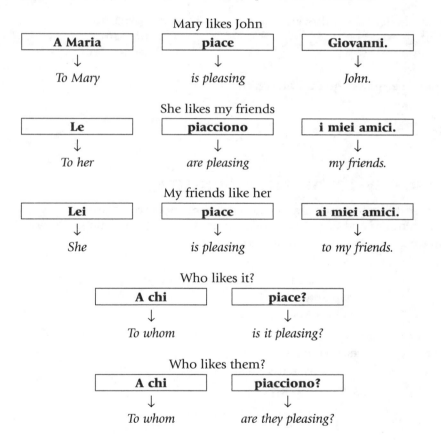

Mary likes John

A Maria	**piace**	**Giovanni.**
↓	↓	↓
To Mary	*is pleasing*	*John.*

She likes my friends

Le	**piacciono**	**i miei amici.**
↓	↓	↓
To her	*are pleasing*	*my friends.*

My friends like her

Lei	**piace**	**ai miei amici.**
↓	↓	↓
She	*is pleasing*	*to my friends.*

Who likes it?

A chi	**piace?**
↓	↓
To whom	*is it pleasing?*

Who likes them?

A chi	**piacciono?**
↓	↓
To whom	*are they pleasing?*

EXERCISE Set 4–4

Choose the appropriate answer, **a** or **b**, to each question.

1. **Marco, ti piace il formaggio italiano?**
   a. **Sì, mi piace molto.**
   b. **Sì, mi piacciono molto.**

2. **Piacete anche a loro?**
   a. **Sì, gli piacciamo.**
   b. **Sì, gli piacete.**

3. **Piacciamo a te?**
   a. **Sì, mi piacete.**
   b. **Sì, mi piacciono.**

4. **A chi piace la musica di Beethoven?**
   a. **Piace a noi.**
   b. **Piacete a noi.**

5. **Signora Dini, Le piace quella macchina nuova?**
   a. **Sì, mi piace.**
   b. **Sì, Le piace.**

6. **Quale macchina vi piace?**
   a. **Vi piace quella macchina.**
   b. **Ci piace quella macchina.**

7. **Tu piaci ai genitori di Paolo?**
   a. **Sì, loro mi piacciono.**
   b. **Sì, io gli piaccio.**

8. **Ti piacciono i genitori di Paolo?**
   a. **No, non gli piaccio.**
   b. **No, non mi piacciono.**

9. **A chi piaci tu?**
   a. **Ti piaccio.**
   b. **Piaccio a lei.**

Other Verbs with Similar Features

The following verbs exhibit the same "grammatical behavior" of **piacere**—that is, they require frequent usage of indirect object pronouns and they have to be rephrased mentally in analogous ways:

affascinare	to fascinate, to be fascinated by
apparire	to appear
bastare	to be sufficient, to suffice, to be enough
dolere	to be painful, to ache
importare	to be important, to matter
interessare	to interest, to be interested by
mancare	to lack, to miss
rimanere	to be left over, to remain
sembrare	to seem

Of these, the following are irregular in the present indicative:

apparire

(io)	appaio	I appear
(tu)	appari	you (fam.) appear
(lui/lei/Lei)	appare	he, she, you (pol.) appear(s)
(noi)	appaiamo	we appear
(voi)	apparite	you appear
(loro)	appaiono	they appear

dolere

(io)	**dolgo**	I suffer
(tu)	**duoli**	you (fam.) suffer
(lui/lei/Lei)	**duole**	he, she, you (pol.) suffer(s)
(noi)	**dogliamo**	we suffer
(voi)	**dolete**	you suffer
(loro)	**dolgono**	they suffer

rimanere

(io)	**rimango**	I remain
(tu)	**rimani**	you (fam.) remain
(lui/lei/Lei)	**rimane**	he, she, you (pol.) remain(s)
(noi)	**rimaniamo**	we remain
(voi)	**rimanete**	you remain
(loro)	**rimangono**	they remain

The best initial learning strategy is, once again, to rephrase the English expression in your mind:

English Expression	Rephrase to	Italian Expression
↓	↓	↓
I am fascinated by that book	"That book is fascinating to me"	**Quel libro mi affascina**
There are two days left	"Two days are lacking"	**Mancano due giorni**
We miss you	"You are lacking to us"	**Tu ci manchi**

Prospettiva personale

Answer each question with **sì** or **no** from your personal perspective:

la festa	holiday, feast, party	**lo sport**	sport
l'osso (le ossa)	bone (bones)	**studiare**	to study
i soldi	money	**ultimo**	last
spesso	often		

_____ 1. Ti affascinano gli sport?

_____ 2. Al tuo amico/alla tua amica appaiono interessanti i film italiani?

_____ 3. Alla tua famiglia basta una macchina?

_____ 4. Ti dolgono spesso le ossa?

_____ 5. Per te, importano le feste?

_____ 6. Alla tua famiglia interessa parlare l'italiano?

_____ 7. Ti mancano soldi in questo momento?

_____ 8. Ti sembra importante studiare molto?

EXERCISE Set 4–5

Say the following things in Italian.

1.   Does that restaurant seem good?

_____

2.   The last thing left is to write to Maria.

_____

3.   That movie doesn't interest me at all.

_____

4.   The spaghetti is enough for me.

_____

5.   My bones are aching.

_____

6.   Those things matter a lot.

_____

7.   Do you (fam., sing.) miss me?

_____

Crossword Puzzle 4

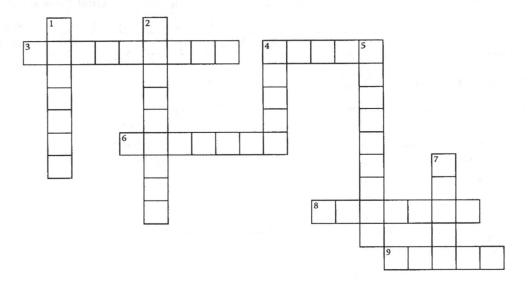

Orizzontali

3. **Ti … gli spaghetti?**
4. **Tu … anche a me.**
6. **Voi … ai miei genitori.**
8. **Non gli … gli spaghetti. Ha molta fame.**
9. **Ti … quel libro?**

Verticali

1. **Io … alla tua amica.**
2. **Noi … ai tuoi amici.**
4. **Gli … la frutta.**
5. **Il cinema non mi … affatto!**
7. **Lei mi … molto.**

5
Common Irregular Verbs

Conjugation and Uses of *Bere, Dare, Dire, Fare*

The verbs **bere**, **dare**, **dire**, and **fare** are common irregular verbs. Here are their forms in the present indicative:

bere / *to drink*

(io)	bevo	I drink, I am drinking, I do drink
(tu)	bevi	you (fam.) drink, you are drinking, you do drink
(lui/lei/Lei)	beve	he, she, you (pol.) drink(s), he, she, you is/are drinking, he, she, you does/do drink
(noi)	beviamo	we drink, we are drinking, we do drink
(voi)	bevete	you drink, you are drinking, you do drink
(loro)	bevono	they drink, they are drinking, they do drink

dare / *to give*

(io)	do	I give, I am giving, I do give
(tu)	dai	you (fam.) give, you are giving, you do give
(lui/lei/Lei)	dà	he, she, you (pol.) give(s), he, she, you is/are giving, he, she, you does/do give
(noi)	diamo	we give, we are giving, we do give
(voi)	date	you give, you are giving, you do give
(loro)	danno	they give, they are giving, they do give

dire / *to say, to tell, to speak*

(io)	dico	I say, I am saying, I do say
(tu)	dici	you (fam.) say, you are saying, you do say
(lui/lei/Lei)	dice	he, she, you (pol.) say(s), he, she, you is/are saying, he, she, you does/do say
(noi)	diciamo	we say, we are saying, we do say
(voi)	dite	you say, you are saying, you do say
(loro)	dicono	they say, they are saying, they do say

fare / *to do, to make*

(io)	faccio	I make, I am making, I do make
(tu)	fai	you (fam.) make, you are making, you do make
(lui/lei/Lei)	fa	he, she, you (pol.) make(s), he, she, you is/are making, he, she, you does/do make
(noi)	facciamo	we make, we are making, we do make
(voi)	fate	you make, you are making, you do make
(loro)	fanno	they make, they are making, they do make

Here are some common expressions in which these verbs are used:

bere alla salute	to drink to health
bere forte	to drink heavily
dare del Lei	to be on polite terms
dare del tu	to be on familiar terms
dare la mano	to shake hands
dare un film	to show a movie
dire di no	to say no
dire di sì	to say yes
dire la verità	to tell the truth
dire una bugia/la bugia	to tell a lie, to lie
fare del bene	to do good (things)
fare del male	to do bad (things)
fare il medico/l'avvocato/...	to be a doctor/a lawyer/...

EXERCISE Set 5–1

bene	good	**male**	bad, evil
la bugia	lie	**la mano (le mani)**	hand (hands)
d'ora in poi	from now on	**mentre**	while
da	from	**la salute**	health
forte	strong, heavily	**su**	on
generalmente	generally	**la verità**	truth

A. Supply the missing present indicative form of the verb **bere**, giving the English equivalent.

EXAMPLE: **lui**____   =   _____
           lui beve   =   *he drinks, he is drinking, he does drink*

1. **io** _____   =   _____

2. **tu** _____   =   _____

3. **noi** _____   =   _____

4. **loro** _____   =   _____

5. **voi** _____   =   _____

6. **Lei** _____   =   _____

Now, supply the missing present indicative form of the verb **dare**, giving the English equivalent.

7. **io** _____   =   _____

8. **tu** _____   =   _____

9. **io e tu** _____   =   _____

10. **loro** _____   =   _____

11. **tu e lei** _____   =   _____

12. **lui** _____   =   _____

Now, supply the missing present indicative form of the verb **dire**, giving the English equivalent.

13. **io** _____   =   _____

14. **tu** _____   =   _____

15. **noi** _____   =   _____

16. **loro** _____   =   _____

17. **voi** _____   =   _____

18. **Lei** _____   =   _____

Finally, supply the missing present indicative form of the verb **fare**, giving the English equivalent.

19. **io** _____   =   _____

20. **tu** _____   =   _____

21. **io e tu** _____   =   _____

22. **loro** _____   =   _____

23. **tu e lei** _____   =   _____

24. **lei** _____   =   _____

B. Say the following things in Italian.

Grammar Summary

The following chart summarizes the different contracted forms of prepositions and definite articles. These will come in handy in the exercises of this and subsequent chapters.

+	il	i	lo	l'	gli	la	le
a	al	ai	allo	all'	agli	alla	alle
da	dal	dai	dallo	dall'	dagli	dalla	dalle
di	del	dei	dello	dell'	degli	della	delle
in	nel	nei	nello	nell'	negli	nella	nelle
su	sul	sui	sullo	sull'	sugli	sulla	sulle

1. We always drink to the health of the family.

   _____

2. My friends always drink heavily at parties.

   _____

3. Mrs. Marchi, why are you on polite terms with me all the time?

   _____

4. Mrs. Marchi and I will be on familiar terms from now on.

   _____

5. I am shaking Mr. Smith's hand.

_____

6. Are they showing that new movie nearby?

_____

7. I always say yes and you _(fam., sing.)_ always say no, right?

_____

8. You _(fam., sing.)_ always tell the truth, while they always lie.

_____

9. My grandfather always does good for people; he never does bad things.

_____

10. My sister is a doctor and I am an engineer.

_____

Prospettiva personale

Answer each question with a complete sentence, indicating if you do or do not do the following things.

EXAMPLE: **Tu fai il medico?**
                **Sì, (io) faccio il medico/No, non faccio il medico.**

1. **Tu fai l'ingegnere?**

_____

2. **Tu dici sempre la verità?**

_____

3. **Tu fai del bene o del male generalmente?**

_____

4. **Tu bevi forte?**

_____

5. **A chi dai del Lei?**

_____

6. **A chi dai del tu?**

_____

7. **Quale film nuovo danno al cinema in questo momento?**

_____

8. **Quando dici le bugie?**

_____

9. **A chi dai la mano generalmente?**

_____

10. **A chi bevi alla salute generalmente?**

_____

Illustrative Dialogue

Marco:	**Maria, è vero che tua sorella _fa_ il medico?**	Mary, is it true that your sister is a doctor?
Maria:	**Sì, e anche la sua amica _fa_ il medico, ma suo fidanzato _fa_ l'avvocato.**	Yes, and so is her friend a doctor, but her fiancé is a lawyer.
Marco:	**E tu che _fai_?**	And what about you?
Maria:	**Sono ancora studentessa. Anche tu sei studente, vero?**	I'm still a student. You're also a student, aren't you?
Marco:	**Sì, purtroppo! Sai che tempo _fa_ oggi?**	Yes, unfortunately! Do you know what the weather is like today?
Maria:	**Forse _fa_ caldo. Perché?**	Maybe it'll be warm. Why?
Marco:	**Perché oggi desidero _fare_ una passeggiata.**	Because today I want to take a stroll/walk.

Grammar Notes

Note the forms of the possessive **suo**, which means both _his_ and _her_ (agreeing in number and gender with the noun it modifies):

His	Her
il suo libro/ his book	**il suo libro**/ her book
i suoi libri/ his books	**i suoi libri**/ her books
la sua macchina/ his car	**la sua macchina**/ her car
le sue machine/ his cars	**le sue machine**/ her cars

The possessive **loro**/ _their_ is invariable:

| **il loro libro**/ their book | **i loro libri**/ their books |
| **la loro rivista**/ their magazine | **le loro riviste**/ their magazines |

The polite forms are identical to the **suo** forms in the singular, and to the **loro** forms in the plural. To keep the two types distinct in writing, the polite forms are often capitalized. But this is _not_ an obligatory rule:

il Suo amico/ your friend   **i Loro amici**/ their friends

Note that the verb **fare** is used to indicate weather conditions:

Che tempo _fa_?/ _How's the weather?_
Oggi _fa_ freddo. / _Today it is cold._
_Fa_ **molto caldo.** / _It is very hot._
_Fa_ **un po' fresco.** / _It's a little cool._

The verb **essere** is used when climate conditions in general are to be inferred:

Il tempo è caldo d'estate in Italia./ _The weather is hot in the summer in Italy._
L'inverno è freddo./ _Winter is cold._

EXERCISE Set 5–2

il bel tempo	beautiful/nice weather	**la passeggiata**	stroll, walk
il brutto tempo	bad weather	**la pioggia**	rain
caldo	hot, warm	**piovere**	to rain
il cattivo tempo	bad weather	**purtroppo**	unfortunately
la fidanzata	fiancée	**lo studente**	student (m.)
il fidanzato	fiancé	**la studentessa**	student (f.)
freddo	cold	**il tempo**	weather
fresco	cool	**tirare vento**	to be windy
la neve	snow	**un po'**	a little
nevicare	to snow	**il vento**	wind

A. Choose the appropriate answer, **a** or **b**, to each question.

1. **Che fa la sorella di Maria?**
   a. **Fa il medico.**
   b. **Fa bel tempo.**

2. **Che fa la sua amica?**
   a. **Fa cattivo tempo.**
   b. **Fa il medico.**

3. **Anche il suo fidanzato fa il medico?**
   a. **No, lui fa l'avvocato.**
   b. **No, lui è studente.**

4. **Che tempo fa oggi?**
   a. **Fa l'ingegnere.**
   b. **Fa caldo.**

5. **Che desidera fare Marco?**
   a. **La pioggia.**
   b. **Una passeggiata.**

6. **Com'è il tempo generalmente?**
   a. **È bello.**
   b. **Fa bel tempo.**

7. **Oggi che tempo fa?**
   a. **È bello**
   b. **Fa bel tempo.**

B. Missing from each of the following sentences is **bere**, **dare**, **dire**, or **fare**. Put each verb, in its correct form, in each sentence according to the sense.

1. **I loro amici _____ sempre alla salute di tutti.**

2. **Oggi tira vento e _____ molto freddo.**

3. **Le loro amiche _____ sempre la verità.**

4. **Purtroppo, tuo cugino _____ sempre le bugie.**

5. **Voi, invece, _____ sempre la verità.**

6. **Dove _____ quel film nuovo?**

7. **Che tempo _____ oggi?**

8. **Loro _____ sempre una passeggiata la domenica.**

9. **Franco, è vero che tu _____ il meccanico?**

Prospettiva personale

Vero o falso? Indicate whether the following statements are true ("V") or false ("F") from your personal perspective.

_____ 1. **Mi piace molto quando fa bel tempo.**

_____ 2. **Non mi piace il brutto tempo affatto.**

_____ 3. **Oggi fa molto caldo.**

_____ 4. **Oggi fa cattivo tempo.**

_____ 5. **Nella mia città il tempo è sempre bello.**

_____ 6. **Oggi fa un po' fresco.**

_____ 7. **Mi piace molto la pioggia.**

_____ 8. **Non mi piace la neve.**

_____ 9. **Oggi tira vento.**

Conjugation and Uses of *Andare*, *Uscire*, *Venire*

Here are three other useful irregular verbs. Their present indicative forms are given below:

andare / *to go*

(io)	vado	I go, I am going, I do go
(tu)	vai	you (fam.) go, you are going, you do go
(lui/lei/Lei)	va	he, she, you (pol.) go(es), he, she, you is/are going, he, she, you does/do go
(noi)	andiamo	we go, we are going, we do go
(voi)	andate	you go, you are going, you do go
(loro)	vanno	they go, they are going, they do go

uscire / *to go out*

(io)	esco	I go out, I am going out, I do go out
(tu)	esci	you (fam.) go out, you are going out, you do go out
(lui/lei/Lei)	esce	he, she, you (pol.) go(es) out, he, she, you is/are going out, he, she, you does/do go out
(noi)	usciamo	we go out, we are going out, we do go out
(voi)	uscite	you go out, you are going out, you do go out
(loro)	escono	they go out, they are going out, they do go out

venire / *to come*

(io)	vengo	I come, I am coming, I do come
(tu)	vieni	you (fam.) come, you are coming, you do come
(lui/lei/Lei)	viene	he, she, you (pol.) come(s), he, she, you is/are coming, he, she, you does/do come
(noi)	veniamo	we come, we are coming, we do come
(voi)	venite	you come, you are coming, you do come
(loro)	vengono	they come, they are coming, they do come

EXERCISE Set 5–3

A. Supply the missing present indicative form of the verb **andare**, giving the English equivalent.

EXAMPLE: **lui** _____ =   _____

                 lui va   =   he goes, he is going, he does go

1. **io**_____   =   _____

2. **tu**_____   =   _____

3. **noi**_____   =   _____

4. **loro**_____   =   _____

5. **voi**_____   =   _____

6. **Lei**_____   =   _____

Now, supply the missing present indicative form of the verb **uscire**, giving the English equivalent.

7. **io**_____   =   _____

8. **tu**_____   =   _____

9. **io e tu**_____   =   _____

10. **loro**_____   =   _____

11. **tu e lei**_____   =   _____

12. **lui**_____   =   _____

Finally, supply the missing present indicative form of the verb **venire**, giving the English equivalent.

13. **io**_____   =   _____

14. **tu**_____   =   _____

15. **noi**_____   =   _____

16. **loro**_____   =   _____

17. **voi**_____   =   _____

18. **lei**_____   =   _____

Grammar Note

Note the forms of the possessives **nostro**/ *our* and **vostro**/ *your (fam., pl.)*:

Our	Your
il nostro amico/ *our friend*	**il vostro amico**/ *your friend*
i nostri amici/ *our friends*	**i vostri amici**/ *your friends*
la nostra macchina/ *our car*	**la vostra macchina**/ *your car*
le nostre macchine/ *our cars*	**le vostre macchine**/ *your cars*

B. Say the following things in Italian:

il bar	espresso bar	**senza**	without
già	already	**stasera**	tonight
il mare	sea, ocean	**tardi**	late
sciare	to ski	**la vacanza**	vacation

1. Our friends are coming to your (fam., pl.) party too.

   _____

2. Franco, are you going out with Maria tonight?

   _____

3. Marco and Maria, where are you going?

_____

4. Maybe their parents are also coming to your (fam., pl.) house.

_____

5. I always go to the espresso bar with my friends.

_____

6. Claudia, are you coming too to the espresso bar?

_____

7. I always go out on Saturdays.

_____

8. Are they going to Italy this summer?

_____

9. I am coming to the party as well.

_____

C. Choose the appropriate verb, **a**, **b**, or **c**, according to sense.

1. **Ogni estate io ... in Italia per le vacanze.**
   a. **vado**
   b. **esco**
   c. **vengo**

2. **Anche tu oggi non ... con gli amici per andare al bar perché fa cattivo tempo, vero?**
   a. **vai**
   b. **esci**
   c. **vieni**

3. **Quando ... il tuo amico? Sono già le otto e mezzo. È tardi!**
   a. **va**
   b. **esce**
   c. **viene**

4. **Noi ... sempre al mare per le vacanze.**
   a. **andiamo**
   b. **usciamo**
   c. **veniamo**

5. **Con chi ... per andare al cinema stasera?**
   a. **andate**
   b. **uscite**
   c. **venite**

6. **A che ora ... qui?**
   a. **vanno**
   b. **escono**
   c. **vengono**

Conjugation and Uses of *Dovere, Potere, Volere*

The verbs **dovere**, **potere**, and **volere** are known as modal verbs. They are irregular in the present indicative. Here are their forms:

dovere/ *to have to ("to must")*

(io)	**devo**	I have to, I must
(tu)	**devi**	you (fam.) have to, you must
(lui/lei/Lei)	**deve**	he, she, you (pol.) has/have to, he, she, you must
(noi)	**dobbiamo**	we have to, we must
(voi)	**dovete**	you have to, you must
(loro)	**devono**	they have to, they must

potere/ *to be able to*

(io)	**posso**	I am able to, I can
(tu)	**puoi**	you (fam.) are able to, you can
(lui/lei/Lei)	**può**	he, she, you (pol.) is/are able to, he, she, you can
(noi)	**possiamo**	we are able to, we can
(voi)	**potete**	you are able to, you can
(loro)	**possono**	they are able to, they can

volere/ *to want to*

(io)	**voglio**	I want to
(tu)	**vuoi**	you (fam.) want to
(lui/lei/Lei)	**vuole**	he, she, you (pol.) want(s) to
(noi)	**vogliamo**	we want to
(voi)	**volete**	you want to
(loro)	**vogliono**	they want to

These verbs allow you to express permission, desire, necessity, and other similar kinds of states:

Posso venire anch'io?/ *Can I come too?*
Non *devi* andare in Italia oggi?/ *Don't you have to go to Italy today?*
Voglio comprare un nuovo computer./ *I want to buy a new computer.*

They are, thus, normally followed by an infinitive.

EXERCISE Set 5–4

A. Supply the missing present indicative form of the verb **dovere**, giving the English equivalent.

EXAMPLE: lui _____ = _____
          lui deve = he has to, he must

1. io _____ = _____
2. tu _____ = _____
3. noi _____ = _____
4. loro _____ = _____
5. voi _____ = _____
6. Lei _____ = _____

Now, supply the missing present indicative form of the verb **potere**, giving the English equivalent.

7. io _____ = _____
8. tu _____ = _____
9. io e tu _____ = _____
10. loro _____ = _____
11. tu e lei _____ = _____
12. lui _____ = _____

Finally, supply the missing present indicative form of the verb **volere**, giving the English equivalent.

13. io _____   =   _____

14. tu _____   =   _____

15. noi _____   =   _____

16. loro _____   =   _____

17. voi _____   =   _____

18. lei _____   =   _____

B. Say the following things in Italian.

1. I must go to the espresso bar.

   _____

2. I want to go to Italy this summer.

   _____

3. I can buy a new car now because I have the money.

   _____

4. Marco, why do you always have to say no?

   _____

5. Claudia, can you come to the party tonight?

   _____

6. Alessandro, do you want to go out tonight?

   _____

7. His uncle must also come to the party.

   _____

8. She wants to go out, but he can't.

   _____

9. We must always tell the truth.

   _____

10. We cannot go to her party because we want to go to the movies.

    _____

11. Alessandro and Sarah, can you go out tonight? Do you want to go out? Or do you have to study?

    _____

12. They always want to go to the movies on Saturdays, but today they have to do something important. So they can't go.

    _____

Prospettiva personale

Answer each question, in an appropriate manner.

EXAMPLE: **Tu vuoi andare al cinema oggi?**
Sì, (io) voglio andare al cinema oggi. / No, non voglio andare al cinema oggi.

1. **Tu vuoi guardare la televisione stasera?**

   _____

2. **La tua famiglia vuole parlare l'italiano bene?**

   _____

3. **Devi studiare di più** (more) **per parlare l'italiano bene?**

   _____

4. **Che cosa vuoi fare quando piove?**

   _____

5. **Che cosa volete fare nella tua famiglia quando fa cattivo tempo?**

   _____

6. **Che cosa vuoi fare generalmente il sabato o la domenica?**

   _____

7. **Che cosa devi fare di solito** (usually) **ogni giorno?**

   _____

Conjugation and Uses of Other Irregular Verbs

morire/ *to die*

(io)	**muoio**	I die, I am dying
(tu)	**muori**	you (fam.) die, you are dying
(lui/lei/Lei)	**muore**	he, she, you (pol.) die(s), he, she, you is/are dying
(noi)	**moriamo**	we die, we are dying
(voi)	**morite**	you die, you are dying
(loro)	**muoiono**	they die, they are dying

nascere/ *to be born*

(io)	**nasco**	I am born
(tu)	**nasci**	you (fam.) are born
(lui/lei/Lei)	**nasce**	he, she, you (pol.) is/are born
(noi)	**nasciamo**	we are born
(voi)	**nascete**	you are born
(loro)	**nascono**	they are born

NOTE

Technically, the verb **nascere** *is conjugated as a regular second-conjugation verb. It is included here because you must change the pronunciation of the "c" as hard or soft depending on the following vowel.*

salire/ *to climb, to go up*

(io)	**salgo**	I climb, I am climbing
(tu)	**sali**	you (fam.) climb, you are climbing
(lui/lei/Lei)	**sale**	he, she, you (pol.) climb(s), he, she, you is/are climbing
(noi)	**saliamo**	· we climb, we are climbing
(voi)	**salite**	you climb, you are climbing
(loro)	**salgono**	they climb, they are climbing

scegliere/ *to choose, to select*

(io)	**scelgo**	I choose, I am choosing, I do choose
(tu)	**scegli**	you (fam.) choose, you are choosing, you do choose
(lui/lei/Lei)	**sceglie**	he, she, you (pol.) choose(s), he, she, you is/are choosing, he, she, you do(es) choose
(noi)	**scegliamo**	we choose, we are choosing, we do choose
(voi)	**scegliete**	you choose, you are choosing, you do choose
(loro)	**scelgono**	they choose, they are choosing, they do choose

tenere/ *to keep, to hold*

(io)	**tengo**	I keep, I am keeping, I do keep
(tu)	**tieni**	you (fam.) keep, you are keeping, you do keep
(lui/lei/Lei)	**tiene**	he, she, you (pol.) keep(s), he, she, you is/are keeping, he, she, you do(es) keep
(noi)	**teniamo**	we keep, we are keeping, we do keep
(voi)	**tenete**	you keep, you are keeping, you do keep
(loro)	**tengono**	they keep, they are keeping, they do keep

TIP

The forms of the verb **tenere** *are similar to those of* **venire:**

(io) vengo	→	(io) tengo
(tu) vieni	→	(tu) tieni
...		

EXERCISE Set 5–5

Choose the appropriate verb according to sense:

di solito	usually	**rapido**	rapid
fortunato	fortunate, lucky	**la scala (le scale)**	stair, staircase
lo stesso	the same	**la tasca**	pocket
il modo	manner, way	**la voglia**	desire, urge

1. **Di solito, io ... i film italiani quando voglio andare al cinema.**
   a. **muoio**
   b. **nasco**
   c. **salgo**
   d. **scelgo**
   e. **tengo**

2. **Tu ... dalla voglia di uscire stasera, non è vero?**
   a. **muori**
   b. **nasci**
   c. **sali**
   d. **scegli**
   e. **tieni**

3. **Il suo amico … le scale in modo rapido.**
   a. muore
   b. nasce
   c. sale
   d. sceglie
   e. tiene
4. **Noi … sempre le mani in tasca quando fa freddo.**
   a. moriamo
   b. nasciamo
   c. saliamo
   d. scegliamo
   e. teniamo
5. **Marco e Maria, perché … sempre gli stessi film?**
   a. morite
   b. nascete
   c. salite
   d. scegliete
   e. tenete
6. **Le persone che … in autunno sono fortunate.**
   a. muoiono
   b. nascono
   c. salgono
   d. scelgono
   e. tengono

Crossword Puzzle 5

Orizzontali

2. **Noi… sempre la verità.**

5. **Loro … studiare di più.**

6. **Loro … sempre alla nostra salute.**

9. **Loro … ogni sabato sera.**

11. **Io … dalla voglia di andare al cinema.**

12. **I suoi amici … sempre i film italiani.**

Verticali

1. **Che cosa … voi stasera?**

2. **Loro si … del tu.**

3. **Noi … in Italia ogni estate.**

4. **… anche voi alla nostra festa?**

7. **Tu … uscire stasera con me?**

8. **Anche loro … comprare una macchina nuova.**

10. **Anche Sarah … di solito il sabato, vero?**

6
Reflexive Verbs

Conjugation of Reflexive Verbs

A verb is reflexive when it has an identical subject and direct object, as in *She dressed herself*. The object is expressed as a reflexive pronoun. Reflexive verbs are thus conjugated in exactly the same manner as nonreflexive verbs, but with reflexive pronouns.

Here are the Italian reflexive pronouns:

Singular		Plural	
1st person	**mi** *myself*	1st person	**ci** *ourselves*
2nd person	**ti** *yourself* (fam.)	2nd person	**vi** *yourselves* (fam.)
3rd person	**si** *himself, herself, yourself* (pol.)	3rd person	**si** *themselves, yourselves* (pol.)

Io *mi lavo* di solito alla mattina. / *I usually wash myself in the morning.*
Tu non *ti diverti* di solito al cinema, vero? / *You do not enjoy yourself usually at the movies, right?*

NOTE

A reflexive infinitive is identifiable by the ending **-si** *(oneself).*

lavarsi / to wash oneself

mettersi / to put on, to wear

divertirsi / to enjoy oneself

Reflexive verbs are conjugated in exactly the same manner as other verbs with, of course, the addition of reflexive pronouns:

1. Drop the reflexive infinitive ending, **-arsi, -ersi, -irsi**:

lavarsi / *to wash oneself*	→	**lav-**
mettersi / *to put on, to wear*	→	**mett-**
divertirsi / *to enjoy oneself*	→	**divert-**

2. Add on the endings in the usual manner (Chapter 1).

3. Don't forget to put the reflexive pronouns in front.

lavarsi

(io)	mi	lavo	I wash myself, I am washing myself
(tu)	ti	lavi	you (fam.) wash yourself, you are washing yourself
(lui/lei/Lei)	si	lava	he, she, you (pol.) wash(es) himself/herself/yourself, he, she, you is/are washing himself/herself/yourself
(noi)	ci	laviamo	we wash ourselves, we are washing ourselves
(voi)	vi	lavate	you wash yourselves, you are washing yourselves
(loro)	si	lavano	they wash themselves, they are washing themselves

mettersi

(io)	mi	metto	I wear, I am wearing
(tu)	ti	metti	you (fam.) wear, you are wearing
(lui/lei/Lei)	si	mette	he, she, you (pol.) wear(s), he, she, you is/are wearing
(noi)	ci	mettiamo	we wear, we are wearing
(voi)	vi	mettete	you wear, you are wearing
(loro)	si	mettono	they wear, they are wearing

divertirsi

(io)	mi	diverto	I enjoy myself, I am enjoying myself
(tu)	ti	diverti	you (fam.) enjoy yourself, you are enjoying yourself
(lui/lei/Lei)	si	diverte	he, she, you (pol.) enjoy(s) himself/herself/yourself, he, she, you is/are enjoying himself/herself/yourself
(noi)	ci	divertiamo	we enjoy ourselves, we are enjoying ourselves
(voi)	vi	divertite	you enjoy yourselves, you are enjoying yourselves
(loro)	si	divertono	they enjoy themselves, they are enjoying themselves

---

REMINDER

Be careful again when you pronounce the third person plural forms! The accent is not placed on the ending, but on a syllable before the ending:

si divertono / *they enjoy themselves*
|
stress

Here are some common reflexive verbs that will come in handy for basic communication purposes:

addormentarsi	to fall asleep
alzarsi	to get up, to stand up
ammalarsi	to get sick
andarsene	to go away
annoiarsi	to become bored
arrabbiarsi	to become angry
chiamarsi	to call oneself, to be named
dimenticarsi	to forget
divertirsi	to enjoy oneself, to have fun
farsi il bagno	to take a bath
farsi la barba	to shave

farsi la doccia	to take a shower
lamentarsi	to complain
lavarsi	to wash oneself
mettersi	to put on, to wear
prepararsi	to prepare oneself
ricordarsi	to remember
sentirsi	to feel
sposarsi	to marry, to get married
svegliarsi	to wake up
vergognarsi	to be ashamed
vestirsi	to get dressed

Notice that a few of the verbs are not equivalently reflexive in English. Be careful!

Two of the above verbs require special commentary. The first one is **andarsene**. Treat this verb as any reflexive verb, adding **ne** (which in this case means *away*) right after the pronouns. However, you must change the reflexive pronouns as shown. Recall that **andare** is an irregular verb (Chapter 5):

andarsene / *to go away*

(io)	me	ne	vado	I go away, I am going away
(tu)	te	ne	vai	you (fam.) go away, you are going away
(lui/lei/Lei)	se	ne	va	he, she, you (pol.) go(es) away, he, she, you is/are going away
(noi)	ce	ne	andiamo	we go away, we are going away
(voi)	ve	ne	andate	you go away, you are going away
(loro)	se	ne	vanno	they go away, they are going away

The second verb that requires commentary is **chiamarsi.** This is rendered in English with expressions such as *my name is, your name is*, etc.:

> **(Io)** *mi chiama* **Marcello.** / *My name is Marcello.*
>
> **Come *ti chiami*?** / *What's your name?*

EXERCISE Set 6–1

A. Supply the missing present indicative form of the verb **alzarsi**, giving the English equivalent.

EXAMPLE: lui _____   =   _____
             lui si alza   =   he gets up, he is getting up

1. **io** _____   =   _____

2. **tu** _____   =   _____

3. **noi** _____   =   _____

4. **loro** _____   =   _____

5. **voi** _____   =   _____

6. **Lei** _____   =   _____

Now, supply the missing present indicative form of the verb **mettersi**, giving the English equivalent.

7. io _____   =   _____

8. tu _____   =   _____

9. io e tu _____   =   _____

10. loro _____   =   _____

11. tu e lei _____   =   _____

12. lui _____   =   _____

Now, supply the missing present indicative form of the verb **sentirsi**, giving the English equivalent.

13. io _____   =   _____

14. tu _____   =   _____

15. noi _____   =   _____

16. loro _____   =   _____

17. voi _____   =   _____

18. Lei _____   =   _____

Finally, supply the missing present indicative form of the verb **andarsene**, giving the English equivalent.

19. io _____   =   _____

20. tu _____   =   _____

21. noi _____   =   _____

22. loro _____   =   _____

23. voi _____   =   _____

24. lei _____   =   _____

B. Choose the correct verb form according to the sense:

altro	other	**il membro**	member
elegante	elegant	**regolare**	regular
facile	easy	**se**	if
fuori	outside	**semplice**	simple
generale	general	**la sera**	evening
la mattina	morning	**verso**	around, toward

1. **Io generalmente ... quando guardo la televisione.**
   a. **mi addormento**
   b. **mi chiamo**
   c. **mi alzo**

2. **Tu ... sempre tutto!**
   a. **ti arrabbi**
   b. **ti diverti**
   c. **ti dimentichi**

3. **Sua cugina ... regolarmente quando va al cinema.**
   a. **si chiama**
   b. **si diverte**
   c. **si sposa**

4. **Noi ... facilmente quando le cose non vanno bene.**
   a. **ci lamentiamo**
   b. **ci vestiamo**
   c. **ci laviamo**

5. **È vero che voi ... facilmente tutto?**
    a. **vi ricordate**
    b. **vi vergognate**
    c. **vi sposate**

6. **Signore, come ... Lei?**
    a. **si chiama**
    b. **si prepara**
    c. **si sveglia**

7. **Loro ... il bagno ogni giorno.**
    a. **si lavano**
    b. **si annoiano**
    c. **si fanno**

Grammar Note

Adverbs of manner end in **-mente**, corresponding (in general) to the English ending -ly. To construct such an adverb, change the **-o** of an adjective to **-a** and then add on **-mente**. If the adjective ends in **-e**, then just add on **-mente**:

> **certo** / certain → **certa** → **certamente** / certainly
>
> **semplice** / simple → **semplicemente** / simply

However, if the adjective ends in **-le** or **-re** and is preceded by a vowel, then the **-e** is dropped:

> **facile** / easy → **facilmente** / easily
>
> **regolare** / regular → **regolarmente** / regularly

C. Say the following things in Italian.

1. Maria, why do you always get dressed elegantly?

    _____

2. I am not ashamed of anything!

    _____

3. Marco, at what time do you get up generally in the morning?

    _____

4. Alessandro and Sarah, is it true that you are getting married this fall?

    _____

5. They always complain about everything!

    _____

6. I usually take a shower and I shave when I get up in the morning.

    _____

7. Why are you becoming angry, Miss Gentile?

    _____

8. They always become bored when they watch TV.

    _____

9. I get sick very easily if it is cold outside.

    _____

Prospettiva personale

Answer each question, in an appropriate manner.

EXAMPLE: **Quando ti addormenti generalmente la sera?**
Generalmente mi addormento verso le dieci/molto tardi/...

1. **A che ora ti alzi la mattina di solito?**

   _____

2. **Ti ammali facilmente se fa freddo?**

   _____

3. **Quando ti annoi facilmente?**

   _____

4. **Quando ti arrabbi generalmente?**

   _____

5. **Come si chiamano i membri della tua famiglia?**

   _____

6. **Quando vi divertite tu e la tua famiglia?**

   _____

Illustrative Dialogue

la camicetta	blouse	**poi**	then
la camicia	shirt	**provarsi**	to try on
il/la cliente (m./f.)	customer	**scusarsi**	to excuse oneself
il commesso/la commessa	store clerk	**secondo**	according to
cortese	courteous	**il tipo**	type
l'orologio	watch	**il vestito**	dress, suit
i pantaloni	pants		

Cliente:	*Mi scusi. Mi posso provare* **questo vestito?**	Excuse me. May I try on this dress?
Commesso:	**Sì, Lei può** *provarsi* **tutti i vestiti che vuole.**	Yes, you can try on all the dresses you want.
Cliente:	**Questo mi piace molto. Non** *mi metto* **mai questo tipo di vestito.**	I like this one a lot. I never wear this type of dress.
Commesso:	**È un bel vestito. Desidera altro?**	It's a beautiful dress. Would you like anything else?
Cliente:	**Una bella camicetta per me e poi voglio una camicia e dei bei pantaloni per mio marito. Lui** *si lamenta* **sempre dei suoi vestiti.**	A nice blouse for me and then I want a shirt and nice pants for my husband. He always complains about his clothes.
Commesso:	**Ecco per Lei.**	Here you are.
Cliente:	**Grazie, Lei è molto cortese.**	Thank you, you are very courteous.

Grammar Notes

With a modal verb (Chapter 5) the reflexive pronoun can be put before the modal or else attached to the infinitive as shown:

Before

        Ti vuoi divertire? / *Do you want to have fun?*

        Vi potete svegliare quando volete. / *You can wake up when you want.*

After

        Vuoi divertirti? / *Do you want to have fun?*

        Potete svegliarvi quando volete. / *You can wake up when you want.*

The adjective **bello** can be used before or after the noun it modifies. If it is put after, then its endings change in the usual fashion. If it is put before, then its singular forms undergo the same kinds of changes that the definite article does:

Masculine Singular	Masculine Plural
un bel vestito / *a beautiful suit*	**bei vestiti** / *beautiful dresses*
un bell'orologio / *a beautiful watch*	**begli orologi** / *beautiful watches*
un bello zio / *a handsome uncle*	**begli zii** / *handsome uncles*

Feminine Singular	Feminine Plural
una bella camicia / *a beautiful shirt*	**belle camicie** / *beautiful shirts*
una bell'amica / *a beautiful friend*	**belle amiche** / *beautiful friends*

EXERCISE Set 6–2

A. Answer the following questions with complete sentences based on the dialogue.

EXAMPLE: **Che cosa vuole fare la cliente?** (What does the customer want to do?)
        La cliente vuole provarsi/si vuole provare un vestito.

    1. Chi si vuole provare un vestito nuovo?

    _____

    2. Quanti vestiti può provarsi la cliente, secondo (according to) **il commesso?**

    _____

    3. Che cosa non si mette mai la cliente?

    _____

    4. Com'è il vestito, secondo il commesso?

    _____

    5. Che cos'altro desidera la cliente?

    _____

    6. Che cosa fa sempre il marito della cliente?

    _____

B. Make up your own dialogue, as indicated.

Cliente:	Excuse me.
Commessa:	May I help you?
Cliente:	May I try on this beautiful watch?
Commessa:	Of course. Maybe I know you **(La conosco)**. What's your name?
Cliente:	My name is Maria Marchi. And you, what's your name?
Commessa:	My name is Claudia Santini. I don't remember your name. Sorry (Excuse me).
Cliente:	No problem **(Non c'è problema)**. I also become ashamed when I forget something.

Uses and Features

Some verbs can be "converted" into reflexives so that one can express "reciprocalness" (*to each other, to one another*, etc.):

vedere / *to see*	→	**vedersi** / *to see one another*
telefonare / *to phone*	→	**telefonarsi** / *to phone one another*
chiamare / *to call*	→	**chiamarsi** / *to call one another*
parlare / *to speak*	→	**parlarsi** / *to speak to each other*
capire / *to understand*	→	**capirsi** / *to understand each other*

Loro non *si vedono* **da anni.** / *They haven't seen each other for years.*
Voi *vi telefonate* **spesso, vero?** / *You phone each other often, right?*
Voi *vi chiamate* **ogni giorno, no?** / *You call each other every day, right?*
Noi non *ci parliamo* **da molti anni.** / *We haven't been talking to each other for many years.*

Grammar Note

The preposition **da** followed by a time word or expression renders the idea of *for*…

Non si parlano *da* **molto tempo.** / *They haven't been talking to each other for a long time.*
Non si vedono *da* **mesi.** / *They haven't seen each other for months.*

As you have seen, many verbs that are reflexive in Italian are not similarly reflexive in English. You will simply have to memorize these.

Sometimes, Italian reflexive verbs correspond to English verbal constructions made up with verbs such as *to get*… and *to become* …:

alzarsi	=	to get up
ammalarsi	=	to get sick
annoiarsi	=	to become bored
sposarsi	=	to get married

EXERCISE Set 6–3

Missing from each of the following sentences is the verb. The missing verbs are given to you in their infinitive forms. Put each verb, in its correct form, in each sentence according to the sense.

Verbs:
annoiarsi, vedersi, capirsi, chiamarsi, sposarsi, parlarsi, alzarsi

1. **Come ti chiami? _____ Claudia Corelli.**

2. **Marco, a che ora _____ generalmente la mattina?**

3. **Noi _____ spesso quando guardiamo la televisione.**

4. **Maria _____ questa primavera.**

5. **Quei due amici non _____ da mesi.**

6. **Io e tu non _____ mai!**

7. **È vero che voi non _____ da molto tempo?**

Crossword Puzzle 6

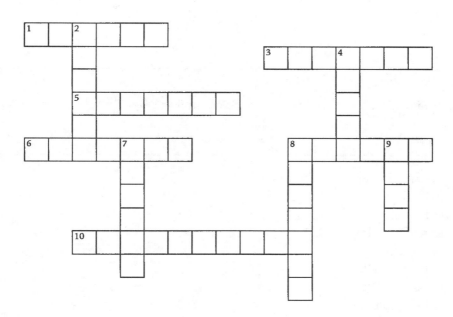

Orizzontali

1. **Io mi ... la doccia ogni mattina.**
3. **Scusi, mi posso ... questo vestito?**
5. **Noi ci ... tardi di solito la mattina.**
6. **Quando si ... tuo fratello e la tua amica?**
8. **A che ora ti ... la mattina?**
10. **Loro si ... ogni giorno.**

Verticali

2. **Io mi ... Giuseppe.**
4. **La sua amica si ... sempre elegantemente.**
7. **Io mi ... facilmente se fa freddo.**
8. **Oggi loro non si ... troppo bene.**
9. **Perché non ti ... più spesso?**

7
The Present Progressive

Conjugation of *Stare*

In order to learn how to use the present progressive you will have to first learn the forms of the verb **stare /** *to stay, to be*:

(io)	**sto**	I am, I stay
(tu)	**stai**	you (fam.) are, you stay
(lui/lei/Lei)	**sta**	he, she, you (pol.) is/are, he, she, you stay(s)
(noi)	**stiamo**	we are, we stay
(voi)	**state**	you are, you stay
(loro)	**stanno**	they are, they stay

TIP

This verb renders the idea of "to be" only in specific kinds of expressions such as when it is used as the auxiliary in progressive tenses:

Sto parlando = *I am speaking*

This verb is used in certain useful idiomatic expressions:

stare attento	to be careful
stare bene	to be well
stare calmo	to remain calm
stare fermo	to stay still
stare male	to be not well
stare per	to be about to
stare zitto	to be/keep quiet

EXERCISE Set 7–1

A. Supply the missing present indicative form of the verb **stare,** giving the English equivalent.

EXAMPLE: **lui** ____ = _____
          lui sta = he is, he stays

1. **io** _____ = _____

2. **tu** _____ = _____

3. **noi** _____   =   _____

4. **loro** _____   =   _____

5. **voi** _____   =   _____

6. **Lei** _____   =   _____

7. **la sua amica**   =   _____

B. Say the following things in Italian:

accendere	to turn on	**per di più**	moreover
attento	careful	**il pericolo**	danger
attraversare	to cross	**specialmente**	especially
calmo	calm	**stare per**	to be about to
così, così	so, so	**la strada**	road
fermo	still, motionless	**il televisore**	television set
non c'è male	not bad	**zitto**	quiet

1.

-Are you (fam., sing.) always careful?

_____

-Yes, I am always careful.

_____

2.

-Mrs. Dini, how are you?

_____

-I am well, thank you.

_____

3.

-Maria, how are you?

_____

-I am not well.

_____

4.

-Are your friends careful when they cross the road?

_____

-Yes, they are always careful.

_____

5.

-We must always remain calm, especially when we are afraid.

_____

-And, moreover, we must also stay still and keep quiet.

_____

6.

-Marco, what are you about to do?

_____

-I'm about to turn on the television set.

_____

Prospettiva personale

Answer the following questions in an appropriate manner from your personal perspective. Use complete sentences.

EXAMPLE: **Come stai in questo momento?**
            In questo momento sto bene/sto male/così, così/...

1. **Come stai in questo momento?**

_____

2. **Tu stai sempre attento/attenta quando attraversi la strada?**

_____

3. **Che cosa stai per fare in questo momento?**

_____

4. **Tu stai calmo/calma quando c'è pericolo?**

_____

5. **Chi non sta mai zitto/zitta nella tua famiglia?**

_____

The Present Progressive

The present progressive, called the **presente progressivo** in Italian, is formed with the present tense of the verb **stare** and the gerund of the verb, in that order.

To form the gerund of regular verbs

1. Drop the infinitive ending of the verb:

   parlare / _to speak_   →   parl-
   vendere / _to sell_   →   vend-
   finire / _to finish_   →   fin-

2. Add the following endings to the resulting stems:

   parlando / _speaking_
   vendendo / _writing_
   finendo / _finishing_

The good news is that most verbs have regular gerunds. Even **essere** has a regular gerund (**essendo**)! Here are the four most common verbs with irregular gerunds:

   bere / _to drink_   →   **bevendo** / _drinking_
   dare / _to give_   →   **dando** / _giving_
   dire / _to tell, to say_ →   **dicendo** / _telling, saying_
   fare / _to do, to make_ →   **facendo** / _doing_

Below are three verbs conjugated in the present progressive:

First conjugation: **parlare** / *to speak*

(io)	sto	parlando	I am speaking
(tu)	stai	parlando	you (fam.) are speaking
(lui/lei/Lei)	sta	parlando	he, she, you (pol.) is/are speaking
(noi)	stiamo	parlando	we are speaking
(voi)	state	parlando	you are speaking
(loro)	stanno	parlando	they are speaking

Second conjugation: **vendere** / *to sell*

(io)	sto	vendendo	I am selling
(tu)	stai	vendendo	you (fam.) are selling
(lui/lei/Lei)	sta	vendendo	he, she, you (pol.) is/are selling
(noi)	stiamo	vendendo	we are selling
(voi)	state	vendendo	you are selling
(loro)	stanno	vendendo	they are selling

Third conjugation: **finire** / *to finish*

(io)	sto	finendo	I am finishing
(tu)	stai	finendo	you (fam.) are finishing
(lui/lei/Lei)	sta	finendo	he, she, you (pol.) is/are finishing
(noi)	stiamo	finendo	we are finishing
(voi)	state	finendo	you are finishing
(loro)	stanno	finendo	they are finishing

This tense is an alternative to the present indicative when the action is ongoing.

Present Indicative	Present Progressive
In questo momento, Maria *studia*. At this moment, Maria is studying.	**In questo momento, Maria *sta studiando*.** At this moment, Maria is studying.
Che *fa* tuo fratello? What is your brother doing?	**Che *sta facendo* tuo fratello?** What is your brother doing?

It cannot be used in any other way in the present! In effect, it translates *exactly* the English present progressive: *I am studying, You are reading,* etc.

EXERCISE Set 7–2

A. Give the present progressive equivalents of the following present indicative forms of **cantare** / *to sing*, providing an appropriate English translation for each one.

EXAMPLE: **lui canta**   =   _____
          lui sta cantando   =   he is singing

1. **io canto**   _____ = _____

2. **tu canti**   _____ = _____

3. **noi cantiamo** _____ = _____

4. **loro cantano** _____ = _____

5. **voi cantate** _____ = _____

6. **Lei canta** _____ = _____

Now, give the present progressive equivalents of the following present indicative forms of **leggere** / *to read*, providing an appropriate English translation for each one.

7. **io leggo** _____ = _____

8. **tu leggi** _____ = _____

9. **io e tu leggiamo** _____ = _____

10. **loro leggono** _____ = _____

11. **tu e lei leggete** _____ = _____

12. **lui legge** _____ = _____

Now, give the present progressive equivalents of the following present indicative forms of **pulire** / *to clean*, providing an appropriate English translation for each one.

13. **io pulisco** _____ = _____

14. **tu pulisci** _____ = _____

15. **noi puliamo** _____ = _____

16. **loro puliscono** _____ = _____

17. **voi pulite** _____ = _____

18. **lei pulisce** _____ = _____

Finally, give the present progressive equivalents of the following present indicative forms of **andare** / *to go*, providing an appropriate English translation for each one.

19. **io vado** _____ = _____

20. **tu vai** _____ = _____

21. **noi andiamo** _____ = _____

22. **loro vanno** _____ = _____

23. **voi andate** _____ = _____

24. **lei va** _____ = _____

B. Say the following things in Italian:

il cappuccino	cappuccino coffee	**la fine**	end
chiacchierare	to chat	**mangiare**	to eat
chiedere	to ask	**rispondere**	to answer
l'espresso	espresso coffee	**il verbo**	verb
la fantascienza	science fiction		

1. Franco, what are you drinking? Are you drinking an espresso coffee?

_____

2. What movie are they showing at this time?

_____

3. Mrs. Marchi, what are you saying?

_____

4. What are they doing?

_____

5. Marco and Maria are going out at this moment.

_____

6. Where is Alessandro? He's sleeping.

_____

7. What are they drinking? Are they drinking a cappuccino?

_____

C. Rewrite the following story by changing the indicated verbs in the present indicative to the present progressive.

In questo momento, Franco e Dina (*vanno*) 1. _____ al Bar Roma, dove ci sono i loro amici che (*prendono*) 2. _____ il caffè. Quando arrivano, Franco e Dina vedono che i loro amici (*chiacchierano*) 3. _____mentre (*bevono*) 4. _____ il caffè. Franco chiede: "Ehi (*Hey*), ragazzi, che (*fate*) 5. _____?" Un'amica risponde: "Ciao, Franco e Dina, non (*facciamo*) 6. _____ niente, solo (*chiacchieriamo*) 7. _____ !" Alla fine, Dina dice: "Perché non andiamo tutti al cinema? (*Danno*) 8. _____ un nuovo film di fantascienza."

Prospettiva personale

Answer the following questions in an appropriate manner from your personal perspective. Use complete sentences.

EXAMPLE: **Che stai facendo in questo momento?**
              In questo momento, sto studiando i verbi italiani/
              In questo momento non sto facendo niente/...

1. **Che stai facendo in questo momento?**

_____

2. **Che stanno facendo gli altri membri della tua famiglia?**

_____

3. **Che libro stai leggendo in questo momento?**

_____

4. **Quali film interessanti stanno dando in questo momento?**

_____

5. **Stai bevendo qualcosa in questo momento? Se sì** (*If yes*), **che cosa stai bevendo?**

_____

6. **Stai mangiando qualcosa in questo momento?**

_____

Illustrative Dialogue

a presto	see you soon	**la mela**	apple
gli alimentari	foods (food store)	**il pesce**	fish
la banca	bank	**il pisello**	pea
la carne	meat	**programmare**	to plan
la ditta	company, firm	**la spesa**	food shopping
incontrarsi	to encounter	**tornare**	to go back, to return
l'informatica	computer science	**l'università**	university
insieme	together	**la volta**	time, occasion

**Due amiche che non si vedono da tempo, s'incontrano in un negozio di alimentari mentre *stanno
facendo* la spesa.** *(Two friends who haven't seen each other for awhile, run into each other at a foodstore while they
are shopping.)*

Claudia:	**Franca, come stai? Che *stai facendo* di bello?**	Franca, how are you? What's up (= What are you doing that's nice)?
Franca:	***Sto* molto bene, Claudia. In questo momento *sto lavorando* per una ditta di informatica. E tu?**	I'm very well, Claudia. Right now, I'm working for a computer firm. And you?
Claudia:	**Io *sto lavorando* in una banca. Anche tu *stai facendo* la spesa?**	I'm working in a bank. Are you also shopping for food?
Franca:	**Sì. Ho bisogno di comprare delle mele, dei piselli e della carne. E tu, che cosa *stai comprando*?**	Yes. I need to buy some apples, some peas, and some meat. And you, what are you buying?
Claudia:	**Del pesce e un po' di frutta. Perché non usciamo insieme qualche volta?**	Some fish and a bit of fruit. Why don't we go out together sometime?
Franca:	**Va bene. Ecco il mio numero di telefono. Ciao!**	OK. Here's my phone number. Bye!
Claudia:	**Ecco il mio. Ciao!**	Here's mine. Bye!

Grammar Note

Partitives are structures placed before nouns that indicate a part of something as distinct from its whole: e.g.,
some apples, a bit of fruit, a few peas, etc.

In Italian, the most commonly used type of partitive consists of the preposition **di** + the appropriate forms of the definite article (see Chapter 5 for the appropriate contractions):

del pesce	=	*some fish, a little fish*
dei piselli	=	*some peas*
degli spaghetti	=	*some spaghetti*
della carne	=	*some meat, a little meat*
delle mele	=	*some apples*

EXERCISE Set 7–3

A. Answer the following questions with complete sentences based on the dialogue.

   1. **Come si chiamano le due amiche?**

   _____

2. **Cosa stanno facendo?**

_____

3. **Dove sta lavorando Franca?**

_____

4. **E Claudia dove sta lavorando?**

_____

5. **Che cosa sta comprando Franca?**

_____

6. **E che cosa sta comprando Claudia?**

_____

7. **Che cosa stanno programmando le due amiche?**

_____

B. Make up your own dialogue, as indicated.

Gianni: Hi, Giorgio. We haven't seen each other for years. What's up?

_____

Giorgio: Hi, Gianni. It's true. Right now, I'm doing nothing. What about you?

_____

Gianni: I'm working in a bank. But I'm planning to go back to the university.

_____

Giorgio: I'm planning the same thing.

_____

Gianni: You know, they are showing a new movie tonight. Do you want to come with my fiancée and me?

_____

Giorgio: No, thanks. Right now, I'm going out with Franca. We are planning to do something else. See you soon!

_____

Gianni: Bye!

_____

Uses and Features

The present progressive is, as you have seen above, an alternative to the present indicative, allowing you to zero in on an ongoing action.

> **In questo momento, mia sorella _sta leggendo_.** / _At this moment, my sister is reading._
> **Marco _sta scrivendo_ un' e-mail.** / _Mark is writing an e-mail._
> **Loro _stanno finendo_ di lavorare.** / _They are finishing work._

The present progressive of reflexive verbs is formed in the usual fashion but, of course, with the addition of reflexive pronouns. Here is the verb **lavarsi** / _to wash oneself_ fully conjugated for you in the present progressive:

(io)	mi	sto	lavando	I am washing myself
(tu)	ti	stai	lavando	you (fam.) are washing yourself
(lui/lei/Lei)	si	sta	lavando	he, she, you (pol.) is/are washing himself/herself/yourself
(noi)	ci	stiamo	lavando	we are washing ourselves
(voi)	vi	state	lavando	you are washing yourselves
(loro)	si	sta	lavando	they are washing themselves

As a stylistic option, the pronoun may be attached to the gerund:

(io) **mi sto lavando**	=	(io) **sto lavandomi**
(tu) **ti stai lavando**	=	(tu) **stai lavandoti**
(lui/lei/Lei) **si sta lavando**	=	(lui/lei/Lei) **sta lavandosi**
(noi) **ci stiamo lavando**	=	(noi) **stiamo lavandoci**
(voi) **vi state lavando**	=	(voi) **state lavandovi**
(loro) **si stanno lavando**	=	(loro) **stanno lavandosi**

This form of the present progressive is, however, less common.

VOCABULARY TIP

The present progressive is often used with words such as

in questo momento	*in/at this moment, at this time*
mentre	*while*
adesso/ora	*now*

EXERCISE Set 7–4

Choose which verb tense is more appropriate, the present indicative or the present progressive of the given verb. Note that in some cases both can be chosen.

1. **Che cosa stai facendo in questo momento, Giorgio?**
   a. **Sto bevendo un cappuccino.**
   b. **Bevo un cappuccino.**

2. **E tu che fai?**
   a. **Sto scrivendo un' e-mail.**
   b. **Scrivo un' e-mail.**

3. **Generalmente che fa Maria quando ha tempo?**
   a. **Sta leggendo dei libri.**
   b. **Legge dei libri.**

4. **Dov'è Marco in questo momento?**
   a. **Si sta alzando.**
   b. **Si alza.**

5. **Ogni estate noi ... in Italia.**
   a. **stiamo andando**
   b. **andiamo**

6. **Come ... loro generalmente per andare al lavoro?**
   a. **stanno vestendosi**
   b. **si vestono**

7. **Anche lui ... dei piselli e della frutta.**
   a. **sta comprando**
   b. **compra**

8. **Di solito noi ... solo un po' di carne in quel negozio di alimentari.**
   a. **stiamo comprando**
   b. **compriamo**

9. **Per che cosa ... ?**
   a. **ti stai preparando**
   b. **ti prepari**

Crossword Puzzle 7

Orizzontali

3. **In questo momento, loro stanno … (dancing).**
4. **Ma che stai … (saying)?**
7. **Che cosa stai … (wearing)?**
8. **Noi … uscendo in questo momento.**

Verticali

1. **Marco, cosa stai … (doing)?**
2. **Claudia, dove stai … (going)?**
3. **Loro stanno … un caffè (drinking).**
5. **Stanno … un film nuovo adesso (giving).**
6. **Giorgio, ma che … dicendo?**

8
Peculiarities

First-Conjugation Spelling Peculiarities

If the first-conjugation infinitive ending is **-ciare** or **-giare**, then drop the **-are** and retain the **-i** of the ending, but do not write a "double -i" when adding on the present indicative endings **-i** and **-iamo**:

cominciare / *to begin* → **cominci-**

(io)	**comincio**	I begin, I am beginning, I do begin
(tu)	**cominci**	you (fam.) begin, you are beginning, you do begin
(lui/lei/Lei)	**comincia**	he, she, you (pol.) begin(s), he, she, you is/are beginning, he, she, you does/do begin
(noi)	**cominciamo**	we begin, we are beginning, we do begin
(voi)	**cominciate**	you begin, you are beginning, you do begin
(loro)	**cominciano**	they begin, they are beginning, they do begin

mangiare / *to eat* → **mangi-**

(io)	**mangio**	I eat, I am eating, I do eat
(tu)	**mangi**	you (fam.) eat, you are eating, you do eat
(lui/lei/Lei)	**mangia**	he, she, you (pol.) eat(s), he, she, you is/are eating, he, she, you does/do eat
(noi)	**mangiamo**	we eat, we are eating, we do eat
(voi)	**mangiate**	you eat, you are eating, you do eat
(loro)	**mangiano**	they eat, they are eating, they do eat

Here are a few common useful verbs ending in **-ciare** and **-giare**:

abbracciare	to hug
allacciare	to fasten
annunciare	to announce
assaggiare	to taste
baciare	to kiss
lanciare	to throw
lasciare	to let, to leave (behind)
noleggiare	to rent (car, movie, etc.)
parcheggiare	to park
pronunciare	to pronounce
viaggiare	to travel

If the infinitive ends in **-iare**, the same pattern of "not doubling the -i" applies, unless the **-i** is stressed during the conjugation, in which case it is retained before the **-i** ending only:

Unstressed	Stressed
cambiare to change	**deviare** to deviate
copiare to copy	**inviare** to send
studiare to study	**sciare** to ski

For example

cambiare / *to change* → **cambi-**

(io)	cambio	I change, I am changing, I do change
(tu)	cambi	you (fam.) change, you are changing, you do change
(lui/lei/Lei)	cambia	he, she, you (pol.) change(s), he, she, you is/are changing, he, she, you does/do change
(noi)	cambiamo	we change, we are changing, we do change
(voi)	cambiate	you change, you are changing, you do change
(loro)	cambiano	they change, they are changing, they do change

sciare / *to ski* → **sci-**

(io)	scio	I ski, I am skiing, I do ski
(tu)	scii	you (fam.) ski, you are skiing, you do ski
(lui/lei/Lei)	scia	he, she, you (pol.) ski(es), he, she, you is/are skiing, he, she, you does/do ski
(noi)	sciamo	we ski, we are skiing, we do ski
(voi)	sciate	you ski, you are skiing, you do ski
(loro)	sciano	they ski, they are skiing, they do ski

TIP

In most verbs ending in **-iare** *the* **-i** *is unstressed. Therefore, the most common conjugation pattern is the one exemplified by* **cambiare.**

If the first-conjugation infinitive ending is **-care** or **-gare,** drop the **-are** but add an **"h"** before the present indicative endings **-i** and **-iamo.** This indicates that the hard sound is to be retained:

cercare / *to look for, to search for* → **cerc-**

(io)	cerco	I search, I am searching, I do search
(tu)	cerchi	you (fam.) search, you are searching, you do search
(lui/lei/Lei)	cerca	he, she, you (pol.) search(es), he, she, you is/are searching, he, she, you does/do search
(noi)	cerchiamo	we search, we are searching, we do search
(voi)	cercate	you search, you are searching, you do search
(loro)	cercano	they search, they are searching, they do search

pagare / *to pay (for)* → **pag-**

(io)	pago	I pay, I am paying, I do pay
(tu)	paghi	you (fam.) pay, you are paying, you do pay
(lui/lei/Lei)	paga	he, she, you (pol.) pay(s), he, she, you is/are paying, he, she, you (pol.) does/do pay

(noi)	**paghiamo**	we pay, we are paying, we do pay
(voi)	**pagate**	you pay, you are paying, you do pay
(loro)	**pagano**	they pay, they are paying, they do pay

Here are a few common useful verbs ending in **-care** and **-gare**:

comunicare	to communicate
criticare	to criticize
dimenticarsi	to forget
giocare	to play
indicare	to indicate
legare	to tie
negare	to deny
pregare	to pray, to beg
spiegare	to explain

Note that **giocare** means *to play* a game, sports, and so on; whereas **suonare** (introduced in Chapter 1) means *to play* an instrument:

Lui *gioca* a calcio molto bene. / *He plays soccer very well.*

Lei *suona* il pianoforte molto bene. / *She plays the piano very well.*

The spelling and pronunciation peculiarities described above apply only to the first conjugation. A second-conjugation verb such as **conoscere** or **leggere,** for instance, is conjugated in the usual way and the **g** or **c** is pronounced as hard or soft as the case may be:

(io) *leggo* / *I know*   →   *pronounce the "g" as hard*

(tu) *leggi* / *you read*   →   *pronounce the "g" as soft*

and so on

REMINDER

As always, be careful when you pronounce the third person plural forms! The accent is not placed on the ending, but on a syllable before the ending:

cominciano / *they begin*   **pagano** / *they pay*

| | | |

stress   stress

EXERCISE Set 8–1

A. Supply the missing present indicative forms of the verbs **baciare** and **viaggiare,** giving the English equivalents.

EXAMPLE: lui ____   =   _____

lui bacia/lui viaggia   =   he kisses/he travels (he is kissing, etc.)

1. **io** _____   =   _____

2. **tu** _____   =   _____

3. **noi** _____   =   _____

4. **loro** _____   =   _____

5. voi _____   =   _____

6. Lei _____   =   _____

Now, supply the missing present indicative forms of the verbs **studiare** and **inviare,** giving the English equivalents.

7. io _____   =   _____

8. tu _____   =   _____

9. io e tu _____   =   _____

10. loro _____   =   _____

11. tu e lei _____ =   _____

12. lui _____   =   _____

Finally, supply the missing present indicative forms of the verbs **comunicare** and **spiegare,** giving the English equivalents.

13. io _____   =   _____

14. tu _____   =   _____

15. noi _____   =   _____

16. loro _____   =   _____

17. voi _____   =   _____

18. lui _____   =   _____

B. Say the following things in Italian:

il calcio	soccer	**il panino**	bun sandwich
la cena	dinner	**il piatto**	plate
la cintura di sicurezza	seatbelt	**il pranzo**	lunch
la colazione	breakfast	**la scarpa**	shoe
il dolce	sweet	**la scuola**	school
l'opinione (f.)	opinion	**lo sport**	sport
la palla	ball	**squisito**	delicious

1. At what time does the movie begin?

_____

2. I always eat sweets at parties. What do you (fam., sing.) eat usually?

_____

3. We always hug each other every time that we meet.

_____

4. Giorgio, are you fastening the seatbelt?

_____

5. What are they announcing?

_____

6. We are tasting the sweets. They are delicious.

_____

7. We throw the ball very well.

_____

8. Why are they leaving school (behind)? Is it because they travel a lot?

_____

9. Where do you (fam., sing.) usually park your car?

_____

10. Marco, why do you always change your opinion?

_____

11. I never deviate from studying Italian verbs.

_____

12. Maria, what e-mail are you sending to your friend Carla?

_____

13. Franco, what are you looking for?

_____

14. Your opinion indicates that you deny the truth.

_____

15. Alessandro what are you doing? Are you tying your shoes?

_____

Prospettiva personale

Answer the following questions in an appropriate manner from your personal perspective. Use complete sentences.

EXAMPLE: **Che cosa mangi generalmente per colazione?**
             Per colazione, generalmente mangio un panino/un piatto di pasta/...

1. **Che cosa mangi di solito per la colazione?**

_____

2. **Che cosa mangi di solito per pranzo?**

_____

3. **Che cosa mangi di solito per cena?**

_____

4. **Chi baci regolarmente? Perché vi baciate?**

_____

5. **Noleggi spesso i film? Quale tipo di film noleggi generalmente?**

_____

6. **Come pronunci la lingua italiana?**

_____

7. **Viaggiate spesso nella tua famiglia? Se sì, dove viaggiate?**

_____

8. **Studi molto i verbi italiani?**

_____

9. **Copi di solito i verbi in questo libro sul tuo computer?**

_____

10. **Ti piace andare a sciare? Se sì, dove scii?**

_____

11. **Quando esci con gli amici, chi paga generalmente?**

_____

12. **Comunichi spesso con i tuoi parenti?**

_____

13. **Chi critichi regolarmente?**

_____

14. **Giochi a qualche sport? Se sì, quale?**

_____

15. **Preghi regolarmente? Perché?**

_____

Illustrative Dialogue

alcuni (-e)	some	**l'idea**	idea
l'appunto	note	**la matita**	pencil, crayon
cambiare idea	to change one's mind	**la penna**	pen
la carta	card	**qualche**	some

Carlo:	**Nora, che _cerchi_?**	Nora, what are you looking for?
Nora:	**_Cerco_ una matita o una penna.**	I'm looking for a pencil or a pen.
Carlo:	**Ne ho alcune io. Perché?**	I have some. Why?
Nora:	**_Sto studiando_ e ho bisogno di scrivere qualche appunto.**	I'm studying and I need to write a few notes.
Carlo:	**Perché non _giochi_ a carte con me?**	Why don't you play cards with me?
Nora:	**Non ho tempo!**	I don't have time!
Carlo:	**Ti _prego_!**	I beg of you!
Nora:	**No. Se _cambio_ idea, ti chiamo.**	No. If I change my mind, I'll call you.

Grammar Notes

The structure **alcuni (-e)** renders the idea of *some*. It is therefore another partitive structure (Chapter 7):

alcuni libri	=	*some books*
alcune matite	=	*some pencils*

The invariable adjective **qualche** can also be used to express partiality. But be careful with this one! It must be followed by a *singular* noun, even though the meaning is plural!

qualche libro	=	*some books*
qualche matita	=	*some pencils*

The particle **ne** renders the idea of *some (of it, of them)*. It is placed before the verb:

Ho due libri / *I have two books.*	**Ne ho due** / *I have two (of them).*
Hai delle matite? / *Do you have any pencils?*	**Ne ho alcune** / *I have some.*

EXERCISE Set 8–2

Answer the following questions with complete sentences based on the dialogue.

1. **Come si chiamano le due persone?**

   _____

2. **Cosa cerca Nora?**

   _____

3. **Perché?**

   _____

4. **Quante penne e matite ha Carlo?**

   _____

5. **Che cosa chiede Carlo a Nora?**

   _____

6. **Perché non vuole giocare Nora?**

   _____

7. **Che fa Nora se cambia idea?**

   _____

A Different Type of Infinitive

Recall that there are three main types of verbs in Italian:

1. First-conjugation verbs ending in **-are: parlare** / *to speak*

2. Second-conjugation verbs ending in **-ere: scrivere** / *to write*

3. Third-conjugation verbs ending in **-ire: capire** / *to understand*

There is a fourth type ending in **-rre**; but this type is quite rare. Here are the most common **-rre** verbs (for practical purposes):

attrarre	to attract
dedurre	to deduce
indurre	to induce
introdurre	to introduce
porre	to pose, to put
produrre	to produce
ridurre	to reduce
sedurre	to seduce
supporre	to suppose
tradurre	to translate
trarre	to draw (pull)

All verbs of this type have irregular conjugations. However, there is a pattern in the case of those ending in **-durre**:

1. Change the ending in your mind to **-cere**:

   dedurre → **deducere**

2. Drop the **-ere** ending of your "hypothetical" verb stem:

   deducere → **deduc-**

3. Add the usual second-conjugation endings:

(io)	**deduco**	I deduce, I am deducing
(tu)	**deduci**	you (fam.) deduce, you are deducing
(lui/lei/Lei)	**deduce**	he, she, you (pol.) deduce(s), he, she, you is/are deducing
(noi)	**deduciamo**	we deduce, we are deducing
(voi)	**deducete**	you deduce, you are deducing
(loro)	**deducono**	they deduce, they are deducing

The verbs **indurre**, **introdurre**, **produrre**, **ridurre**, **sedurre**, and **tradurre** are conjugated in this way.

To form the present participle of these verbs, use the same hypothetical verb stem, gerund and add the usual **-endo**:

deducere → **deduc-** → **deducendo**

You can now use these verbs in the present progressive (Chapter 7):

(io) sto deducendo / *I am deducing*

(tu) stai introducendo / *you are introducing*

The other verbs are conjugated as follows:

trarre / *to draw* and **attrarre** / *to attract*

(io)	**traggo**	I draw, I am drawing
(tu)	**trai**	you (fam.) draw, you are drawing
(lui/lei/Lei)	**trae**	he, she, you (pol.) draw(s), he, she, you is/are drawing
(noi)	**traiamo**	we draw, we are drawing
(voi)	**traete**	you draw, you are drawing
(loro)	**traggono**	they draw, they are drawing

porre / *to pose* and **supporre** / *to suppose*

(io)	**pongo**	I pose, I am posing
(tu)	**poni**	you (fam.) pose, you are posing
(lui/lei/Lei)	**pone**	he, she, you (pol.) pose(s), he, she, you is/are posing

(noi)	**poniamo**	we pose, we are posing
(voi)	**ponete**	you pose, you are posing
(loro)	**pongono**	they pose, they are posing

The gerund of these verbs is

porre → **ponendo**   **trarre** → **traendo**

EXERCISE Set 8–3

A. Supply the missing present indicative form of the verb **attrarre**, giving the English equivalent.

EXAMPLE: lui _____   =   _____
            lui attrae   =   he attracts, he is attracting

1. **io** _____   =   _____

2. **tu** _____   =   _____

3. **noi** _____   =   _____

4. **loro** _____   =   _____

5. **voi** _____   =   _____

6. **Lei** _____   =   _____

Now, supply the missing present indicative form of the verb **indurre**, giving the English equivalent.

7. **io** _____   =   _____

8. **tu** _____   =   _____

9. **io e tu** _____   =   _____

10. **loro** _____   =   _____

11. **tu e lei** _____   =   _____

12. **lui** _____   =   _____

Finally, supply the missing present indicative form of the verb **supporre**, giving the English equivalent.

13. **io** _____   =   _____

14. **tu** _____   =   _____

15. **noi** _____   =   _____

16. **loro** _____   =   _____

17. **voi** _____   =   _____

18. **lei** _____   =   _____

B. Match the items in each column in an appropriate manner.

1. **Marco, che cosa ...**	a. **sto ponendo**
2. **La signora Dini ... quella cosa.**	b. **seducete**
3. **Io ... la penna sul tavolo** (*table*).	c. **stai traducendo?**
4. **Ma perché voi mi ... sempre?**	d. **sta traendo**
5. **Che cosa ... quelle ditte?**	e. **riduce**
6. **Lui ... sempre tutto a niente!**	f. **producono**

Differences with Respect to English

The predicate of affirmative sentences may or may not have an object. An *object* is the noun, substantive, or noun phrase that receives the action. It normally follows the verb. A pronoun can also function as an object.

There are two types of object: *direct* and *indirect*. Each one can be identified very easily as follows:

1. A noun, substantive, or noun phrase that directly follows the verb is a direct object.

   Lui suona *il violino*. / *He plays the violin.*

2. A noun, substantive, or noun phrase that follows the verb but is introduced by a preposition such as **a** (*to, at*) or **per** (*for*) is an indirect object.

   Lui va *al negozio*. / *He is going to the store.*

Whether an object is direct or indirect depends on the verb. Some verbs must be followed only by one type of object or the other. Most verbs in Italian match their English equivalents when it comes to whether or not a direct or indirect object should follow.

However, there are differences! Here are the most important ones.

Verbs Requiring a Direct Object in Italian

Italian → Direct object	English → Indirect object
ascoltare **Mia madre ascolta la radio ogni sera.**	*to listen to* My mother listens to the radio every evening.
aspettare **Giorgio sta aspettando Maria.**	*to wait for* Giorgio is waiting for Mary.
cercare **Tina cerca la sua penna.**	*to look for, to search for* Tina is looking for her pen.

By the way, verbs that require a direct object are known, technically, as *transitive*.

Verbs Requiring an Indirect Object in Italian

Italian → Indirect object	English → Direct object
chiedere (a) **Gino chiede al professore di venire.**	*to ask* Gino asks the professor to come.
telefonare (a) **Gina telefona a sua madre ogni sera.**	*to phone* Gina phones her mother every evening.
rispondere (a) **Perché non rispondi alla mia domanda?**	*to answer* Why aren't you answering my question?

Verbs that require an indirect object are known, technically, as *intransitive*.

As a final word on the Italian present indicative, note that when used with the preposition **da** (which in this case means both *since* and *for*), it renders the English present progressive tense.

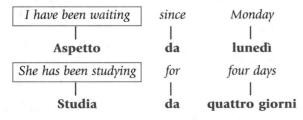

EXERCISE Set 8–4

Say the following things in Italian:

la domanda	question	**la radio (f.)**	radio
per favore	please	**subito**	right away
il programma (m.)	program	**il violino**	violin

1. Maria, why are you listening to that radio program *(programma radio)*?

   _____

2. Carlo is waiting for Mrs. Smith.

   _____

3. What is she looking for? She is looking for her violin.

   _____

4. Marco, ask your sister to come to the party.

   _____

5. Bruno, please phone your professor (m.) right away.

   _____

6. I do not know how to answer your (pol., sing.) question.

   _____

7. We have been living in this city for ten years.

   _____

8. I have been working here since Monday.

   _____

9. He has been studying music for many years.

   _____

Crossword Puzzle 8

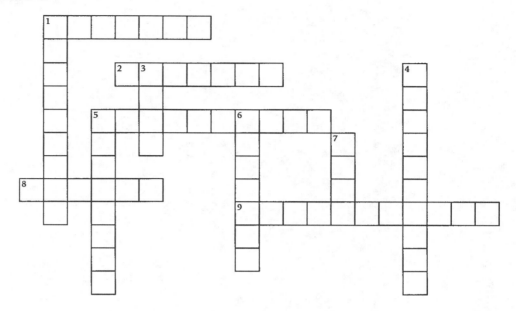

Orizzontali

1. they pose
2. you (fam., sing.) taste
5. we explain
8. you (fam., sing.) induce
9. we criticize

Verticali

1. they produce
3. you (fam., sing.) ski
4. we rent
5. you (pl.) seduce
6. you (fam., sing.) indicate
7. you (fam., sing.) kiss

Part Two

The Past Indicative Tenses

The Past: An Overview

What Is a Past Tense?

A past tense is any tense indicating time gone by or some former action or state. There are four main indicative past tenses in Italian:

1. The present perfect, called the **passato prossimo**

   > **Maria *ha telefonato* ieri.** / *Mary phoned yesterday.*
   > **Abbiamo** appena *finito* **di lavorare.** / *We have just finished working.*

   This verb tense is used to show that an event was completed at the time of speaking. It is equivalent to the English forms *I have spoken, you have written*, etc.

2. The imperfect indicative, called the **imperfetto dell'indicativo**

   > **Maria *telefonava* spesso una volta.** / *Mary used to phone often once.*
   > **Noi *andavamo* spesso in Italia da bambini.** / *We used to go to Italy often as children.*

   This tense allows you to indicate incomplete, continued, or customary past actions. English has no "true" imperfect tense, but some constructions, such as *she was studying* and *he used to study*, render the meaning of imperfect verbs of Italian in a fairly accurate way.

3. The preterite or past absolute, called the **passato remoto**

   > **Loro *arrivarono* in America molti anni fa.** / *They arrived in America many years ago.*
   > **Dante *nacque* a Firenze.** / *Dante was born in Florence.*

   This tense is used to refer to a completed action, state, or event in the distant past. It is equivalent to the English forms *I spoke, you wrote*, etc.

4.   The pluperfect indicative, called the **trapassato prossimo**

   Loro *avevano* già *telefonato*, quando sei rientrato. / *They had already phoned when you got back.*

   Lui mi ha detto che le *aveva* già *parlato*. / *He told me that he had already spoken to her.*

   The pluperfect is used to show that an event was completed before a given past time. It is equivalent to the English compound tense forms *I had spoken, you had written,* etc.

Compound Tenses

The present perfect and the pluperfect are compound tenses. This means simply that they are verbs constructed with two parts, an auxiliary verb and a past participle in that order:

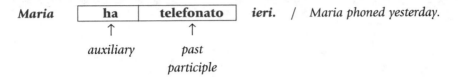

In Italian, the auxiliary verb in compound tenses is either **avere** or **essere**, as you will learn in the next chapter.

9
The Present Perfect

Past Participles

The present perfect of regular verbs, called the **passato prossimo** in Italian, is a compound tense. As you learned in the previous chapter, it is formed with the appropriate form of the auxiliary verb plus the past participle, called the **participio passato** of the verb, in that order.

To form the past participle of regular verbs

1. Drop the infinitive ending of the verb, **-are, -ere, -ire**:

    parlare / *to speak* → **parl-**
    vendere / *to sell* → **vend-**
    finire / *to finish* → **fin-**

2. Add the endings **-ato, -uto,** and **-ito** respectively to the stems:

    parlato / *spoken*
    venduto / *written*
    finito / *finished*

Of the verbs introduced in this book so far, the following have irregular past participles:

accendere / *to turn on*	→	**acceso** / *turned on*
apparire / *to appear*	→	**apparso** / *appeared*
aprire / *to open*	→	**aperto** / *opened*
bere / *to drink*	→	**bevuto** / *drunk*
chiedere / *to ask*	→	**chiesto** / *asked*
chiudere / *to close*	→	**chiuso** / *closed*
conoscere / *to know*	→	**conosciuto** / *known*
coprire / *to cover*	→	**coperto** / *covered*
correre / *to run*	→	**corso** / *run*
dare / *to give*	→	**dato** / *given*
dire / *to tell, to say*	→	**detto** / *told, said*
essere / *to be*	→	**stato** / *been*
fare / *to do, to make*	→	**fatto** / *done, made*
leggere / *to read*	→	**letto** / *read*
mettere (mettersi) / *to put*	→	**messo** / *put (put on)*
morire / *to die*	→	**morto** / *died*
nascere / *to be born*	→	**nato** / *born*
piacere / *to like*	→	**piaciuto** / *liked*
prendere / *to take*	→	**preso** / *taken*
ridere / *to laugh*	→	**riso** / *laughed*
rimanere / *to remain*	→	**rimasto** / *remained*

rispondere / to answer	→	**risposto** / answered
rompere / to break	→	**rotto** / broken
scegliere / to choose	→	**scelto** / chosen
scoprire / to discover	→	**scoperto** / discovered
scrivere / to write	→	**scritto** / written
soffrire / to suffer	→	**sofferto** / suffered
vedere / to see	→	**visto/veduto** / seen
venire / to come	→	**venuto** / come
vivere / to live	→	**vissuto** / lived

The past participles of **conoscere** and **piacere** are not really "irregular." The **"i"** has been added simply to indicate retention of the soft **"c"** sound. The **"i"** of verbs such as **cominciare** and **mangiare** (Chapter 8) is also retained in the formation of the past participle for the same reason:

cominciare / to begin	→	**cominci-**	→	**cominciato** / begun
mangiare / to eat	→	**mangi-**	→	**mangiato** / eaten

The past participle of verbs ending in **-durre** (Chapter 8) is formed as follows:

1. Drop the **-urre**:

dedurre / to deduce	→	**ded-**
produrre / to produce	→	**prod-**

2. Add the suffix (ending) **-otto**:

    dedotto / deduced
    prodotto / produced

The other verbs ending in **-rre** introduced in Chapter 8 have the following irregular past participles:

trarre / to draw	→	**tratto** / drawn
porre / to pose	→	**posto** / posed

Notice, finally, that **vedere** has both a regular and irregular past participle form. Each one is used with equal frequency.

EXERCISE Set 9–1

A. Give the past participles of the following verbs.

    1. **arrivare**   =   _____

    2. **dormire**   =   _____

    3. **capire**   =   _____

    4. **vedere**   =   _____

    5. **credere**   =   _____

    6. **lasciare**   =   _____

    7. **noleggiare**   =   _____

    8. **produrre**   =   _____

9. **supporre** = _____

10. **apparire** = _____

11. **bere** = _____

12. **chiudere** = _____

13. **chiedere** = _____

14. **scegliere** = _____

15. **piacere** = _____

16. **scrivere** = _____

17. **vivere** = _____

18. **venire** = _____

B. Now, can you do the opposite? Given the following past participles, reconstruct their infinitives.

EXAMPLE: **messo**
          mettere

1. **acceso** = _____

2. **letto** = _____

3. **fatto** = _____

4. **stato** = _____

5. **detto** = _____

6. **dato** = _____

7. **corso** = _____

8. **coperto** = _____

9. **risposto** = _____

10. **morto** = _____

11. **rotto** = _____

12. **riso** = _____

13. **rimasto** = _____

14. **preso** = _____

15. **scoperto**   =   _____

16. **sofferto**   =   _____

17. **aperto**   =   _____

Verbs Conjugated with *Avere*

There are two auxiliary verbs in Italian: **avere** / *to have* and **essere** / *to be*. In the present perfect, they are in the present indicative.

Most verbs are conjugated with **avere**:

First conjugation: **parlare** / *to speak*

(io)	ho	parlato	I have spoken, I spoke
(tu)	hai	parlato	you (fam.) have spoken, you spoke
(lui/lei/Lei)	ha	parlato	he, she, you (pol.) has/have spoken, he, she, you spoke
(noi)	abbiamo	parlato	we have spoken, we spoke
(voi)	avete	parlato	you have spoken, you spoke
(loro)	hanno	parlato	they have spoken, they spoke

Second conjugation: **vendere** / *to sell*

(io)	ho	venduto	I have sold, I sold
(tu)	hai	venduto	you (fam.) have sold, you sold
(lui/lei/Lei)	ha	venduto	he, she, you (pol.) has/have sold, he, she, you sold
(noi)	abbiamo	venduto	we have sold, we sold
(voi)	avete	venduto	you have sold, you sold
(loro)	hanno	venduto	they have sold, they sold

Third conjugation: **finire** / *to finish*

(io)	ho	finito	I have finished, I finished
(tu)	hai	finito	you (fam.) have finished, you finished
(lui/lei/Lei)	ha	finito	he, she, you (pol.) has/have finished, he, she, you finished
(noi)	abbiamo	finito	we have finished, we finished
(voi)	avete	finito	you have finished, you finished
(loro)	hanno	finito	they have finished, they finished

EXERCISE Set 9–2

A. Supply the missing present perfect forms of the verbs **cominciare**, **credere**, and **dormire**, giving the English equivalents.

EXAMPLE:	lui ____	=	_____
	lui ha cominciato	=	he has begun, he began
	lui ha creduto	=	he has believed, he believed
	lui ha dormito	=	he has slept, he slept

1. **io** _____ = _____
    = _____
    = _____

2. **tu** _____ = _____
    = _____
    = _____

3. **noi** _____ = _____
    = _____
    = _____

4. **loro** _____ = _____
    = _____
    = _____

5. **voi** _____ = _____
    = _____
    = _____

6. **lei** _____ = _____
    = _____
    = _____

Now supply the missing present perfect forms of the verbs **mettere**, **leggere**, and **scoprire**, giving the English equivalents.

EXAMPLE: **lui** ____   = _____
    lui ha messo = he has put, he put
    lui ha letto = he has read, he read
    lui ha scoperto = he has discovered, he discovered

7. **io** _____ = _____
    = _____
    = _____

8. **tu** _____ = _____
    = _____
    = _____

9. **noi** _____ = _____
    = _____
    = _____

10. **loro** _____ = _____
    = _____
    = _____

11. **voi** _____ = _____
    = _____
    = _____

12. **Lei** _____ = _____
    = _____
    = _____

B. Say the following things in Italian.

il conto	bill	**qualcuno**	someone
la giornata	day (all day)	**quasi**	almost
ieri	yesterday	**la storia**	story
normale	normal	**televisivo**	(of) television
poiché	since	**il vino**	wine

1. Maria and I have never watched that television program together.

_____

2. They didn't understand the story that you (fam., sing.) read to them.

_____

3. Paolo asked Carla to go out with him, but she only laughed.

_____

4. Mr. Dini rented a new movie, but he didn't like it.

_____

5. We paid the bill yesterday, since we drank almost all the coffee.

_____

6. Marco, who gave you that book?

_____

7. Yesterday, it rained. It was bad weather all day long.

_____

8. I have already written that e-mail. Carla saw the e-mail.

_____

9. Franca, did you turn on the television (set)? Yesterday, I saw a new program.

_____

10. What did they say? I didn't understand anything.

_____

Verbs Conjugated with *Essere*

The past participle of verbs conjugated with **essere** agrees in number and gender with the subject, in the same way an adjective does:

Alessandro è *partito* stamani. / *Alexander left this morning.*
Anche Sarah è *partita* stamani. / *Sarah also left this morning.*

Here are examples of verbs conjugated with **essere**:

First Conjugation: **arrivare** / *to arrive*

(io)	sono	arrivato/a	I have arrived, I arrived
(tu)	**sei**	**arrivato/a**	you(fam.) have arrived, you arrived
(lui)	**è**	**arrivato**	he has arrived, he arrived
(lei)	**è**	**arrivata**	she has arrived, she arrived
(Lei)	**è**	**arrivato/a**	you (pol.) have arrived, you arrived

(noi)	siamo	arrivati/e	we have arrived, we arrived
(voi)	siete	arrivati/e	you have arrived, you arrived
(loro)	sono	arrivati/e	they have arrived, they arrived

Second Conjugation: **cadere** / *to fall*

(io)	sono	caduto/a	I have fallen, I fell
(tu)	sei	caduto/a	you (fam.) have fallen, you fell
(lui)	è	caduto	he has fallen, he fell
(lei)	è	caduta	she has fallen, she fell
(Lei)	è	caduto/a	you (pol.) have fallen, you fell
(noi)	siamo	caduti/e	we have fallen, we fell
(voi)	siete	caduti/e	you have fallen, you fell
(loro)	sono	caduti/e	they have fallen, they fell

Third Conjugation: **uscire** / *to go out*

(io)	sono	uscito/a	I have gone out, I went out
(tu)	sei	uscito/a	you (fam.) have gone out, you went out
(lui)	è	uscito	he has gone out, he went out
(lei)	è	uscita	she has gone out, she went out
(Lei)	è	uscito/a	you (pol.) have gone out, you went out
(noi)	siamo	usciti/e	we have gone out, we went out
(voi)	siete	usciti/e	you have gone out, you went out
(loro)	sono	usciti/e	they have gone out, they went out

When do you use **avere** or **essere**? The best strategy is to assume that most verbs are conjugated with **avere** (which is true!), and then memorize the verbs that are conjugated with **essere**. However, as a rule of thumb it works as follows: if the verb answers the question *what*, it requires **avere**, while if it answers the question *where* or *when* it requires **essere**. A complete list of the verbs introduced in this book that are conjugated with **essere** can be found in Appendix B at the back. The most common verbs conjugated with **essere** are as follows:

andare	to go
apparire	to appear
arrivare	to arrive
cadere	to fall
correre	to run
diventare	to become
entrare	to enter
essere	to be
morire	to die
nascere	to be born
partire	to leave
salire	to climb, to go up
sembrare	to seem
stare	to stay
tornare	to go back, to return
uscire	to go out
venire	to come
vivere	to live

With a modal verb, the general rule is to select the auxiliary required the following infinitive:

Verb Conjugated with *Avere*	Verb Conjugated with *Essere*
ho voluto chiamare I wanted to call	**sono voluto/a andare** I wanted to go
hanno potuto chiamare they were able to call	**sono potuti/e andare** they were able to go
hai dovuto chiamare you had to call	**sei dovuto/a andare** you had to go

However, in contemporary conversational usage, the tendency is to use only **avere** with modal verbs:

    ho voluto andare   *rather than*   **sono voluto/a andare**

In the case of the verbs **correre** and **vivere** the auxiliary is **essere**, unless they are used as transitive verbs (Chapter 8), in which case they are conjugated with **avere**:

    Ho corso **tutto il giorno.** / *I ran the whole day.*
    Sono corso **per aiutare.** / *I ran to help.*

    Ho vissuto **una vita intera in Italia.** / *I lived an entire life in Italy.*
    Sono vissuto **in America.** / *I lived in America.*

With the verbs **nevicare** / *to snow* and **piovere** / *to rain* either auxiliary can be used:

    Ieri *ha/è* **nevicato.** / *It snowed yesterday.*

Finally, "impersonal" verbs are all conjugated with **essere**. These are verbs that have only third person forms.

    durare / *to last*
    Quel film è *durato* **tre ore.** / *That movie lasted three hours.*

    costare / *to cost*
    Quanto *sono costate* **le mele?** / *How much did the apples cost?*

    succedere / *to happen* (Past participle: **successo**)
    Quando è *successo?* / *When did it happen?*

TIP

The present perfect is generally translated in three ways as follows:

Ho mangiato la pizza   =   ⎡ *I have eaten pizza*
                               ⎢ *I ate pizza*
                               ⎣ *I did eat pizza*

Sono già arrivati   =   ⎡ *They have already arrived*
                               ⎢ *They arrived already*
                               ⎣ *They did arrive already*

EXERCISE **Set 9–3**

A. Supply the missing present perfect forms of the verbs **andare**, **cadere**, and **partire**, giving the English equivalents.

EXAMPLE:	**lui** ____	=	_____
	lui è andato	=	he has gone, he went
	lui è caduto	=	he has fallen, he fell
	lui è partito	=	he has left, he left

1. **io** _____ = _____

   = _____

   = _____

2. **tu** _____ = _____

   = _____

   = _____

3. **noi** _____ = _____

   = _____

   = _____

4. **loro** ____ = _____

   = _____

   = _____

5. **voi** _____ = _____

   = _____

   = _____

6. **lei** _____ = _____

   = _____

   = _____

Now supply the missing present perfect forms of the verbs **essere**, **nascere**, and **venire**, giving the English equivalents.

EXAMPLE:	**lui** ____	=	_____
	lui è stato	=	he has been, he was
	lui è nato	=	he was born
	lui è venuto	=	he has come, he came

7. **io** _____ = _____

   = _____

   = _____

8. tu _____ =   _____

           =   _____

           =   _____

9. noi _____ =   _____

           =   _____

           =   _____

10. loro _____ =   _____

           =   _____

           =   _____

11. voi _____ =   _____

           =   _____

           =   _____

12. Lei _____ =   _____

           =   _____

           =   _____

B. Fill in the blanks with the appropriate auxiliary verb, in its correct form, and the final vowel of the past participle.

EXAMPLES: **Lui _____ chiamat_ due giorni fa.**
              Lui ha chiamato due giorni fa.

              Anche mia sorella _____ venut_ alla festa.
              Anche mia sorella è venuta alla festa.

aiutare	to help	**scorso**	last (last week, month)
il cittadino	citizen	**stamani**	this morning
fa	ago	**tutto**	entire, whole

1. **I tuoi amici _____ arrivat__ stamani, vero?**

2. **È vero, Maria, che tu _____ stat__ a casa tutta la giornata ieri?**

3. **Loro _____ aiutat__ i loro amici l'intera settimana scorsa.**

4. **I suoi amici _____ andat__ in Italia due anni fa. La loro vacanza _____ durat__ poco.**

5. **Noi _____ diventat__ cittadini americani qualche anno fa.**

6. **La sua amica _____ telefonat__ qualche minuto fa.**

7. **Le sue amiche _____ entrat__ qualche minuto fa.**

8. **Signora Smith, quando _____ stat__ in Italia, Lei?**

9. **Voi _____ vist__ Marco?**

10. **A che ora _____ tornat__ voi ieri?**

11. **Quei libri _____ costat__ molto!**

12. **Alessandro, quanti libri _____ comprat__**

13. **Che cosa_____ success__ ieri a tua cugina?**

14. **Marco _____ uscit__ qualche minuto fa.**

Grammar Note

If the gender of the person or persons referred to is not specified, then the masculine form of the past participle is used:

Specified	Unspecified
Le ragazze sono uscite. The girls went out.	**Loro sono usciti.** They went out.

Prospettiva personale

Sì o no? Answer the questions from your personal perspective. Use complete sentences.

EXAMPLES: **Sei uscito/a?**
              Sì, sono uscito/a/No, non sono uscito/a.

              Ha nevicato?
              Sì, ha nevicato/No, non ha nevicato.

   Ieri...

   1. **Sei uscito/a?**

   _____

   2. **Se sì, dove sei andato/a?**

   _____

   3. **Ha fatto bel tempo?**

   _____

   4. **Che tempo ha fatto?**

   _____

   5. **È venuto qualcuno a casa tua?**

   _____

   6. **Se sì, chi è venuto?**

   _____

   7. **Tu e la tua famiglia/i tuoi amici siete andati al cinema?**

   _____

   8. **Se sì, quale film avete visto?**

   _____

   9. **Sei stato/a a casa?**

   _____

Illustrative Dialogue

Buon divertimento!   Have fun!
il divertimento   enjoyment

il mondo   world
la visita   visit

Linda:	**Lucia, *sono arrivati* i tuoi nipoti ieri in visita?**	Lucia, have your grandchildren arrived yesterday to visit?
Lucia:	**Sì, *sono arrivati* ieri. *È stata* la giornata più felice della mia vita!**	Yes, they arrived yesterday. It was the happiest day of my life!
Linda:	**Come *sono diventati*?**	How have they become?
Lucia:	**Mio nipote *è diventato* più alto di suo padre e mia nipote *è diventata* la ragazza più intelligente del mondo!**	My grandson has become taller than his father and my granddaughter has become the most intelligent girl in the world!
Linda:	**Quando *sono nati*?**	When were they born?
Lucia:	**Mio nipote *è nato* quasi dieci anni fa e mia nipote *è nata* quasi sei anni fa.**	My grandson was born nearly ten years ago and my granddaughter was born nearly six years ago.
Linda:	**Buon divertimento!**	Have fun!
Lucia:	**Grazie!**	Thanks!

Grammar Notes

To compare adjectives or adverbs, the following structures are used:

1. **così…come/tanto…quanto** / *as…as*

     Paola è così felice come sua sorella. / *Paula is as happy as her sister.*
     Loro sono tanto felici quanto noi. / *They are as happy as we are.*

2. **più…di** / *more*   **meno…di** / *less*

     Paola è più felice di sua sorella. / *Paula is happier than her sister.*
     Loro sono meno felici di noi. / *They are less happy than we are.*

3. **più…che** / *more*   **meno…che** / *less*

     Paola è più felice che ricca. / *Paula is happier than she is rich.*
     Loro sono meno felici che ricchi. / *They are less happy than they are rich.*

The difference between (2) and (3) is, essentially, that **di** is used when different people or things are being compared and **che** when different characteristics apply to the same person or thing.

     For the *superlative degree* use the definite article (in its proper form, of course!) followed by **più** or **meno**, as the case may be.

     Paola è la più alta della sua classe. / *Paula is the tallest in her class.*
     Loro sono i più simpatici della classe. / *They are the nicest in the class.*

EXERCISE Set 9–4

Answer the following questions based on the dialogue. Use complete sentences.

     1. **Quali persone sono arrivate in visita?**

_____

2. **Quando sono arrivate?**

_____

3. **Che tipo di giornata è stata per Lucia?**

_____

4. **Come sono diventati i nipoti di Lucia?**

_____

5. **Quando sono nati?**

_____

Piacere, Esserci, and Reflexive Verbs

In compound tenses, **piacere** is conjugated with **essere**. This means, of course, that the past participle agrees with the subject—no matter where it occurs in the sentence:

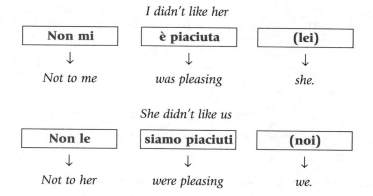

And do not forget that you might need to use the stressed forms of the indirect object pronouns (Chapter 4). These come after the verb for reasons of emphasis or clarity.

> **Quella musica è piaciuta solo a me, non a loro!** / *Only I liked that music, not they!*

Recall the verb form **esserci** / *to be there* (Chapter 2), which is used in the past to acknowledge that something or someone has been or was somewhere. It has the following two forms in the present perfect:

Singular	Plural
C'è stato l'insegnante? Has the teacher been here/there?	*Ci sono stati* gli insegnanti? Have the teachers been here/there?

In compound tenses, reflexive verbs are conjugated only with the auxiliary verb **essere**.

> **Lui *si è divertito* in Italia.** / *He enjoyed himself in Italy.*
>
> **Maria *si è alzata* tardi questa mattina.** / *Mary got up late this morning.*

Here is **lavarsi** / *to wash oneself* completely conjugated for you:

(io)	mi	sono	lavato/a	I have washed myself, I washed myself
(tu)	ti	sei	lavato/a	you (fam.) have washed yourself, you washed yourself

(lui)	si	è	lavato	he has washed himself, he washed himself
(lei)	si	è	lavata	she has washed herself, she washed herself
(Lei)	si	è	lavato/a	you (pol.) have washed yourself, you washed yourself
(noi)	ci	siamo	lavati/e	we have washed ourselves, we washed ourselves
(voi)	vi	siete	lavati/e	you have washed yourselves, you washed yourselves
(loro)	si	sono	lavati/e	they have washed themselves, they washed themselves

EXERCISE Set 9–5

A. Supply the missing present perfect forms of the verb **divertirsi**, giving the English equivalents.

EXAMPLE: lui _____   =   _____
            lui si è divertito   =   he has enjoyed himself, he enjoyed himself

1. io _____ = _____
2. tu _____ = _____
3. noi _____ = _____
4. loro _____ = _____
5. voi _____ = _____
6. lei _____ = _____

B. Say the following things in Italian.

di più	more, most	**la sciarpa**	scarf
il guanto	glove	**lo stile**	style
invitare	to invite	**lo stivale**	boot
recente	recent		

1. Maria, did you like that new movie? I didn't like it at all!

   _____

2. I have always liked spaghetti!

   _____

3. She liked Paolo a lot, but he didn't like her.

   _____

4. They liked me, but they didn't like my sister.

   _____

5. Has Marco been here?

   _____

6. Has Claudia been here?

_____

7. Have Marco and Claudia been here?

_____

8. Yesterday I put on a jacket, gloves, and boots. It was very cold!

_____

9. I got dressed in a new style because they invited me to their party.

_____

Prospettiva personale

Answer each question from your personal perspective. Use complete sentences.

EXAMPLES: **A che ora ti sei alzato/a stamani?**
                Mi sono alzato/a alle sette/alle otto/...

1. **A che ora ti sei alzato/a stamani?**

_____

2. **A che ora si sono alzati gli altri membri della tua famiglia?**

_____

3. **Hai visto qualche film recentemente? Quale film ti è piaciuto di più?**

_____

4. **Che cosa hai mangiato ieri per cena? Ti è piaciuto?**

_____

5. **Sei mai stato/a in Italia? Ti sei divertito/a?**

_____

With Direct Object Pronouns

In Chapter 4 you learned about the indirect object pronouns. It is now necessary to learn about the direct object pronouns. As in the case of the former, these come *before* the verb:

	Singular		Plural
1st person	**mi** / *me*	1st person	**ci** / *us*
2nd person	**ti** / *you* (fam.)	2nd person	**vi** / *you* (fam. and in general)
3rd person	**lo** / *him, it* (m.)	3rd person	**li** / *them* (m.)
	la / *her, it* (f.)		**le** / *them* (f.)
	La / *you* (pol.)		

These pronouns replace direct objects (Chapter 8):

Maria chiama *suo fratello*. / *Mary is calling her brother.*

Maria *lo* chiama. / *Mary is calling him.*

    direct object
    pronoun

The English direct object pronoun *it* (plural *them*) is expressed by the third person direct object pronoun forms on page 119. Be careful! Choose the pronoun according to the gender and number of the noun that has been replaced.

Giovanni compra *il biglietto*. / *John is buying the ticket.*

Giovanni *lo* compra. / *John is buying it.*

Giovanni compra *i biglietti*. / *John is buying the tickets.*

Giovanni *li* compra. / *John is buying them.*

Giovanni compra *la rivista*. / *John is buying the magazine.*

Giovanni *la* compra. / *John is buying it.*

Giovanni compra *le riviste*. / *John is buying the magazines.*

Giovanni *le* compra. / *John is buying them.*

In compound tenses, the past participle of the verb must be made to agree in gender and number with these four pronouns (**lo, la, li, le**):

Giovanni ha comprato *il biglietto*. / *John bought the ticket.*

Giovanni *lo* ha *comprato*. / *John bought it.*

Giovanni ha comprato *i biglietti*. / *John bought the tickets.*

Giovanni *li* ha *comprati*. / *John bought them.*

Giovanni ha comprato *la rivista*. / *John bought the magazine.*

Giovanni *la* ha *comprata*. / *John bought it.*

Giovanni ha comprato *le riviste*. / *John bought the magazines.*

Giovanni *le* ha *comprate*. / *John bought them.*

Note that only the singular forms **lo** and **la** can be elided with the auxiliary forms of **avere: ho, hai, ha, hanno**:

    Giovanni *lo* ha comprato.   *or*   **Giovanni *l'ha* comprato.** / *John bought it.*

    Giovanni *la* ha comprata.   *or*   **Giovanni *l'ha* comprata.** / *John bought it.*

Agreement with the other direct object pronouns **mi, ti, ci, vi** is optional:

    Giovanni *ci* ha *chiamato*. / *John called us.*

    or

    Giovanni *ci* ha *chiamati*. / *John called us.*

There is *no* agreement with indirect object pronouns.

> **Giovanni *gli* ha scritto.** / *John wrote (to) him, (to) them.*
> **Giovanni *le* ha scritto.** / *John wrote (to) her.*

EXERCISE Set 9–6

Replace the indicated objects with direct object pronouns and then make all necessary adjustments to the past participles.

EXAMPLES: **Maria ha chiamato noi.**
Maria, ci ha chiamato/Maria, ci ha chiamati.

Maria ha comprato gli stivali.
Maria li ha comprati.

1. **Paolo ha sempre detto la verità!**

   _____

2. **Bruno ha chiamato voi ieri, vero?**

   _____

3. **Hanno invitato me alla festa!**

   _____

4. **Paola ha chiamato te poco tempo fa.**

   _____

5. **Io ho comprato quel vestito in quel negozio in via Nazionale.**

   _____

6. **Anche tu hai comprato quei guanti nello stesso negozio, vero?**

   _____

7. **Lui ha mangiato quella mela volentieri** (gladly).

   _____

8. **Lei ha già assaggiato quelle mele.**

   _____

9. **Noi abbiamo letto quella rivista.**

   _____

Uses and Features

The present perfect tense is used to refer to simple actions that occurred in the recent past. It is the most common of all past tenses in conversational Italian:

> **Maria *ha venduto* la sua macchina due mesi fa.** / *Mary sold her car two months ago.*
> **Ieri *ho parlato* al signor Verdi.** / *Yesterday I spoke to Mr. Verdi.*
> **Loro *hanno dormito* troppo stamani.** / *They slept too much this morning.*
> ***Ho già mangiato.*** / *I have already eaten.*

VOCABULARY TIP

The present perfect is often used with words and expressions such as

appena	just
fa	ago
già	already
ieri	yesterday
ieri sera	last night
questo pomeriggio	this afternoon
scorso (-a)	last (week, month, etc.)
stamani	this morning

A few verbs change their meaning when used in this tense. The two most common ones are

	Present	Past
conoscere	*to know (a person/place)* **Io conosco Maria molto bene.** *I know Mary very well.*	*to meet (for the first time)* **Io ho conosciuto Maria ieri per la prima volta.** *I met Mary yesterday for the first time.*
sapere	*to know* **Io so che vieni alla festa.** *I know that you are coming to the party.*	*to find out/learn* **Io ho saputo che vieni alla festa.** *I found out that you are coming to the party.*

EXERCISE Set 9–7

Say the following things in Italian.

1. We know that he is going out with Maria.

   _____

2. We found out that he is going out with Maria.

   _____

3. I met my Italian teacher last year.

   _____

4. I know your brother very well. I met him many years ago.

   _____

5. They left for Italy this morning.

   _____

6. Your friend (f.) called this afternoon.

   _____

7. They went to the movies last night.

   _____

8. I have already done that.

_____

9. My brother has just arrived.

_____

10. My parents came to America a few years ago.

_____

Crossword Puzzle 9

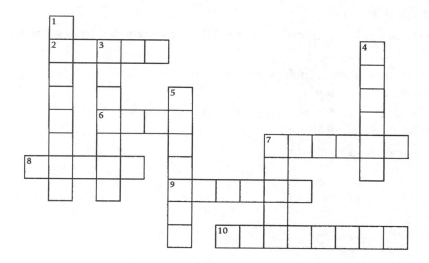

Orizzontali

2. **Chi ha ...** *(rompere)* **quello?**
6. **Quando sono ...** *(nascere)* **i tuoi fratelli?**
7. **A che ora hai ...** *(finire)* **di lavorare?**
8. **Maria, sei mai ...** *(essere)* **a Roma?**
9. **Claudia, a che ora sei ...** *(uscire)* **ieri sera?**
10. **Ho ...** *(scoprire)* **la verità.**

Verticali

1. **Le ragazze sono ...** *(arrivare)* **ieri.**
3. **Loro sono ...** *(tornare)* **in italia.**
4. **Quando è ...** *(venire)* **tua sorella?**
5. **Loro sono ...** *(vivere)* **in Italia.**
7. **Che tempo ha ...** *(fare)* **ieri?**

10
The Imperfect

Regular Verbs

To form the imperfect indicative of regular verbs, called the **imperfetto dell'indicativo** in Italian, do the following:

1. Drop the **-re** from the infinitive endings **-are, -ere, -ire**:

   parlare / *to speak* → **parla-**
   scrivere / *to write* → **scrive-**
   finire / *to finish* → **fini-**

2. Add the following endings to the stem:

(io)	-vo
(tu)	-vi
(lui/lei/Lei)	-va
(noi)	-vamo
(voi)	-vate
(loro)	-vano

3. Here's the result:

   First conjugation: **parlare** / *to speak*

(io)	parlavo	I was speaking, I used to speak
(tu)	parlavi	you (fam.) were speaking, you used to speak
(lui/lei/Lei)	parlava	he, she, you (pol.) was/were speaking, he, she, you used to speak
(noi)	parlavamo	we were speaking, we used to speak
(voi)	parlavate	you were speaking, you used to speak
(loro)	parlavano	they were speaking, they used to speak

   Second conjugation: **scrivere** / *to write*

(io)	scrivevo	I was writing, I used to write
(tu)	scrivevi	you (fam.) were writing, you used to write
(lui/lei/Lei)	scriveva	he, she, you (pol.) was/were writing, he, she, you used to write
(noi)	scrivevamo	we were writing, we used to write
(voi)	scrivevate	you were writing, you used to write
(loro)	scrivevano	they were writing, they used to write

Third conjugation: **finire** / *to finish*

(io)	**finivo**	I was finishing, I used to finish
(tu)	**finivi**	you (fam.) were finishing, you used to finish
(lui/lei/Lei)	**finiva**	he, she, you (pol.) was/were finishing, he, she, you used to finish
(noi)	**finivamo**	we were finishing, we used to finish
(voi)	**finivate**	you were finishing, you used to finish
(loro)	**finivano**	they were finishing, they used to finish

TIP

Be careful again when you pronounce third person plural forms! The accent is not *placed on the ending, but on the syllable before the ending:*

parlavano	**scrivevano**	**finivano**
|	|	|
stress	stress	stress

In the case of verbs such as **cominciare** and **mangiare** (Chapter 8) the **"i"** is retained in the formation of the stem:

cominciare / *to begin*   →   **comincia-**

(io)	**cominciavo**	I was beginning, I used to begin
(tu)	**cominciavi**	you (fam.) were beginning, you used to begin
(lui/lei/Lei)	**cominciava**	he, she, you (pol.) was/were beginning, he, she, you used to begin
(noi)	**cominciavamo**	we were beginning, we used to begin
(voi)	**cominciavate**	you were beginning, you used to begin
(loro)	**cominciavano**	they were beginning, they used to begin

mangiare / *to eat*   →   **mangia-**

(io)	**mangiavo**	I was eating, I used to eat
(tu)	**mangiavi**	you (fam.) were eating, you used to eat
(lui/lei/Lei)	**mangiava**	he, she, you (pol.) was/were eating, he, she, you used to eat
(noi)	**mangiavamo**	we were eating, we used to eat
(voi)	**mangiavate**	you were eating, you used to eat
(loro)	**mangiavano**	they were eating, they used to eat

Reflexive verbs are conjugated (of course!) with reflexive pronouns. Here is **lavarsi** completely conjugated for you:

lavarsi / *to wash oneself*   →   **lava-**

(io)	**mi**	**lavavo**	I was washing myself, I used to wash myself
(tu)	**ti**	**lavavi**	you (fam.) were washing yourself, you used to wash yourself
(lui/lei/Lei)	**si**	**lavava**	he, she, you (pol.) was/were washing himself/herself/yourself, he, she, you used to wash himself/herself/yourself
(noi)	**ci**	**lavavamo**	we were washing ourselves, we used to wash ourselves
(voi)	**vi**	**lavavate**	you were washing yourselves, you used to wash yourselves
(loro)	**si**	**lavavano**	they were washing themselves, they used to wash themselves

Essentially, the imperfect allows you to refer to incomplete, habitual, or recurring actions in the past: *I used to sing well, he was always hungry*, etc.

TIP

Notice that the **imperfetto** *is rendered in English generally by the forms "I was speaking," "I used to speak," and so on:*

$$\text{mangiavo} = \begin{bmatrix} \textit{I was eating} \\ \textit{I used to eat} \end{bmatrix}$$

The verb form **esserci** / *to be there* (Chapter 2) has again only two forms, which are used in the imperfect to acknowledge that something or someone *was* somewhere:

Singular	Plural
C'era *Alessandro?* Was Alexander here/there?	**C'erano Alessandro e Sarah?** Were Alexander and Sarah there?

EXERCISE Set 10–1

A. Supply the missing imperfect forms of the verbs **andare**, **mettere**, and **dormire**, giving the English equivalents.

EXAMPLE: lui _____   =   _____

            lui andava, metteva, dormiva   =   he was going, putting, sleeping,
                                                   he used to go, put, sleep

1. io _____   =   _____

2. tu _____   =   _____

3. noi _____   =   _____

4. loro _____   =   _____

5. voi _____   =   _____

6. Lei _____   =   _____

Now, supply the missing imperfect forms of the verbs **baciare**, **noleggiare**, and **vestirsi**, giving the English equivalents.

7. io _____   =   _____

8. tu _____   =   _____

9. noi _____   =   _____

10. loro _____   =   _____

11. voi _____   =   _____

12. lei _____   =   _____

B. Say the following things in Italian.

ansioso	anxious	**i fumetti**	comic books
il bambino (la bambina)	child	**il latte**	milk
la faccenda	house chore	**la spiaggia**	beach
il fagiolo	bean	**gli spinaci**	spinach

Da bambino/a *(As a child)*/**Da bambini/e** *(As children)*…

1. I used to play the piano.

_____

2. you (fam., sing.) used to sing very well.

_____

3. my brother used to go the movies often.

_____

4. we used to get up late on Saturdays.

_____

5. you (fam., pl.) used to watch TV a lot.

_____

6. his friends (m.) used to play soccer.

_____

7. I used to eat pasta often.

_____

8. Mr. Tartini used to go often to the beach.

_____

9. they used to have fun after school.

_____

10. there was always a lot to do *(da fare)*.

_____

11. there were many things to do.

_____

12. I used to wait anxiously for my favorite TV programs on Saturdays.

_____

Prospettiva personale

Answer each question from your personal perspective. Use complete sentences.

EXAMPLE: **Da bambino/a…mangiavi spesso gli spinaci?**
Sì, da bambino/a mangiavo spesso gli spinaci/No, da bambino/a non mangiavo mai gli spinaci/…

Da bambino/a...

1. a che ora ti alzavi la mattina generalmente?

   _____

2. che cosa mangiavi regolarmente?

   _____

3. dove andavi spesso?

   _____

4. quali programmi televisivi guardavi?

   _____

5. che macchina avevate?

   _____

6. mangiavi spesso i fagioli?

   _____

7. volevi spesso il latte?

   _____

8. dovevi fare le faccende?

   _____

9. leggevi i fumetti?

   _____

Illustrative Dialogue

a presto	see you soon	**il passato**	past
assai	quite, rather	**pensare**	to think
la donna	woman	**pronto**	hello (answering the phone)
passare	to pass, to go by	**volentieri**	gladly

Franca:	**Pronto, chi parla?**	Hello, who is it (who is speaking)?
Rina:	**Sono Rina, Franca. Come stai?**	It's Rina (literally "I am Rina"), Franca. How are you?
Franca:	**Non c'è male. E tu?**	Not bad. And you?
Rina:	**Assai bene.** _Pensavo_ **a te ieri perché si** _parlava_ **in famiglia di quando** _vivevamo_ **vicino di casa.**	Quite well. I was thinking of you yesterday because we were talking in my family about when we used to live near each other (literally: "when we lived near of house").
Franca:	**Sono passati troppi anni, vero?**	Too many years have gone by, right?
Rina:	**Eh, già! Ti ricordi quante volte** _uscivamo_ **insieme?**	Oh yeah! Do you remember how many times we used to go out together?
Franca:	**Certo! Perché non ci vediamo per parlare del passato?**	Of course! Why don't we see each other to talk about the past?
Rina:	**Volentieri! Ti chiamo tra qualche giorno. Ciao!**	Gladly! I'll call you in a few days. Bye!
Franca:	**A presto!**	See you soon!

Grammar Note

The impersonal pronoun **si** (*one in general, we, they,* etc.) has the following peculiar characteristics:

1. The verb agrees with what appears to be the predicate!

    Si compra quel libro solo in Italia. / *One buys that book only in Italy.*

    Si comprano quei libri solo in Italia. / *One buys those books only in Italy.*

2. All compound tenses using **si** (Chapter 9) are conjugated with **essere**, with the past participle agreeing, apparently, with the predicate!

    Si sono veduti quei film solo in Italia. / *One saw those films only in Italy.*

3. When followed by a predicate adjective, the adjective is always in the plural:

    Sì è felici in Italia. / *One is happy in Italy.*

EXERCISE Set 10–2

Answer the following questions based on the dialogue. Use complete sentences.

1. **Chi ha telefonato a Franca?**

    _____

2. **Come sta Franca?**

    _____

3. **E Rina come sta?**

    _____

4. **A chi pensava Rina ieri?**

    _____

5. **Di che cosa parlavano nella sua famiglia?**

    _____

6. **Quanti anni sono passati?**

    _____

7. **Che cosa facevano** (used to do) **le due donne insieme?**

    _____

Irregular Verbs

The good news is that in the Italian verb system very few verbs are irregular in the imperfect indicative. Here are the most common ones:

bere / *to drink*

(io)	**bevevo**	I was drinking, I used to drink
(tu)	**bevevi**	you (fam.) were drinking, you used to drink
(lui/lei/Lei)	**beveva**	he, she, you (pol.) was/were drinking, he, she, you used to drink
(noi)	**bevevamo**	we were drinking, we used to drink
(voi)	**bevevate**	you were drinking, you used to drink
(loro)	**bevevano**	they were drinking, they used to drink

TIP

If you change the infinitive of **bere** *in your mind to* **"bevere"** *(as a hypothetical form), then the previous conjugation can be considered regular:*

> **bere** → "bevere" → beve- → **add endings**

---

dare / *to give*

(io)	**davo**	I was giving, I used to give
(tu)	**davi**	you (fam.) were giving, you used to give
(lui/lei/Lei)	**dava**	he, she, you (pol.) was/were giving, he, she, you used to give
(noi)	**davamo**	we were giving, we used to give
(voi)	**davate**	you were giving, you used to give
(loro)	**davano**	they were giving, they used to give

dire / *to tell, to say*

(io)	**dicevo**	I was saying, I used to say
(tu)	**dicevi**	you (fam.) were saying, you used to say
(lui/lei/Lei)	**diceva**	he, she, you (pol.) was/were saying, he, she, you used to say
(noi)	**dicevamo**	we were saying, we used to say
(voi)	**dicevate**	you were saying, you used to say
(loro)	**dicevano**	they were saying, they used to say

TIP

If you change the infinitive of **dire** *in your mind to* **"dicere"** *(as a hypothetical form), then the conjugation above can be considered regular:*

> **dire** → "dicere" → dice- → **add endings**

---

essere / *to be*

(io)	**ero**	I was, I used to be
(tu)	**eri**	you (fam.) were, you used to be
(lui/lei/Lei)	**era**	he, she, you (pol.) was/were, he, she, you used to be
(noi)	**eravamo**	we were, we used to be
(voi)	**eravate**	you were, you used to be
(loro)	**erano**	they were, they used to be

fare / *to do, to make*

(io)	**facevo**	I was making, I used to make
(tu)	**facevi**	you (fam.) were making, you used to make
(lui/lei/Lei)	**faceva**	he, she, you (pol.) was/were making, he, she, you used to make
(noi)	**facevamo**	we were making, we used to make
(voi)	**facevate**	you were making, you used to make
(loro)	**facevano**	they were making, they used to make

TIP

If you change the infinitive of **fare** *in your mind to* **"facere"** *(as a hypothetical form), then the conjugation above can be considered regular:*

> **fare** → "facere" → face- → **add endings**

stare / *to stay, to be*

(io)	**stavo**	I was staying, I used to stay
(tu)	**stavi**	you (fam.) were staying, you used to stay
(lui/lei/Lei)	**stava**	he, she, you (pol.) was/were staying, he, she, you used to stay
(noi)	**stavamo**	we were staying, we used to stay
(voi)	**stavate**	you were staying, you used to stay
(loro)	**stavano**	they were staying, they used to stay

Recall that verbs ending in **-durre** can be rendered hypothetically "regular" as follows:

1. Change the ending in your mind to **-cere**:

   dedurre   →   "deducere"

2. Drop the **-re** ending of the "hypothetical" verb stem:

   deducere   →   deduce-

3. Add the usual endings (above):

(io)	**deducevo**	I was deducing, I used to deduce
(tu)	**deducevi**	you (fam.) were deducing, you used to deduce
(lui/lei/Lei)	**deduceva**	he, she, you (pol.) was/were deducing, he, she, you used to deduce
(noi)	**deducevamo**	we were deducing, we used to deduce
(voi)	**deducevate**	you were deducing, you used to deduce
(loro)	**deducevano**	they were deducing, they used to deduce

Here are the conjugations of **trarre** and **porre**, which do not follow this pattern:

trarre / *to draw (pull)* and **attrarre** / *to attract*

(io)	**traevo**	I was drawing, I used to draw
(tu)	**traevi**	you (fam.) were drawing, you used to draw
(lui/lei/Lei)	**traeva**	he, she, you (pol.) was/were drawing, he, she, you used to draw
(noi)	**traevamo**	we were drawing, we used to draw
(voi)	**traevate**	you were drawing, you used to draw
(loro)	**traevano**	they were drawing, they used to draw

porre / *to pose* and **supporre** / *to suppose*

(io)	**ponevo**	I was posing, I used to pose
(tu)	**ponevi**	you (fam.) were posing, you used to pose
(lui/lei/Lei)	**poneva**	he, she, you (pol.) was/were posing, he, she, you used to pose
(noi)	**ponevamo**	we were posing, we used to pose
(voi)	**ponevate**	you were posing, you used to pose
(loro)	**ponevano**	they were posing, they used to pose

TIP

If you change the infinitive of **porre** *in your mind to* "ponere" *(as a hypothetical form), then the conjugation above can be considered regular:*

   porre   →   "ponere"   →   pone- → add endings

EXERCISE Set 10–3

A. Supply the missing imperfect indicative form of the verbs **bere**, **dare**, and **dire** giving the English equivalents.

EXAMPLE: **lui** _____   =   _____

    lui beveva, dava, diceva   =   he was drinking, giving, saying,
                                                      he used to drink, give, say

1. **io** _____   =   _____

2. **tu** _____   =   _____

3. **noi** _____   =   _____

4. **loro** _____   =   _____

5. **voi** _____   =   _____

6. **lei** _____   =   _____

Now, supply the missing imperfect indicative form of the verbs **essere**, **fare**, and **stare** giving the English equivalents.

7. **io** _____   =   _____

8. **tu** _____   =   _____

9. **noi** _____   =   _____

10. **loro** _____   =   _____

11. **voi** _____   =   _____

12. **lei** _____   =   _____

Finally, supply the missing imperfect indicative form of the verbs **produrre**, **attrarre**, and **supporre**, giving the English equivalents.

13. **io** _____   =   _____

14. **tu** _____   =   _____

15. **noi** _____   =   _____

16. **loro** _____   =   _____

17. **voi** _____   =   _____

18. **lui** _____   =   _____

B. Say the following things in Italian:

dare via	to give away	**strano**	strange
il giocattolo	toy	**studioso**	studious
ingenuo	naïve, ingenuous	**vivace**	lively, active

Da bambino/a *(As a child)*/**Da bambini/e** *(As children)*…

1. I used to drink milk every day.

2. you (fam., sing.) used to give away lots of toys.

_____

3. my brother always told (used to tell) the truth.

_____

4. my friends and I were very happy.

_____

5. you (pl., fam.) used to stay at home often.

_____

6. it used to be beautiful almost every day.

_____

7. my sisters used to do many strange things.

_____

8. I used to be very studious.

_____

9. you (fam., sing.) were frequently sad.

_____

Imperfect Progressive

The imperfect progressive, called the **imperfetto progressivo** in Italian, is an alternative to the imperfect indicative. It corresponds, basically, to the present progressive (Chapter 7), allowing you to zero in on an action in the past that was ongoing at the time (usually relative to another action):

> **Ieri mentre mia sorella _stava mangiando_, io _stavo guardando_ la TV.** / _Yesterday, while my sister was eating, I was watching TV._

It is formed with the imperfect tense of the verb **stare** and the gerund of the verb, in that order. Review Chapter 7 for the formation of the gerund and for irregular forms of the gerund.

Here are three verbs conjugated in the present progressive:

First conjugation: **parlare** / _to speak_

(io)	stavo	parlando	I was speaking
(tu)	stavi	parlando	you (fam.) were speaking
(lui/lei/Lei)	stava	parlando	he, she, you (pol.) was/were speaking
(noi)	stavamo	parlando	we were speaking
(voi)	stavate	parlando	you were speaking
(loro)	stavano	parlando	they were speaking

Second conjugation: **vendere** / _to sell_

(io)	stavo	vendendo	I was selling
(tu)	stavi	vendendo	you (fam.) were selling
(lui/lei/Lei)	stava	vendendo	he, she, you (pol.) was/were selling
(noi)	stavamo	vendendo	we were selling
(voi)	stavate	vendendo	you were selling
(loro)	stavano	vendendo	they were selling

Third conjugation: **finire** / *to finish*

(io)	**stavo**	**finendo**	I was finishing
(tu)	**stavi**	**finendo**	you (fam.) were finishing
(lui/lei/Lei)	**stava**	**finendo**	he, she, you (pol.) was/were finishing
(noi)	**stavamo**	**finendo**	we were finishing
(voi)	**stavate**	**finendo**	you were finishing
(loro)	**stavano**	**finendo**	they were finishing

EXERCISE Set 10–4

Replace the imperfect indicative forms of the given verbs with corresponding imperfect progressive forms.

EXAMPLE: **lui mangiava**
                lui stava mangiando

1. **io andavo**   =   _____

2. **tu cominciavi**   =   _____

3. **noi scrivevamo** =   _____

4. **loro leggevano** =   _____

5. **voi preferivate** =   _____

6. **lei dormiva**   =   _____

7. **io producevo**   =   _____

8. **tu bevevi**   =   _____

9. **noi davamo**   =   _____

10. **loro facevano** =   _____

11. **voi supponevate** =   _____

12. **lui studiava**   =   _____

Uses and Features

"Imperfect" means incomplete. The imperfect indicative is, thus, a tense used to express or describe an action, event, or state of being that was incomplete, continuous, or habitual in the past. Specifically, it is used

1. To express an action in the past that went on simultaneously with another action.
   Mentre mia madre *leggeva*, mio padre *guardava* la TV. / *While my mother was reading, my father watched TV.*

   or

   Mentre mia madre *stava leggendo*, mio padre *guardava* la TV. / *While my mother was reading, my father watched TV.*

2. To express an action that was ongoing as another action occurred in the past.
   Mia sorella *ascoltava* un CD, quando hai chiamato. / *My sister was listening to a CD, when you called.*

   or

   Mia sorella *stava ascoltando* un CD, quando hai chiamato. / *My sister was listening to a CD, when you called.*

3. To indicate a past action, desire, condition, etc. that took place habitually.

> **Quando *eravamo* in Italia, *andavamo* spesso al mare.** / *When we were in Italy, we often used to go to the sea.*
>
> **Da bambino *volevo* sempre mangiare gli spaghetti.** / *As a child I always wanted to eat spaghetti.*

4. To describe a former, earlier, or bygone mental, emotional, or physical condition, situation, or feature. The verbs most commonly used in this way are **avere** / *to have*, **credere** / *to believe*, **essere** / *to be*, **pensare** / *to think*, **potere** / *to be able to*, **preferire** / *to prefer*, **sapere** / *to know*, **sentire** / *to feel*, **volere** / *to want*.

> **Da giovane lei *aveva* i capelli biondi.** / *As a young woman she had blonde hair.*
>
> **Da bambino *sapevo* già parlare due lingue.** / *As a child I already knew how to speak two languages.*

5. To refer to routine time of day in the past.

> **A che ora *avevi* lezione d'italiano di solito?** / *At what time did you use to have your Italian class usually?*

6. To quote someone indirectly in the past.

> **Alessandro ha detto che *veniva* anche lui alla festa.** / *Alexander said that he too was coming to the party.*

VOCABULARY TIP

The imperfect indicative is often used with words and phrases such as

da bambino/da giovane/ecc.	as a child/as a youth/etc.
di solito	usually
durante	during
mai	never
mentre	while
ogni giorno/mese/...	every day/month/...
qualche volta	sometimes, once in a while
sempre	always
spesso	often, frequently

Needless to say, reflexive verbs are conjugated in the usual way in both the imperfect indicative and imperfect progressive tenses but, of course, with the addition of reflexive pronouns:

> **Lei *si alzava* tardi di solito.** / *She used to get up late usually.*
>
> **Mentre lui *si stava vestendo*, io leggevo il giornale.** / *While he was getting dressed, I read the newspaper.*

Also, keep in mind what that pesky verb **piacere** means in Italian, even when it is used in the imperfect:

> **Da bambino non *mi piaceva* il latte.** / *As a child, I didn't like milk ("milk was not pleasing to me").*
>
> **Da bambina non *le piacevano* le caramelle.** / *As a child she didn't like candies ("candies were not pleasing to her").*

EXERCISE **Set 10–5**

A. Say the following things in Italian.

biondo	blond	**il mare**	sea
i capelli	hair (head)	**presto**	early
la caramella	candy	**verso**	around
dunque	thus, therefore		

1. While your brother was playing the cello, I slept (was sleeping).

   _____

2. When they were in Italy, they wanted always to go to the sea.

   _____

3. As a youth, I knew how to speak Spanish.

   _____

4. My sister was blonde as a child.

   _____

5. When I was very young, I believed everything that *(quello che)* my brother told (used to tell) me.

   _____

6. They always preferred going to the movies years ago, but I never wanted to go.

   _____

7. We usually ate at 6 PM every evening.

   _____

8. Sarah never said that she wanted to come to the party.

   _____

9. We used to get up early every morning, and thus we always used to fall asleep around 7 PM in the evenings.

   _____

Crossword Puzzle 10

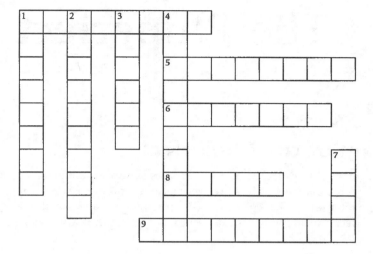

Orizzontali

1. Da giovani loro … sempre al mare.
5. Due anni fa, io … per una ditta italiana.
6. Mio fratello … a calcio da bambino.
8. Mia sorella … l'Italia da bambina.
9. Loro … sempre vestiti alla moda.

Verticali

1. Ogni mattina loro si … presto.
2. Il sabato noi … sempre fino a tardi.
3. Marco ha detto che anche lui … alla festa.
4. Anni fa io … solo i film di fantascienza.
7. Io … via sempre i miei giocattoli da bambino/a.

11
The Pluperfect

Conjugation of the Pluperfect

The pluperfect of regular verbs, called the **trapassato prossimo** in Italian, is a compound tense. Therefore, it is conjugated with an auxiliary verb, either **avere** or **essere**, and the past participle of the verb, in that order. See Chapter 9 for the relevant details regarding past participles and the use of one or the other auxiliary verb.

In the pluperfect, the auxiliary verbs are in the imperfect indicative. Here are examples of verbs conjugated with **avere**:

First conjugation: **parlare** / *to speak*

(io)	**avevo**	**parlato**	I had spoken
(tu)	**avevi**	**parlato**	you (fam.) had spoken
(lui/lei/Lei)	**aveva**	**parlato**	he, she, you (pol.) had spoken
(noi)	**avevamo**	**parlato**	we had spoken
(voi)	**avevate**	**parlato**	you had spoken
(loro)	**avevano**	**parlato**	they had spoken

Second conjugation: **vendere** / *to sell*

(io)	**avevo**	**venduto**	I had sold
(tu)	**avevi**	**venduto**	you (fam.) had sold
(lui/lei/Lei)	**aveva**	**venduto**	he, she, you (pol.) had sold
(noi)	**avevamo**	**venduto**	we had sold
(voi)	**avevate**	**venduto**	you had sold
(loro)	**avevano**	**venduto**	they had sold

Third conjugation: **finire** / *to finish*

(io)	**avevo**	**finito**	I had finished
(tu)	**avevi**	**finito**	you (fam.) had finished
(lui/lei/Lei)	**aveva**	**finito**	he, she, you (pol.) had finished
(noi)	**avevamo**	**finito**	we had finished
(voi)	**avevate**	**finito**	you had finished
(loro)	**avevano**	**finito**	they had finished

Here are examples of verbs conjugated with **essere**:

First Conjugation: **arrivare** / *to arrive*

(io)	**ero**	**arrivato/a**	I had arrived
(tu)	**eri**	**arrivato/a**	you (fam.) had arrived
(lui)	**era**	**arrivato**	he arrived
(lei)	**era**	**arrivata**	she arrived
(Lei)	**era**	**arrivato/a**	you (pol.) arrived
(noi)	**eravamo**	**arrivati/e**	we had arrived
(voi)	**eravate**	**arrivati/e**	you had arrived
(loro)	**erano**	**arrivati/e**	they had arrived

Second Conjugation:	**cadere** / *to fall*		
(io)	ero	**caduto/a**	I had fallen
(tu)	eri	**caduto/a**	you (fam.) had fallen
(lui)	era	**caduto**	he had fallen
(lei)	era	**caduta**	she had fallen
(Lei)	era	**caduto/a**	you (pol.) had fallen
(noi)	eravamo	**caduti/e**	we had fallen
(voi)	eravate	**caduti/e**	you had fallen
(loro)	erano	**caduti/e**	they had fallen

Third Conjugation:	**uscire** / *to go out*		
(io)	ero	**uscito/a**	I had gone out
(tu)	eri	**uscito/a**	you (fam.) had gone out
(lui)	era	**uscito**	he had gone out
(lei)	era	**uscita**	she had gone out
(Lei)	era	**uscito/a**	you (pol.) had gone out
(noi)	eravamo	**usciti/e**	we had gone out
(voi)	eravate	**usciti/e**	you had gone out
(loro)	erano	**usciti/e**	they had gone out

For a list of common verbs conjugated with **essere** see Chapter 9. Again, all reflexive verbs are conjugated with **essere**. Here's **lavarsi** / *to wash oneself* completely conjugated for you:

(io)	mi	ero	**lavato/a**	I had washed myself
(tu)	ti	eri	**lavato/a**	you (fam.) had washed yourself
(lui)	si	era	**lavato**	he had washed himself
(lei)	si	era	**lavata**	she had washed herself
(Lei)	si	era	**lavato/a**	you (pol.) had washed yourself
(noi)	ci	eravamo	**lavati/e**	we had washed ourselves
(voi)	vi	eravate	**lavati/e**	you had washed yourselves
(loro)	si	erano	**lavati/e**	they had washed themselves

TIP

Notice that the **trapassato** *is rendered in English generally by expressions such as* I had spoken, you had written, *and so on.*

avevo mangiato = I had eaten

erano già arrivati = they had already arrived

Recall from Chapter 9 that in compound tenses **piacere** is conjugated with **essere**. This means, of course, that the past participle agrees with the subject—no matter where it occurs in the sentence:

I hadn't liked the pizza.

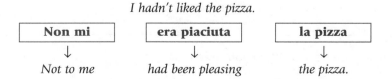

Non mi	**era piaciuta**	**la pizza**
↓	↓	↓
Not to me	*had been pleasing*	*the pizza.*

Finally, recall from Chapter 9 that the past participle of the verb in a compound tense agrees in gender and number with the preceding direct object pronoun:

Maria aveva già comprato *quelle riviste.* / *Maria had already bought those magazines.*

Maria *le* **aveva già** *comprate.* / *Maria had already bought them.*

EXERCISE Set 11–1

A. Supply the missing pluperfect forms of the verbs **mangiare**, **credere**, and **capire**, giving the English equivalents.

EXAMPLE:	**lui** _____	=	_____
	lui aveva mangiato, aveva creduto,	=	*he had eaten, believed,*
	aveva capito		*understood*

1. **io** _____   =   _____

2. **tu** _____   =   _____

3. **noi** _____   =   _____

4. **loro** _____   =   _____

5. **voi** _____   =   _____

6. **Lei** _____   =   _____

Finally, supply the missing pluperfect forms of the verbs **andare**, **nascere**, and **vestirsi**, giving the English equivalents.

7. **io** _____   =   _____

8. **tu** _____   =   _____

9. **noi** _____   =   _____

10. **loro** _____   =   _____

11. **voi** _____   =   _____

12. **lei** _____   =   _____

B. Say the following things in Italian:

(pp. = past participle, * = conjugated with **essere**)

assicurare	to ensure	**finalmente**	finally
contento	happy	**preferito**	favorite
decidere (pp: deciso)	to decide	**sicuro**	sure
dopo che	after	**valere* la pena (pp.: valso)**	to be worthwhile
fare delle spese	to shop	**veramente**	truly

1. They had already eaten, when she arrived.

_____

2. I had already gotten up, when you called me.

_____

3. As a child she could (was able to) watch TV only after she had studied.

_____

4. After you (fam., pl.) had gone out, he finally arrived.

_____

5. I was sure that you (fam., sing.) had already done it **(lo)**.

_____

6. Bruno said that he had already seen those movies. And, it's true. He had seen them.

_____

7. Nora wanted to go out only after she had finished **(di)** watching her favorite program.

_____

8. Mrs. Santini indicated that she had just read that novel. She said it had not been worthwhile.

_____

9. Everyone was happy that you (fam., pl.) had decided **(di)** to come to the party.

_____

10. After they had gone shopping, the two friends (f.) went to the movies.

_____

Prospettiva personale

List (1) three things you used to like as a child and still do, (2) three things you liked yesterday, and (3) three things you want to assure someone else that you had indeed liked. Use the glossary at the back of this book to help you with vocabulary, or else consult a dictionary. Write complete sentences as in the model answers below.

EXAMPLES: (1) **Mi piacevano gli spaghetti da bambino.**
(2) **Mi è piaciuta la pizza che ho mangiato ieri.**
(3) **Ti assicuro** (_I assure you_) **che mi era veramente piaciuta la pizza.**

1. Da bambino/a...

_____

_____

_____

2. Ieri ...

_____

_____

_____

3. Ti assicuro che...

_____

_____

_____

Illustrative Dialogue

Carla:	**Maria, è vero che anche tu ed Elena *eravate uscite* insieme ieri?**	Maria, is it true that you and Elena went out together yesterday?
Maria:	**Sì, siamo andate al cinema. Ma ti assicuro che quello che tutti *avevano detto* del film è vero. Non vale niente.**	Yes, we went to the movies. But I can assure you that what everyone had said about the movie is true. It isn't worth anything.
Carla:	**Ma non *avevi detto* che volevi uscire con me per fare delle spese?**	But hadn't you said that you wanted to go out shopping with me?
Maria:	**È vero! Mi sono dimenticata! Scusa!**	It's true! I forgot! Sorry!
Carla:	**Non c'è problema!**	No problem!

Grammar Notes

A relative clause is introduced into a main sentence by means of a relative pronoun, which serves as a subject or an object in the clause. The main relative pronouns in Italian are

> **che** / *that, which, who*
> **Ti assicuro *che* anche lui è italiano.** / *I can assure you that he too is Italian.*
> **Il ragazzo *che* ha conosciuto ieri si chiama Alessandro.** / *The name of the boy who you met*
> > *yesterday is Alessandro.*

> **cui** / *which, of whom, to whom, etc.*
> **La persona *a cui* ho dato la penna è mia sorella.** / *The person to whom I gave the pen is my sister.*

> **quello che, quel che, ciò che** / *that which (= "what")*
> **Quello che/Quel che/Ciò che hai detto è vero.** / *What you said is true.*

The conjunction **e** / *and* and the preposition **a** / *to* are often pronounced **ed** and **ad** if the following word starts with a vowel. This allows for a "smoother" pronunciation:

> **Maria *ed* Elena** / *Mary and Helen*
> **Ho dato la penna *ad* un amico.** / *I have given the pen to a friend.*

EXERCISE Set 11–2

Answer the following questions based on the dialogue. Use complete sentences.

1. **È vero che Maria ed Elena erano uscite insieme ieri?**

_____

2. **Dove erano andate?**

_____

3. **Che cosa avevano detto tutti?**

_____

4. **Che cosa aveva detto Elena a Carla?**

_____

5. **Di che cosa si era dimenticata Maria?**

_____

Uses and Features

The pluperfect indicative is used to express an action that occurred before another past action:

> **Dopo che _era arrivata_, mi ha telefonato.** /After she had arrived, she phoned me.
> **Lui mi ha detto che le _aveva_ già _parlato_.** / He told me that he had already spoken to her.

This tense corresponds to the English pluperfect. But be careful! Sometimes the pluperfect is only implied in English colloquial usage:

> **Sono andati in Italia dopo che _avevano finito_ gli esami.** / They went to Italy after they (had) finished their exams.

EXERCISE Set 11–3

Choose the verb form, **a** or **b**, that best completes each sentence according to sense.

1. **Quando sono arrivato, loro ... già.**
   a. **si erano addormentati**
   b. **si sono addormentati**

2. **Quando lei ha chiamato, noi ... già di andare al cinema.**
   a. **avevamo deciso**
   b. **abbiamo deciso**

3. **È proprio vero che tu ... di lavorare alle sei ieri sera?**
   a. **avevi finito**
   b. **hai finito**

4. **Dopo che mia sorella ... dall'Italia, ha deciso di studiare la lingua italiana.**
   a. **era tornata**
   b. **è tornata**

5. **Che tempo ... ieri?**
   a. **aveva fatto**
   b. **ha fatto**

6. **Maria, ti ... quella pasta?**
   a. **era piaciuta**
   b. **è piaciuta**

7. **Hanno detto che ... già quel film.**
   a. **avevano visto**
   b. **hanno visto**

Crossword Puzzle 11

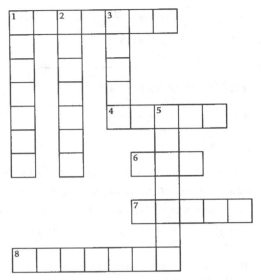

(Missing from each compound tense is the auxiliary. Supply it according to the corresponding English translation.)

Orizzontali

1. **loro … mangiato** (they had eaten)
4. **loro … andati** (they had gone)
6. **tu … arrivato** (you have arrived)
7. **loro … cercato** (they have tried to)
8. **noi ci … alzati** (we had gotten up)

Verticali

1. **noi … mangiato** (we have eaten)
2. **voi … venuti** (you had come)
3. **voi … detto** (you have said)
5. **loro … fatto** (they had done)

12
The Past Absolute

Regular Verbs

To form the past absolute (preterit) of regular verbs, called the **passato remoto** in Italian, do the following:

First conjugation:

1. Drop the infinitive ending **-are**:

     parl*are* / *to speak* →   **parl-**

2. Add the following endings to the stem:

(io)	**-ai**
(tu)	**-asti**
(lui/lei/Lei)	**-ò**
(noi)	**-ammo**
(voi)	**-aste**
(loro)	**-arono**

3. Here's the result:

(io)	**parlai**	I spoke
(tu)	**parlasti**	you (fam.) spoke
(lui/lei/Lei)	**parlò**	he, she, you (pol.) spoke
(noi)	**parlammo**	we spoke
(voi)	**parlaste**	you spoke
(loro)	**parlarono**	they spoke

Second conjugation:

1. Drop the infinitive ending **-ere**:

     vend*ere* / *to sell* →   **vend-**

2. Add the following endings to the stem:

(io)	**-ei/-etti**
(tu)	**-esti**
(lui/lei/Lei)	**-é/-ette**
(noi)	**-emmo**
(voi)	**-este**
(loro)	**-erono/-ettero**

3. Here's the result:

(io)	**vendei/vendetti**	I sold
(tu)	**vendesti**	you (fam.) sold
(lui/lei/Lei)	**vendé/vendette**	he, she, you (pol.) sold

(noi)	**vendemmo**	we sold
(voi)	**vendeste**	you sold
(loro)	**venderono/vendettero**	they sold

Third conjugation:

1. Drop the infinitive ending **-ire**:

   fin*ire* / *to finish* →   **fin-**

2. Add the following endings to the stem:

(io)	**-ii**
(tu)	**-isti**
(lui/lei/Lei)	**-ì**
(noi)	**-immo**
(voi)	**-iste**
(loro)	**-irono**

3. Here's the result:

(io)	**finii**	I finished
(tu)	**finisti**	you (fam.) finished
(lui/lei/Lei)	**finì**	he, she, you (pol.) finished
(noi)	**finimmo**	we finished
(voi)	**finiste**	you finished
(loro)	**finirono**	they finished

In the case of verbs such as **cominciare** and **mangiare** (Chapter 8) the **"i"** is retained in the formation of the stem:

comin*ciare* / *to begin*   →   **cominci-**

(io)	**cominciai**	I began
(tu)	**cominciasti**	you (fam.) began
(lui/lei/Lei)	**cominciò**	he, she, you (pol.) began
(noi)	**cominciammo**	we began
(voi)	**cominciaste**	you began
(loro)	**cominciarono**	they began

man*giare* / *to eat*   →   **mangi-**

(io)	**mangiai**	I ate
(tu)	**mangiasti**	you (fam.) ate
(lui/lei/Lei)	**mangiò**	he, she, you (pol.) ate
(noi)	**mangiammo**	we ate
(voi)	**mangiaste**	you ate
(loro)	**mangiarono**	they ate

Reflexive verbs are conjugated (of course!) with reflexive pronouns. Here is **lavarsi** completely conjugated for you:

lavarsi / *to wash oneself*   →   **lava-**

(io)	mi	**lavai**	I washed myself
(tu)	ti	**lavasti**	you (fam.) washed yourself
(lui/lei/Lei)	si	**lavò**	he, she, you (pol.) washed himself/herself/yourself
(noi)	ci	**lavammo**	we washed ourselves
(voi)	vi	**lavaste**	you washed yourselves
(loro)	si	**lavarono**	they washed themselves

In essence, the past absolute is used to refer to an action, event, or state that occurred in the relatively distant past. Otherwise, the present perfect (Chapter 9) is preferred in common usage:

Relatively Recent Past	Relatively Distant Past
Ieri *sono andato* **al cinema.** Yesterday I went to the movies.	**Nel 1952 loro** *andarono* **in America.** In 1952 they went to America.
Ho mangiato **la pizza qualche minuto fa.** I ate the pizza a few minutes ago.	*Partirono* **per l'Italia molti anni fa.** They left for Italy many years ago.

EXERCISE Set 12–1

A. Supply the missing past absolute forms of the verbs **viaggiare**, **credere**, and **capire**, giving the English equivalents.

EXAMPLE: lui ____   =   _____
             lui viaggiò, credé (credette),   =   he traveled, believed, understood
             capì

1. **io** _____   =   _____
2. **tu** _____   =   _____
3. **noi** _____   =   _____
4. **loro** _____   =   _____
5. **voi** _____   =   _____
6. **Lei** _____   =   _____

Now, supply the missing past absolute forms of the verb **vestirsi**, giving the English equivalent.

7. **io** _____   =   _____
8. **tu** _____   =   _____
9. **noi** _____   =   _____
10. **loro** _____   =   _____
11. **voi** _____   =   _____
12. **lei** _____   =   _____

B. Say the following things in Italian:

> **NOTE**
>
> *to, in* + a country   =   **in** + country
> **Sono andato/a *in* Italia.** / *I went to Italy.*
> **Vivono *in* Francia.** / *They live in France.*
>   *Except :*
>   **Vivono *negli* Stati Uniti.** / *They live in the U.S.*
> *to, in* + a city   =   **a** + city
> **Sono andato/a *a* Roma.** / *I went to Rome.*
> **Vivono *a* Parigi.** / *They live in Paris.*

Molti anni fa...

1. my parents arrived from Italy.

   _____

2. I spent **(passare)** a year in Rome.

   _____

3. you (fam., sing.) went to Italy.

   _____

4. her son became an engineer.

   _____

5. his daughter finished studying medicine **(medicina)**.

   _____

6. we discovered Italy.

   _____

7. they married in Florence.

   _____

8. our friends worked for that company.

   _____

9. I became an American citizen **(cittadino/a)**.

   _____

C. Quiz! Do you know your history? Answer each question and then look up the answer at the back. Use complete sentences. Have fun!

EXAMPLE: **Chi inventò il telescopio?** (*Who invented the telescope?*)
               Galileo Galilei inventò il telescopio.

l'automobile (f.)	automobile	**il Polo Nord**	North Pole
comporre	to compose (conj. like **porre**)	**primo**	first
inventare	to invent	**il telescopio**	telescope
l'opera	opera		

1. **Chi compose** (composed) **l'opera** *Il Barbiere di Siviglia*?

_____

2. **Chi inventò la radio?**

_____

3. **Chi scoprì il "Nuovo Mondo"?**

_____

4. **Quando scoprì il "Nuovo Mondo"?**

_____

5. **Chi andò al Polo Nord per la prima volta?**

_____

6. **Chi compose l'opera** *La Traviata*?

_____

Illustrative Dialogue

l'annunciatore (m.)	TV announcer, host	**il premio**	prize
l'annunciatrice (f.)	TV announcer, host	**la risposta**	answer
costruire	to build, to make	**la stampa**	printing, printing press
la domanda	question	**la tappa**	stage
indovinare	to guess	**il telequiz**	TV quiz show
la lampadina	light bulb	**il telespettatore**	TV viewer
il Polo Sud	South Pole	**vincere (pp.: vinto)**	to win

Annunciatore:	**Buonasera, gentili telespettatori. Stasera, siamo all'ultima tappa del nostro telequiz.**	Good evening, kind viewers. Tonight, we are at the last stage of our TV quiz.
Annunciatrice:	**Ecco le ultime tre domande. Chi le indovina vince il nostro premio. Eccole!**	Here are the last three questions. Whoever guesses them will win our prize. Here they are!
Annunciatore:	**Prima domanda. Chi *andò* al Polo Sud per la prima volta?**	First question. Who went to the South Pole for the first time?

Annunciatore:	**Seconda domanda. Chi** *costruì* **la prima lampadina?**	Second question. Who made the first light bulb?
Annunciatore:	**Terza ed ultima domanda. Chi** *inventò* **la stampa?**	Third and last question. Who invented the printing press?
Annunciatore:	**A domani sera per le risposte.**	See you tomorrow night for the answers.
Annunciatrice:	**Buonasera.**	Good evening

Grammar Notes

Note the first ten ordinal numbers:

primo / *first*	**sesto** / *sixth*
secondo / *second*	**settimo** / *seventh*
terzo / *third*	**ottavo** / *eighth*
quarto / *fourth*	**nono** / *ninth*
quinto / *fifth*	**decimo** / *tenth*

The remaining ordinals are constructed by dropping the final vowel of the corresponding cardinal and adding -**esimo**:

| **undici** / *eleven* | → | **undic-** + **esimo** | → | undicesimo / *eleventh* |
| **cinquanta** / *fifty* | → | **cinquant-** + **esimo** | → | cinquantesimo / *fiftieth* |

Since these are adjectives, they agree in number and gender with the noun:

il primo giorno / *the first day*   **la prima domanda** / *the first question*

EXERCISE Set 12–2

Answer the following questions based on the dialogue. Use complete sentences.

1. **A quale tappa è il telequiz stasera?**

   _____

2. **Quante domande ci sono?**

   _____

3. **Che cosa succede a chi indovina le tre domande?**

   _____

4. **Chi andò al Polo Sud per la prima volta?**

   _____

5. **Chi costruì la prima lampadina?**

   _____

6. **Chi inventò la stampa?**

   _____

Irregular Verbs

There are quite a number of irregular verbs in the past absolute. For many of these the general pattern goes as follows. Take, for example, **avere** / *to have*

1. The first person singular is always irregular and provides the "irregular stem":

   ebbi / *I had*   →   stem = **ebb-**

2. This stem applies to the third person singular and plural forms as well:

   ebbe / *he, she, you (pol.) had*
   ebbero / *they had*

3. The other forms are regular. Here's the complete conjugation:

(io)	**ebbi**	I had
(tu)	**avesti** (regular)	you (fam.) had
(lui/lei/Lei)	**ebbe**	he, she, you (pol.) had
(noi)	**avemmo** (regular)	we had
(voi)	**aveste** (regular)	you had
(loro)	**ebbero**	they had

Here are other common verbs following this pattern that are completely conjugated for you:

conoscere / *to know, to be familiar with, to meet (for the first time)*

(io)	**conobbi**	I knew
(tu)	**conoscesti** (regular)	you (fam.) knew
(lui/lei/Lei)	**conobbe**	he, she, you (pol.) knew
(noi)	**conoscemmo** (regular)	we knew
(voi)	**conosceste** (regular)	you knew
(loro)	**conobbero**	they knew

leggere / *to read*

(io)	**lessi**	I read
(tu)	**leggesti** (regular)	you (fam.) read
(lui/lei/Lei)	**lesse**	he, she, you (pol.) read
(noi)	**leggemmo** (regular)	we read
(voi)	**leggeste** (regular)	you read
(loro)	**lessero**	they read

piacere / *to be pleasing to*

(io)	**piacqui**	I was pleasing to
(tu)	**piacesti** (regular)	you (fam.) were pleasing to
(lui/lei/Lei)	**piacque**	he, she, you (pol.) was/were pleasing to
(noi)	**piacemmo** (regular)	we were pleasing to
(voi)	**piaceste** (regular)	you were pleasing to
(loro)	**piacquero**	they were pleasing to

sapere / *to know*

(io)	**seppi**	I knew
(tu)	**sapesti** (regular)	you (fam.) knew
(lui/lei/Lei)	**seppe**	he, she, you (pol.) knew
(noi)	**sapemmo** (regular)	we knew
(voi)	**sapeste** (regular)	you knew
(loro)	**seppero**	they knew

scrivere / *to write*

(io)	**scrissi**	I wrote
(tu)	**scrivesti** (regular)	you (fam.) wrote
(lui/lei/Lei)	**scrisse**	he, she, you (pol.) wrote
(noi)	**scrivemmo** (regular)	we wrote
(voi)	**scriveste** (regular)	you wrote
(loro)	**scrissero**	they wrote

venire / *to come*

(io)	**venni**	I came
(tu)	**venisti** (regular)	you (fam.) came
(lui/lei/Lei)	**venne**	he, she, you (pol.) came
(noi)	**venimmo** (regular)	we came
(voi)	**veniste** (regular)	you came
(loro)	**vennero**	they came

volere / *to want*

(io)	**volli**	I wanted to
(tu)	**volesti** (regular)	you (fam.) wanted to
(lui/lei/Lei)	**volle**	he, she, you (pol.) wanted to
(noi)	**volemmo** (regular)	we wanted to
(voi)	**voleste** (regular)	you wanted to
(loro)	**vollero**	they wanted to

Other common verbs following this pattern are the following. Only their first person singular forms are given here, since you can now figure out the remaining forms on your own:

apparire / *to appear*	→	**apparvi (apparii)** / *I appeared*
aprire / *to open*	→	**apersi (aprii)** / *I opened*
chiudere / *to close*	→	**chiusi** / *I closed*
comprendere / *to comprehend*	→	**compresi** / *I comprehended*
coprire / *to cover*	→	**copersi (coprii)** / *I covered*
correre / *to run*	→	**corsi** / *I ran*
dipingere / *to paint*	→	**dipinsi** / *I painted*
dolere / *to ache*	→	**dolsi** / *I ached*
decidere / *to decide*	→	**decisi** / *I decided*
mettere / *to put*	→	**misi** / *I put*
nascere / *to be born*	→	**nacqui** / *I was born*
prendere / *to take*	→	**presi** / *I took*
ridere / *to laugh*	→	**risi** / *I laughed*
rimanere / *to remain*	→	**rimasi** / *I remained*
rompere / *to break*	→	**ruppi** / *I broke*
scegliere / *to choose*	→	**scelsi** / *I chose*
scoprire / *to discover*	→	**scopersi (scoprii)** / *I discovered*
soffrire / *to suffer*	→	**soffersi (soffrii)** / *I suffered*
tenere / *to keep, to hold*	→	**tenni** / *I kept, I held*
valere / *to be worthwhile*	→	**valsi** / *I was worth (something)*
vedere / *to see*	→	**vidi** / *I saw*
vincere / *to win*	→	**vinsi** / *I won*
vivere / *to live*	→	**vissi** / *I lived*

Verbs ending in **-durre** also follow this pattern if you change them, once again, to their hypothetical forms:

dedurre	→	**"deducere"**	→	**dedussi** / *I deduced*
(io)		**dedussi**		I deduced
(tu)		**deducesti** ("regular")		you (fam.) deduced
(lui/lei/Lei)		**dedusse**		he, she, you (pol.) deduced
(noi)		**deducemmo** ("regular")		we deduced
(voi)		**deduceste** ("regular")		you deduced
(loro)		**dedussero**		they deduced

The following common verbs are irregular in this way as well if their "hypothetical" infinitives are used (see Chapter 11).

bere / *to drink*	→	**"bevere"**	→	**bevvi** / *I drank*
(io)		**bevvi (bevetti)**		I drank
(tu)		**bevesti** ("regular")		you (fam.) drank
(lui/lei/Lei)		**bevve (bevette)**		he, she, you (pol.) drank
(noi)		**bevemmo** ("regular")		we drank
(voi)		**beveste** ("regular")		you drank
(loro)		**bevvero (bevettero)**		they drank

dire / *to tell, to say*	→	**"dicere"**	→	**dissi** / *I said*
(io)		**dissi**		I said
(tu)		**dicesti** ("regular")		you (fam.) said
(lui/lei/Lei)		**disse**		he, she, you (pol.) said
(noi)		**dicemmo** ("regular")		we said
(voi)		**diceste** ("regular")		you said
(loro)		**dissero**		they said

fare / *to do, to make*	→	**"facere"**	→	**feci** / *I made*
(io)		**feci**		I made
(tu)		**facesti** ("regular")		you (fam.) made
(lui/lei/Lei)		**fece**		he, she, you (pol.) made
(noi)		**facemmo** ("regular")		we made
(voi)		**faceste** ("regular")		you made
(loro)		**fecero**		they made

porre / *to pose,* **supporre** / *to suppose,* **comporre** / *to compose*	→	**"ponere"**	→	**posi** / *I posed*
(io)		**posi**		I posed
(tu)		**ponesti** ("regular")		you (fam.) posed
(lui/lei/Lei)		**pose**		he, she, you (pol.) posed
(noi)		**ponemmo** ("regular")		we posed
(voi)		**poneste** ("regular")		you posed
(loro)		**posero**		they posed

trarre / *to draw (pull)* and **attrarre** / *to attract*	→	**"traere"**	→	**trassi** / *I drew*
(io)		**trassi**		I drew
(tu)		**traesti** ("regular")		you (fam.) drew
(lui/lei/Lei)		**trasse**		he, she, you (pol.) drew
(noi)		**traemmo** ("regular")		we drew
(voi)		**traeste** ("regular")		you drew
(loro)		**trassero**		they drew

This leaves only **dare**, **essere**, and **stare** as irregular in all forms:

dare / *to give*

(io)	**diedi**	I gave
(tu)	**desti**	you (fam.) gave
(lui/lei/Lei)	**diede**	he, she, you (pol.) gave
(noi)	**demmo**	we gave
(voi)	**deste**	you gave
(loro)	**diedero**	they gave

essere / *to be*

(io)	**fui**	I was
(tu)	**fosti**	you (fam.) were
(lui/lei/Lei)	**fu**	he, she, you (pol.) was/were
(noi)	**fummo**	we were
(voi)	**foste**	you were
(loro)	**furono**	they were

stare / *to stay*

(io)	**stetti**	I stayed
(tu)	**stesti**	you (fam.) stayed
(lui/lei/Lei)	**stette**	he, she, you (pol.) stayed
(noi)	**stemmo**	we stayed
(voi)	**steste**	you stayed
(loro)	**stettero**	they stayed

EXERCISE Set 12–3

A. Supply the past absolute forms as indicated.

1. I had = _____
2. you (fam., sing.) had = _____
3. he met = _____
4. we met = _____
5. she read = _____
6. we read = _____
7. I liked it = _____
8. you (pl.) knew = _____
9. they knew = _____
10. I wrote = _____
11. you (fam., sing.) wrote = _____
12. he came = _____
13. we came = _____
14. she wanted = _____
15. you (pl.) wanted = _____

16. they appeared	=	_____
17. they opened	=	_____
18. I closed	=	_____
19. he comprehended	=	_____
20. they covered	=	_____

B. Give the equivalent past absolute form of each present perfect form.

EXAMPLE: **I ragazzi sono stati qui.**
    I ragazzi furono/stettero qui.

la barzelletta	joke	**lo scudetto**	sports cup, prize
il campionato	championship	**secondo**	according to
ciascuno	each one	**la squadra**	team
la decisione	decision	**il vaso**	vase
la luna	moon		

1. Io sono stato/a in Italia due anni fa.

_____

2. Lui ha deciso di andare in Italia l'anno scorso.

_____

3. Lei si è messa la giacca ieri.

_____

4. Loro sono nati in Italia.

_____

5. Io ho preso una nuova decisione.

_____

6. Lui è rimasto tre giorni con noi.

_____

7. Maria ha rotto il vaso.

_____

8. Marco non ha riso quando hai detto quella barzelletta.

_____

9. Loro hanno scelto di andare in Italia.

_____

10. Io ho tenuto quel bambino per mano tutto il giorno.

_____

11. Non è valso la pena di vedere quel film.

_____

12. Quella squadra ha vinto lo scudetto nel 2001.

_____

13. Lei ha tradotto tutto quel libro.

_____

14. Noi abbiamo bevuto solo un caffè ciascuno.

_____

15. Loro hanno detto la verità, secondo me.

_____

16. Ha fatto brutto tempo l'inverno scorso.

_____

17. A chi hai dato quel libro?

_____

18. Siamo stati in Italia molti anni fa.

_____

Uses and Features

The past absolute, as its name implies, is used to express an action that was completed in the distant or remote past. It is thus used commonly as an "historical" past tense:

I miei nonni _emigrarono_ **molti anni fa.** / _My grandparents emigrated many years ago._

Galileo _inventò_ **il telescopio.** / _Galileo invented the telescope._

The past absolute cannot be used with temporal adverbs such as **già** / _already_, **poco fa** / _a little while ago_, etc. which limit the action to the immediate past (occurring within less than twenty-four hours). Only the present perfect can be used in such cases (Chapter 9).

Incidentally, there is a second pluperfect tense, called the **trapassato remoto** in Italian, that is used to express an action that occurred before a past absolute action. It can be used in place of the **trapassato prossimo** (Chapter 11):

Dopo che _fu arrivata_, **mi telefonò.** / _After she had arrived, she phoned me._

This tense is used rarely, being limited mainly to literary and historical usage. It is formed with the past absolute of the auxiliary verb. Here are two verbs fully conjugated in this tense:

parlare / _to speak_

(io)	ebbi	parlato	I had spoken
(tu)	avesti	parlato	you (fam.) had spoken
(lui/lei/Lei)	ebbe	parlato	he, she, you (pol.) had spoken
(noi)	avemmo	parlato	we had spoken
(voi)	aveste	parlato	you had spoken
(loro)	ebbero	parlato	they had spoken

arrivare / *to arrive*

(io)	fui	arrivato/a	I had arrived
(tu)	fosti	arrivato/a	you (fam.) had arrived
(lui)	fu	arrivato	he had arrived
(lei)	fu	arrivata	she had arrived
(Lei)	fu	arrivato/a	you (pol.) had arrived
(noi)	fummo	arrivati/e	we had arrived
(voi)	foste	arrivati/e	you had arrived
(loro)	furono	arrivati/e	they had arrived

EXERCISE Set 12–4

Rewrite each sentence with the past absolute as indicated.

EXAMPLE: *Ieri* Maria è andata in Italia/*Molti anni fa*
Molti anni fa Maria andò in Italia.

1. Quella squadra ha vinto lo scudetto *la settimana scorsa/nel 1948*

   _____

2. Lui ha detto quello *poco fa/tanti anni fa*

   _____

3. Loro sono venuti in America *qualche anno fa/da bambini*

   _____

4. Ha scritto un romanzo *recentemente/nel 1994*

   _____

5. Loro sono andati in Italia *domenica/l'estate scorsa*

   _____

6. Bruno ha letto *già* quel libro/*nel 1998*

   _____

7. Quelle due amiche si sono conosciute *recentemente/nell'estate del 1980*

   _____

Grammar Note

The verb **conoscere** is, of course, conjugated with the auxiliary **avere** in compound tenses. But in sentence 7 above it is used as a reciprocal verb **conoscersi** / *to meet one another* and is thus conjugated with **essere**.

Crossword Puzzle 12

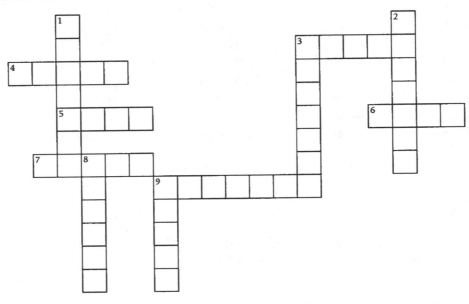

Give the corresponding past absolute forms of the given present perfect forms.

Orizzontali

3. **ho detto**

4. **ha rotto**

5. **ha avuto**

6. **ha fatto**

7. **siete stati**

9. **sono venuti**

Verticali

1. **hanno saputo**

2. **sono vissuti**

3. **hanno dato**

8. **ha scelto**

9. **ho voluto**

Part Three

The Future and Conditional Tenses

The Future and Conditional: An Overview

What Is the Future Tense?

In English the *future* tense is expressed by the "modal" form *will* in order to indicate something that will take place in time to come. In Italian the same tense is constructed with endings added on to the stem:

> **Domani *telefonerò* a Maria.** / *Tomorrow I will phone Mary.*
>
> **Tra due anni *andremo* in Italia.** / *We'll be going to Italy in two years.*

There is also a *future perfect* tense in English and Italian that is used to express or indicate past time with respect to some point in future time, as in

> **Il prossimo mese *saranno* già *partiti*.** / *Next month they will have already left.*
>
> **Quando *avrai finito* di mangiare, andremo al cinema.** / *When you will have finished eating, we will go to the movies.*

As you can see, it is a compound tense made up of an auxiliary verb in the future and the past participle of the verb.

What Is the Conditional Tense?

In English the *conditional* tense is expressed by the modal form *would* in order to indicate or make reference to conditions. In Italian the same tense is constructed with endings added on to the stem:

> ***Telefonerei* a Maria, ma non è a casa.** / *I would phone Mary, but she's not at home.*
>
> ***Andremmo* volentieri in Italia, ma non abbiamo soldi.** / *We would gladly go to Italy, but we don't have any money.*

There is also a *conditional perfect* tense in English and Italian that is used to express or indicate an action or event that *would have* taken place under certain conditions:

> **Sarebbero andati in Italia, ma non avevano soldi.** / *They would have gone to Italy, but they didn't have any money.*

> **Avrei pagato volentieri, ma non avevo il portafoglio.** / *I would have gladly paid, but I didn't have my wallet.*

As you can see, it is also a compound tense made up of an auxiliary verb in the conditional and the past participle of the verb.

13
The Future

Regular Verbs

To form the future tense, called the **futuro semplice** in Italian, do the following:
First conjugation:

1. Change the **-are** ending of the infinitive to **-er**,

    parlare / *to speak* →   **parler-**

2. Add the following endings to the stem:

(io)	-ò
(tu)	-ai
(lui/lei/Lei)	-à
(noi)	-emo
(voi)	-ete
(loro)	-anno

3. Here's the result:

(io)	**parlerò**	I will speak
(tu)	**parlerai**	you (fam.) will speak
(lui/lei/Lei)	**parlerà**	he, she, you (pol.) will speak
(noi)	**parleremo**	we will speak
(voi)	**parlerete**	you will speak
(loro)	**parleranno**	they will speak

4. If the infinitive ending is **-ciare** or **-giare** change it to **-cer** and **-ger**:

    cominciare / *to begin*   →   **comincer-**
    mangiare / *to eat*   →   **manger-**

5. Add the same endings to the resulting stem:

(io)	**comincerò**	I will begin
	mangerò	I will eat
(tu)	**comincerai**	you (fam.) will begin
	mangerai	you (fam.) will eat
(lui/lei/Lei)	**comincerà**	he, she, you (pol.) will begin
	mangerà	he, she, you (pol.) will eat
(noi)	**cominceremo**	we will begin
	mangeremo	we will eat
(voi)	**comincerete**	you will begin
	mangerete	you will eat
(loro)	**cominceranno**	they will begin
	mangeranno	they will eat

6. If the infinitive ending is **-care** or **-gare** change it to **-cher** and **-gher**:

     cercare / *to search for*   →   **cercher-**

     pagare / *to pay*   →   **pagher-**

7. Add the same endings to the resulting stem:

(io)	cercherò	I will search for
	pagherò	I will pay
(tu)	cercherai	you (fam.) will search for
	pagherai	you (fam.) will pay
(lui/lei/Lei)	cercherà	he, she, you (pol.) will search for
	pagherà	he, she, you (pol.) will pay
(noi)	cercheremo	we will search for
	pagheremo	we will pay
(voi)	cercherete	you will search for
	pagherete	you will pay
(loro)	cercheranno	they will search for
	pagheranno	they will pay

Second and Third Conjugations:

1. Drop the **-e** of the infinitive ending:

     scrivere / *to write* → **scriver-**

     finire / *to finish* → **finir-**

2. Add the following endings to both stems:

(io)	-ò
(tu)	-ai
(lui/lei/Lei)	-à
(noi)	-emo
(voi)	-ete
(loro)	-anno

3. Here's the result:

(io)	scriverò	I will write
(tu)	scriverai	you (fam.) will write
(lui/lei/Lei)	scriverà	he, she, you (pol.) will write
(noi)	scriveremo	we will write
(voi)	scriverete	you will write
(loro)	scriveranno	they will write
(io)	finirò	I will finish
(tu)	finirai	you (fam.) will finish
(lui/lei/Lei)	finirà	he, she, you (pol.) will finish
(noi)	finiremo	we will finish
(voi)	finirete	you will finish
(loro)	finiranno	they will finish

4. The same pattern applies to verbs discussed in Chapter 8:

tradurre / *to translate*	→	**tradurr-**
(io)	**tradurrò**	I will translate
(tu)	**tradurrai**	you (fam.) will translate
(lui/lei/Lei)	**tradurrà**	he, she, you (pol.) will translate
(noi)	**tradurremo**	we will translate
(voi)	**tradurrete**	you will translate
(loro)	**tradurranno**	they will translate

Reflexive verbs are conjugated as described above but, of course, with the addition of reflexive pronouns. Here's an example:

alzarsi / *to get up*	→	**alzar-** →	**alzer-**
(io)	**mi**	**alzerò**	I will get up
(tu)	**ti**	**alzerai**	you (fam.) will get up
(lui/lei/Lei)	**si**	**alzerà**	he, she, you (pol.) will get up
(noi)	**ci**	**alzeremo**	we will get up
(voi)	**vi**	**alzerete**	you will get up
(loro)	**si**	**alzeranno**	they will get up

And, of course, let's not forget about that pesky verb **piacere**! In the future it continues to have the same features (Chapter 4):

I will not like that restaurant.

Non mi	**piacerà**	**quel ristorante**
↓	↓	↓
Not to me	*will be pleasing*	*that restaurant.*

She will not like us.

Non le	**piaceremo**	**(noi)**
↓	↓	↓
Not to her	*will be pleasing*	*we.*

Recall, finally, the verb form **esserci** / *to be there* (Chapter 2), which is used in the future to acknowledge that something or someone will be somewhere. It has the following two forms:

Singular	Plural
Ci sarà l'insegnante? Will the teacher be here/there?	*Ci saranno* gli insegnanti? Will the teachers be here/there?

TIP

*Notice that the **futuro** is rendered in English generally by the following two translations:*

Lui **arriverà** domani. = ⎡ *He will arrive tomorrow.* ⎤
⎣ *He will be arriving tomorrow.* ⎦

EXERCISE Set 13-1

A. Supply the missing future forms of the verbs **arrivare**, **credere**, and **dormire**, giving the English equivalents.

EXAMPLE: lui ____   =   _____
           lui arriverà =   he will arrive
           lui crederà   =   he will believe
           lui dormirà   =   he will sleep

1. io _____ =   _____

   =   _____

   =   _____

2. tu _____ =   _____

   =   _____

   =   _____

3. noi _____ =   _____

   =   _____

   =   _____

4. loro _____ =   _____

   =   _____

   =   _____

5. voi _____ =   _____

   =   _____

   =   _____

6. lei _____ =   _____

   =   _____

   =   _____

Now, supply the missing future forms of the verbs **baciare**, **noleggiare**, **comunicare**, and **spiegare**, giving the English equivalents.

7. io _____ =   _____

   =   _____

   =   _____

   =   _____

8. tu _____ =   _____

   =   _____

   =   _____

   =   _____

9. noi _____ = _____

= _____

= _____

= _____

10. loro _____ = _____

= _____

= _____

= _____

11. voi _____ = _____

= _____

= _____

= _____

12. Lei _____ = _____

= _____

= _____

= _____

Finally, supply the missing future forms of the verbs **leggere**, **capire**, **produrre**, and **divertirsi**, giving the English equivalents.

13. io _____ = _____

= _____

= _____

= _____

14. tu _____ = _____

= _____

= _____

= _____

15. noi _____ = _____

= _____

= _____

= _____

16. loro _____ = _____

= _____

= _____

= _____

17. voi _____   =   _____

                   =   _____

                   =   _____

                   =   _____

18. lui _____   =   _____

                   =   _____

                   =   _____

                   =   _____

B. How do you say the following things in Italian?

1. That television program will start at 6PM and end at 9PM.

   _____

2. There will be many people at the party.

   _____

3. I know that she will not like that movie.

   _____

4. I'm sure that they will like you, Alessandro.

   _____

5. We will pay at the Bar Roma, if you (fam., sing.) will eat what we say.

   _____

6. He said that she too will be there.

   _____

7. Tomorrow Maria and I will go out together.

   _____

8. I know for sure that the two of you will get married.

   _____

9. I will be getting up late tomorrow because it is Sunday.

   _____

Prospettiva personale

Can you predict the future? Indicate what you think will happen, using the future tense.

EXAMPLE: -Chi vincerà il "World Series" di baseball quest'anno?
                -*Secondo me (in my opinion) i Milwaukee Brewers vinceranno il "World Series."*

famoso	famous	**probabile**	probable
il futuro	future	**prossimo**	next (week, year, etc.)

1. **Chi vincerà il "World Series" di baseball quest'anno?**

   _____

2. **Chi giocherà per i New York Yankees l'anno prossimo probabilmente?**

   _____

3. **Che cosa succederà agli Stati Uniti nel futuro?**

   _____

4. **Quali persone famose si sposeranno l'anno prossimo?**

   _____

5. **Quanto durerà l'inverno quest'anno?**

   _____

Illustrative Dialogue

la chiromante	fortuneteller	**il sogno**	dream
Mamma mia!	Egad! (lit.: My mother!)	**trovare**	to find
promettere (conj. like **mettere**)	to promise	**trovarsi**	to find oneself
rivelare	to reveal		

Marco:	**Signora, come _sarà_ il futuro per me? Me lo _dirà_?**	Madam, how will the future be for me? Will you tell it to me?
Chiromante:	**Certo. Lei _amerà_ solo una donna nella sua vita.**	Certainly. You will love only one woman in your life.
Marco:	**Chi _sarà_ la donna dei miei sogni?**	Who will be the woman of my dreams?
Chiromante:	**Non gliela _rivelerò_.**	I will not reveal her to you.
Marco:	**Perché? Le prometto che l'_amerò_ fedelmente!**	Why? I promise you that I will love her faithfully!
Chiromante:	**Non importa! Lei la _conoscerà_ fra qualche giorno.**	It doesn't matter! You will meet her in a few days.
Marco:	**Come _si chiamerà_?**	What will her name be?
Chiromante:	**Glielo _dirò_ domani!**	I will tell you tomorrow!
Marco:	**Mamma mia! Conoscere il futuro mi _costerà_ molto!**	Egad! Knowing the future will cost me a lot!

Grammar Notes

Sequencing direct and indirect pronouns is a bit complicated! Just remember the following:

1. The indirect object always precedes the direct object (_lo, la, li,_ or _le_).

2. The indirect forms **mi, ti, ci,** and **vi** are changed to **me, te, ce,** and **ve,** respectively.

Maria mi dà la penna. / _Maria gives the pen to me._

↓

Maria me la dà. / _Maria gives it to me._

3. The indirect forms **gli** and **le** are both changed to **glie-** and the direct forms **lo**, **la**, **li**, and **le** are attached to form one word:

Maria gli dà la penna. / *Maria gives the pen to him.*
↓
Maria gliela dà. / *Maria gives it to him.*

Maria le dà la penna. / *Maria gives the pen to her.*
↓
Maria gliela dà. / *Maria gives it to her.*

EXERCISE **Set 13–2**

Answer the following questions based on the dialogue. Use complete sentences.

GRAMMAR TIP

Use the preposition **da** *to render the concept of* at/to *the doctor's, fortuneteller's, etc.*
dal medico / *at/to the doctor's*   **dalla chiromante** / *at/to the fortuneteller's*

---

1. **Dove si trova Marco?**

   _____

2. **Quante donne *amerà* Marco nella sua vita, secondo la chiromante?**

   _____

3. **La chiromante gli rivelerà il nome della donna a Marco?**

   _____

4. **Come amerà la donna dei suoi sogni, Marco?**

   _____

5. **Quando la conoscerà, secondo la chiromante?**

   _____

6. **Quanto costerà conoscere il futuro, secondo Marco?**

   _____

Irregular Verbs

Most irregular verbs in the future are formed by dropping the first and last vowels of the infinitive ending. Take, for example, **andare** / *to go*:

1. Drop both vowels of the ending:

   andare   →   **andr-**

2. Add the usual future endings:

(io)	**andrò**	I will go
(tu)	**andrai**	you (fam.) will go
(lui/lei/Lei)	**andrà**	he, she, you (pol.) will go
(noi)	**andremo**	we will go
(voi)	**andrete**	you will go
(loro)	**andranno**	they will go

Other common verbs conjugated in this way are as follows:

avere / *to have*

(io)	**avrò**	I will have
(tu)	**avrai**	you (fam.) will have
(lui/lei/Lei)	**avrà**	he, she, you (pol.) will have
(noi)	**avremo**	we will have
(voi)	**avrete**	you will have
(loro)	**avranno**	they will have

cadere / *to fall*

(io)	**cadrò**	I will fall
(tu)	**cadrai**	you (fam.) will fall
(lui/lei/Lei)	**cadrà**	he, she, you (pol.) will fall
(noi)	**cadremo**	we will fall
(voi)	**cadrete**	you will fall
(loro)	**cadranno**	they will fall

dovere / *to have to*

(io)	**dovrò**	I will have to
(tu)	**dovrai**	you (fam.) will have to
(lui/lei/Lei)	**dovrà**	he, she, you (pol.) will have to
(noi)	**dovremo**	we will have to
(voi)	**dovrete**	you will have to
(loro)	**dovranno**	they will have to

potere / *to be able to*

(io)	**potrò**	I will be able to
(tu)	**potrai**	you (fam.) will be able to
(lui/lei/Lei)	**potrà**	he, she, you (pol.) will be able to
(noi)	**potremo**	we will be able to
(voi)	**potrete**	you will be able to
(loro)	**potranno**	they will be able to

sapere / *to know*

(io)	**saprò**	I will know
(tu)	**saprai**	you (fam.) will know
(lui/lei/Lei)	**saprà**	he, she, you (pol.) will know
(noi)	**sapremo**	we will know
(voi)	**saprete**	you will know
(loro)	**sapranno**	they will know

vedere / *to see*

(io)	**vedrò**	I will see
(tu)	**vedrai**	you (fam.) will see
(lui/lei/Lei)	**vedrà**	he, she, you (pol.) will see
(noi)	**vedremo**	we will see
(voi)	**vedrete**	you will see
(loro)	**vedranno**	they will see

With the verbs **dare**, **dire**, **fare**, and **stare**, do what you have learned to do previously with regular verbs. Drop the final vowel of the infinitive and add the usual endings:

dare	→	**dar-**
dire	→	**dir-**
fare	→	**far-**
stare	→	**star-**

dare / *to give*

(io)	**darò**	I will give
(tu)	**darai**	you (fam.) will give
(lui/lei/Lei)	**darà**	he, she, you (pol.) will give
(noi)	**daremo**	we will give
(voi)	**darete**	you will give
(loro)	**daranno**	they will give

dire / *to say, to tell, to speak*

(io)	**dirò**	I will say
(tu)	**dirai**	you (fam.) will say
(lui/lei/Lei)	**dirà**	he, she, you (pol.) will say
(noi)	**diremo**	we will say
(voi)	**direte**	you will say
(loro)	**diranno**	they will say

fare / *to do, to make*

(io)	**farò**	I will make
(tu)	**farai**	you (fam.) will make
(lui/lei/Lei)	**farà**	he, she, you (pol.) will make
(noi)	**faremo**	we will make
(voi)	**farete**	you will make
(loro)	**faranno**	they will make

stare / *to stay*

(io)	**starò**	I will stay
(tu)	**starai**	you (fam.) will stay
(lui/lei/Lei)	**starà**	he, she, you (pol.) will stay
(noi)	**staremo**	we will stay
(voi)	**starete**	you will stay
(loro)	**staranno**	they will stay

Similarly, treat **porre**, **trarre**, etc. as regular verbs:

porre	→	**porr-**
trarre	→	**trarr-**

porre / *to pose*

(io)	**porrò**	I will pose
(tu)	**porrai**	you (fam.) will pose
(lui/lei/Lei)	**porrà**	he, she, you (pol.) will pose
(noi)	**porremo**	we will pose
(voi)	**porrete**	you will pose
(loro)	**porranno**	they will pose

trarre / *to draw (pull)*

(io)	**trarrò**	I will draw
(tu)	**trarrai**	you (fam.) will draw
(lui/lei/Lei)	**trarrà**	he, she, you (pol.) will draw
(noi)	**trarremo**	we will draw
(voi)	**trarrete**	you will draw
(loro)	**trarranno**	they will draw

This leaves only a few verbs that are completely irregular in the future:

bere / *to drink*

(io)	**berrò**	I will drink
(tu)	**berrai**	you (fam.) will drink
(lui/lei/Lei)	**berrà**	he, she, you (pol.) will drink
(noi)	**berremo**	we will drink
(voi)	**berrete**	you will drink
(loro)	**berranno**	they will drink

essere / *to be*

(io)	**sarò**	I will be
(tu)	**sarai**	you (fam.) will be
(lui/lei/Lei)	**sarà**	he, she, you (pol.) will be
(noi)	**saremo**	we will be
(voi)	**sarete**	you will be
(loro)	**saranno**	they will be

rimanere / *to remain*

(io)	**rimarrò**	I will remain
(tu)	**rimarrai**	you (fam.) will remain
(lui/lei/Lei)	**rimarrà**	he, she, you (pol.) will remain
(noi)	**rimarremo**	we will remain
(voi)	**rimarrete**	you will remain
(loro)	**rimarranno**	they will remain

venire / *to come*

(io)	**verrò**	I will come
(tu)	**verrai**	you (fam.) will come
(lui/lei/Lei)	**verrà**	he, she, you (pol.) will come
(noi)	**verremo**	we will come
(voi)	**verrete**	you will come
(loro)	**verranno**	they will come

volere / *to want to*

(io)	**vorrò**	I will want to
(tu)	**vorrai**	you (fam.) will want to
(lui/lei/Lei)	**vorrà**	he, she, you (pol.) will want to
(noi)	**vorremo**	we will want to
(voi)	**vorrete**	you will want to
(loro)	**vorranno**	they will want to

EXERCISE Set 13–3

A. Supply the missing future forms of the verbs **avere**, **dare**, **porre**, and **rimanere**, giving the English equivalents.

EXAMPLE:

lui ____	=	_____
lui avrà	=	he will have
lui darà	=	he will give
lui porrà	=	he will pose
lui rimarrà	=	he will remain

1. **io** _____ = _____
   = _____
   = _____
   = _____

2. **tu** _____ = _____
   = _____
   = _____
   = _____

3. **noi** _____ = _____
   = _____
   = _____
   = _____

4. **loro** _____ = _____
   = _____
   = _____
   = _____

5. **voi** _____ = _____
   = _____
   = _____
   = _____

6. lei _____   =   _____

=   _____

=   _____

=   _____

Now, supply the missing future forms of the verbs **volere**, **venire**, **essere**, and **bere**, giving the English equivalents.

7. io _____   =   _____

=   _____

=   _____

=   _____

8. tu _____   =   _____

=   _____

=   _____

=   _____

9. noi _____   =   _____

=   _____

=   _____

=   _____

10. loro _____   =   _____

=   _____

=   _____

=   _____

11. voi _____   =   _____

=   _____

=   _____

=   _____

12. lui _____   =   _____

=   _____

=   _____

=   _____

B. Supply only the first person singular future form of each verb. And then use it in any way you want.

EXAMPLE: **andare**
                io andrò
                Domani io andrò al cinema/Tra un mese io andrò in Italia/...

1. **sapere**   =   _____

2. **attrarre**   =   _____

3. **comporre**   =   _____

4. **stare**   =   _____

5. **fare**   =   _____

6. **dire**   =   _____

7. **vedere**   =   _____

8. **potere**   =   _____

9. **dovere**   =   _____

Uses and Features

The simple future tense is used most of the time as follows.

1. To express an action or state of being that will take place at some time in the future.

    Domani *andremo* al cinema. / *Tomorrow we will be going to the movies.*
    Lo *farò* quando ho tempo. / *I will do it when I have time.*

2. To express probability.

    Quanto *costerà* quell'automobile? / *How much does that car (probably) cost?*
    Saranno le cinque. / *It's (probably) five o'clock.*

3. To express conjecture (wondering, guessing).

    Chi *sarà* che chiama a quest'ora? / *(I wonder) who is calling at this hour?*

VOCABULARY TIP

The future is often used with words and expressions such as

a otto	*a week from*
domani	*tomorrow*
domani a otto	*a week from tomorrow*
dopo	*later, afterward*
nel futuro	*in the future*
prossimo	*next*
tra/fra	*in*
tra un mese	*in a month (in a month's time)*

EXERCISE Set 13–4

A. Match the two columns logically.

1. Chi ... che telefona così tardi?   a. **verranno**

2. Tra un mese noi ... in vacanza al mare.   b. **daranno**

3. Loro ... domani a otto.   c. **farà**

4. Maria, ti ... più tardi.   d. **arriveranno**

5. Alessandro, quanto pensi che ... quella macchina?   e. **sarà**

6. Signorina, che cosa ..., un caffè o un cappuccino?   f. **andremo**

7. Quale film ... domani al cinema?   g. **chiamerò**

8. Che tempo ... domani?   h. **costerà**

9. Sei sicuro che loro ... alla festa?   i. **prenderà**

B. Translate the following passage into Italian:

affittare	to rent (a place)	**il lavoro**	job
ancora di più	even better	**nel frattempo**	for the time being
l'appartamento	apartment	**il posto**	place
attuale	current	**traslocare**	to move (house)
comunque	however	**visitare**	to visit

Carla will start working for a new firm in a few weeks. She likes her current job, but she will like her new job even better. Unfortunately, she will have to move. Where will she go? She will probably move near her place of work.

For the time being, she will rent an apartment near her work. She will need to buy a new car and she will probably not be able to visit us very often. We know, however, that she will enjoy herself in her new life.

_____

_____

_____

_____

_____

_____

Crossword Puzzle 13

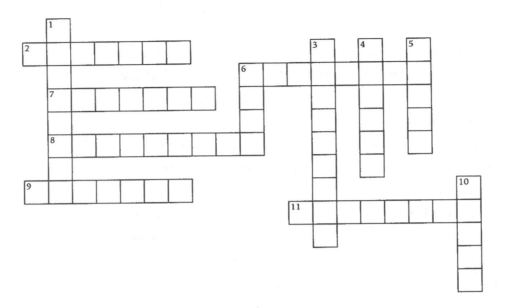

Orizzontali

2. Noi … solo il caffè.
6. Loro … parlare l'italiano solo quando andranno in Italia.
7. Oggi io … a casa tutta la giornata.
8. Fa molto freddo. Forse, ….
9. Anche voi … fare quello che volete.
11. Anche loro … a casa domani.

Verticali

1. Anche loro … alla festa domani.
3. Dove vi … domani (*find yourselves*)?
4. Sarah, quando … in Italia?
5. Anche lui … venire alla festa.
6. Ci … anche ler alla festa.
10. Io … fare delle spese oggi.

14
The Future Perfect

Conjugation of the Future Perfect

The future perfect, called the **futuro anteriore** in Italian, is a compound tense. Therefore, it is conjugated with an auxiliary verb, either **avere** / *to have* or **essere** / *to be*, and the past participle of the verb, in that order. See Chapter 9 for the relevant details regarding past participles and the use of one or the other auxiliary verb.

In this case, the auxiliary verbs are in the simple future. Here are examples of verbs conjugated with **avere**:

First conjugation: **parlare** / *to speak*

(io)	avrò	parlato	I will have spoken
(tu)	avrai	parlato	you (fam.) will have spoken
(lui/lei/Lei)	avrà	parlato	he, she, you (pol.) will have spoken
(noi)	avremo	parlato	we will have spoken
(voi)	avrete	parlato	you will have spoken
(loro)	avranno	parlato	they will have spoken

Second conjugation: **vendere** / *to sell*

(io)	avrò	venduto	I will have sold
(tu)	avrai	venduto	you (fam.) will have sold
(lui/lei/Lei)	avrà	venduto	he, she, you (pol.) will have sold
(noi)	avremo	venduto	we will have sold
(voi)	avrete	venduto	you (fam.) will have sold
(loro)	avranno	venduto	they will have sold

Third conjugation: **finire** / *to finish*

(io)	avrò	finito	I will have finished
(tu)	avrai	finito	you (fam.) will have finished
(lui/lei/Lei)	avrà	finito	he, she, you (pol.) will have finished
(noi)	avremo	finito	we will have finished
(voi)	avrete	finito	you will have finished
(loro)	avranno	finito	they will have finished

Here are examples of verbs conjugated with **essere**:

First Conjugation: **arrivare** / *to arrive*

(io)	sarò	arrivato/a	I will have arrived
(tu)	sarai	arrivato/a	you (fam.) will have arrived
(lui)	sarà	arrivato	he will have arrived
(lei)	sarà	arrivata	she will have arrived
(Lei)	sarà	arrivato/a	you (pol.) will have arrived
(noi)	saremo	arrivati/e	we will have arrived
(voi)	sarete	arrivati/e	you will have arrived
(loro)	saranno	arrivati/e	they will have arrived

Second Conjugation: **cadere** / *to fall*

(io)	sarò	**caduto/a**	I will have fallen
(tu)	sarai	**caduto/a**	you (fam.) will have fallen
(lui)	sarà	**caduto**	he, she, you (pol.) will have fallen
(lei)	sarà	**caduta**	
(Lei)	sarà	**caduto/a**	
(noi)	saremo	**caduti/e**	we will have fallen
(voi)	sarete	**caduti/e**	you will have fallen
(loro)	saranno	**caduti/e**	they will have fallen

Third Conjugation: **uscire** / *to go out*

(io)	sarò	**uscito/a**	I will have gone out
(tu)	sarai	**uscito/a**	you (fam.) will have gone out
(lui)	sarà	**uscito**	he, she, you (pol.) will have gone out
(lei)	sarà	**uscita**	
(Lei)	sarà	**uscito/a**	
(noi)	saremo	**usciti/e**	we will have gone out
(voi)	sarete	**usciti/e**	you will have gone out
(loro)	saranno	**usciti/e**	they will have gone out

For a list of common verbs conjugated with **essere** see Chapter 9. Again, all reflexive verbs are conjugated with **essere**:

divertirsi / *to enjoy oneself*

(io)	mi	sarò	**divertito/a**	I will have enjoyed myself
(tu)	ti	sarai	**divertito/a**	you (fam.) will have enjoyed yourself
(lui)	si	sarà	**divertito**	he will have enjoyed himself
(lei)	si	sarà	**divertita**	she will have enjoyed herself
(Lei)	si	sarà	**divertito/a**	you (pol.) will have enjoyed yourself
(noi)	ci	saremo	**divertiti/e**	we will have enjoyed ourselves
(voi)	vi	sarete	**divertiti/e**	you will have enjoyed yourselves
(loro)	si	saranno	**divertiti/e**	they will have enjoyed themselves

---

TIP

Notice that the conditional perfect is generally translated as follows:

Avrà studiato.	=	*He will have studied.*
Sarà andata.	=	*She will have gone.*

The main use of this tense is in temporal subordinate clauses—clauses that start with **dopo che** / *after*, **quando** / *when*, and **appena** / *as soon as*—connected to clauses in the simple future:

>   **Uscirò quando** *sarai arrivato.* / *I will go out when you (will) have arrived.*

>   **Appena** *avrò finito* **di lavorare,** *andrò* **al cinema.** / *As soon as I (will) have finished working, I'll go to the movies.*

Like the simple future, it is also used to express probability:

>   ***Saranno usciti* già.** / *They must have already gone out.*

>   **Quanto** *sarà costata* **quella casa?** / *How much did that house (probably) cost?*

EXERCISE Set 14–1

A. Supply the missing future perfect forms of the verbs **cominciare**, **credere**, **capire**, and **fare**, giving the English equivalents.

Example: **lui** _____   =   _____
             lui avrà cominciato   =   he will have begun
             lui avrà creduto   =   he will have believed
             lui avrà capito   =   he will have understood
             lui avrà fatto   =   he will have made

1. **io** _____ =   _____

             =   _____

             =   _____

             =   _____

2. **tu** _____ =   _____

             =   _____

             =   _____

             =   _____

3. **noi** _____ =   _____

             =   _____

             =   _____

             =   _____

4. **loro** _____ =   _____

             =   _____

             =   _____

             =   _____

5. **voi** _____ =   _____

             =   _____

             =   _____

             =   _____

6. **lei** _____ =   _____

             =   _____

             =   _____

             =   _____

Now, supply the missing future perfect forms of the verbs **andare**, **venire**, **essere**, and **mettersi**, giving the English equivalents.

7. io _____ =   _____

=   _____

=   _____

=   _____

8. tu _____ =   _____

=   _____

=   _____

=   _____

9. noi _____ =   _____

=   _____

=   _____

=   _____

10. loro _____ =   _____

=   _____

=   _____

=   _____

11. voi _____ =   _____

=   _____

=   _____

=   _____

12. Lei _____ =   _____

=   _____

=   _____

=   _____

B. Say the following things in Italian.

GRAMMAR TIP

To say some, another one, *etc. use the particle* **ne** *before the verb:*

Quanti libri hai? / *How many books do you have?*

Ne ho quattro. / *I have four.*

Vuoi un'altra mela? / *Do you want another apple?*

Sì, *ne* **voglio un'altra.** / *Yes, I want another one.*

---

1. After they will have arrived, we will go to the movies together.

   _____

2. When they (will) have married, they will go to Italy.

   _____

3. I will go out today, only after I (will) have studied a bit.

   _____

4. As soon as he (will) have finished reading that book, I am sure that he will start another one.

   _____

5. After that team (will) probably have won the championship, I will be very happy.

   _____

6. When you will have moved into your new apartment, where will you be working, Mr. Smith?

   _____

7. That car must have cost (*will have cost*) a lot of money!

   _____

8. He must have already gone out.

   _____

9. When he comes, they will have already gone home.

   _____

Illustrative Dialogue

altrimenti	otherwise		**imparare**	to learn
l'appetito	appetite		**l'invitato**	guest
chissà	who knows, I wonder		**la pazienza**	patience
il cibo	food		**smettere** (conj. like **mettere**)	to stop, to quit
controllare	to control			

Franca: **Chissà a che ora arriveranno stasera gli invitati alla nostra festa? Pensi che *si saranno dimenticati*?**

Who knows at what time the guests will arrive tonight at our party? Do you think that they have forgotten?

Paola: **No, *avranno smesso* di lavorare tardi. Saranno qui tra poco. Devi imparare ad avere pazienza.**

No, they must have stopped working late. They'll be here shortly. You must learn to have patience.

Franca: **Lo so, ma *avremo* già *mangiato* tutto, quando arriveranno.**

I know, but we might (will) have already eaten everything, when they arrive.

Paola: **Sì, è vero. Dovremo cercare di controllare il nostro appetito, altrimenti tutto il cibo *sarà* veramente *finito*.**

Yes, it's true. We must try to control our appetite, otherwise all the food will be truly finished.

Franca: **Già!**

Yeah!

EXERCISE **Set 14–2**

Answer the following questions based on the dialogue. Use complete sentences.

1. **Che cosa pensa Franca?**

   _____

2. **Che cosa le risponde Paola?**

   _____

3. **Che cosa deve imparare Franca, secondo Paola?**

   _____

4. **Che cosa avranno fatto le due amiche (probabilmente)?**

   _____

5. **Che cosa dovranno controllare?**

   _____

6. **Perché?**

   _____

Uses and Features

As you have seen, the future perfect is used to refer to an action that occurred before another simple future action (Chapter 13):

> _Andremo_ **al cinema, appena** _avrai finito_ **di lavorare.** / _We will go to the movies, as soon as you (will) have finished work._

And, like the simple future, it can also be used to convey probability:

> **Quanto** _sarà costata_ **quella macchina?** / _How much did that car probably cost?_
> **Lui** _avrà telefonato_ **alle sei.** / _He must have phoned at six._

VOCABULARY TIP

The future perfect, like the present perfect (Chapter 9) is often used with words and expressions such as

appena	_just, as soon as_
dopo che	_after_
già	_already_
quando	_when_

EXERCISE **Set 14–3**

Put the verb in parenthesis into the future or future perfect according to sense.

il/la regista	director	**tardo**	late (adj)
simile	similar	**veloce**	fast, quick
stanco	tired		

1. **Mangerò anche la pizza, appena io (finire)** _____ **gli spaghetti.**

2. **Sono sicura che lui (uscire)** _____ **già.**

3. **Mario (arrivare)** _____ **domani verso il tardo pomeriggio.**

4. **Quando (andare)** _____ **in Italia, tu e Sarah?**

5. **È vero che (venire)** _____ **anche loro alla festa?**

6. **A quest'ora Maria (andare)** _____ **già a dormire.**

7. **Appena (alzarsi)** _____, **loro dovranno vestirsi velocemente, anche se sono stanchi.**

8. **Quando loro (vedere)** _____ **quel film, vorranno certamente vedere film simili di quel regista.**

9. **Dopo che tu (assaggiare)** _____ **questo cibo, sono sicuro che ne vorrai di più.**

Crossword Puzzle 14

Future or future perfect?

Orizzontali

1. **voi ... andati** (*you will have gone*)

5. **io ...** (*I will answer*)

6. **loro ...** (*they will go*)

8. **loro ...** (*they will remain*)

10. **noi ... usciti** (*we will have gone out*)

Verticali

2. **loro ... mangiato** (*they will have eaten*)

3. **tu ... venuto** (*you will have come*)

4. **loro ... fatto** (*they will have done*)

7. **noi ... guardato** (*we will have watched*)

9. **io ... finito** (*I will have finished*)

15
The Conditional

Regular Verbs

The conditional of regular verbs, called the **condizionale** in Italian, is formed in a similar manner to the future (Chapter 13):

First conjugation:

1. Change the **-are** ending of the infinitive to **-er**,

   parlare / *to speak* → **parler-**

2. Add the following endings to the stem:

(io)	**-ei**
(tu)	**-esti**
(lui/lei/Lei)	**-ebbe**
(noi)	**-emmo**
(voi)	**-este**
(loro)	**-ebbero**

3. Here's the result:

(io)	**parlerei**	I would speak
(tu)	**parleresti**	you (fam.) would speak
(lui/lei/Lei)	**parlerebbe**	he, she, you (pol.) would speak
(noi)	**parleremmo**	we would speak
(voi)	**parlereste**	you would speak
(loro)	**parlerebbero**	they would speak

4. If the infinitive ending is **-ciare** or **-giare**, change it to **-cer** or **-ger**:

   cominciare / *to begin* → **comincer-**

   mangiare / *to eat* → **manger-**

5. Add the same endings to the stem:

(io)	**comincerei**	I would begin
	mangerei	I would eat
(tu)	**cominceresti**	you (fam.) would begin
	mangeresti	you (fam.) would eat
(lui/lei/Lei)	**comincerebbe**	he, she, you (pol.) would begin
	mangerebbe	he, she, you (pol.) would eat
(noi)	**cominceremmo**	we would begin
	mangeremmo	we would eat
(voi)	**comincereste**	you would begin
	mangereste	you would eat
(loro)	**comincerebbero**	they would begin
	mangerebbero	they would eat

6. If the infinitive ending is **-care** or **-gare** change it to **-cher** or **-gher**:

cercare / *to search for*   →   **cercher-**

pagare / *to pay*   →   **pagher-**

7. Add the same endings to the resulting stem:

(io)	**cercherei**	I would search for
	pagherei	I would pay
(tu)	**cercheresti**	you (fam.) would search for
	pagheresti	you (fam.) would pay
(lui/lei/Lei)	**cercherebbe**	he, she, you (pol.) would search for
	pagherebbe	he, she, you (pol.) would pay
(noi)	**cercheremmo**	we would search for
	pagheremmo	we would pay
(voi)	**cerchereste**	you would search for
	paghereste	you would pay
(loro)	**cercherebbero**	they would search for
	pagherebbero	they would pay

Second and Third Conjugations:

1. Drop the **-e** of the infinitive ending:

scrivere / *to write*   →   **scriver-**

finire / *to finish*   →   **finir-**

2. Add the same endings to the stem:

(io)	**-ei**
(tu)	**-esti**
(lui/lei/Lei)	**-ebbe**
(noi)	**-emmo**
(voi)	**-este**
(loro)	**-ebbero**

3. Here's the result:

(io)	**scriverei**	I would write
(tu)	**scriveresti**	you (fam.) would write
(lui/lei/Lei)	**scriverebbe**	he, she, you (pol.) would write
(noi)	**scriveremmo**	we would write
(voi)	**scrivereste**	you would write
(loro)	**scriverebbero**	they would write
(io)	**finirei**	I would finish
(tu)	**finiresti**	you (fam.) would finish
(lui/lei/Lei)	**finirebbe**	he, she, you (pol.) would finish
(noi)	**finiremmo**	we would finish
(voi)	**finireste**	you would finish
(loro)	**finirebbero**	they would finish

4. The same pattern applies to verbs discussed in Chapter 8:

tradurre / *to translate*   →   **tradurr-**

(io)	**tradurrei**	I would translate
(tu)	**tradurresti**	you (fam.) would translate

(lui/lei/Lei)	**tradurrebbe**	he, she, you (pol.) would translate
(noi)	**tradurremmo**	we would translate
(voi)	**tradurreste**	you would translate
(loro)	**tradurrebbero**	they would translate

Reflexive verbs are conjugated as described above but, as always, with the addition of reflexive pronouns. Here's an example:

alzarsi/ *to get up* → alzar- → alzer-

(io)	**mi**	**alzerei**	I would get up
(tu)	**ti**	**alzeresti**	you (fam.) would get up
(lui/lei/Lei)	**si**	**alzerebbe**	he, she, you (pol.) would get up
(noi)	**ci**	**alzeremmo**	we would get up
(voi)	**vi**	**alzereste**	you would get up
(loro)	**si**	**alzerebbero**	they would get up

And, of course, let's not forget about that pesky verb **piacere**! In the conditional it continues, of course, to have the same features (Chapter 4):

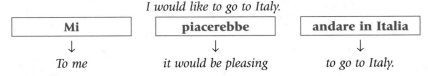

I would like to go to Italy.

Mi	**piacerebbe**	**andare in Italia**
↓	↓	↓
To me	*it would be pleasing*	*to go to Italy.*

TIP

*Notice that the **conditional** is rendered in English generally by the following two translations:*

Lui *chiamerebbe*, **ma...** = ⎡ *He would call, but ...* ⎤
⎣ *He would be calling, but ...* ⎦

The conditional is used, in essence, to convey a conjecture, hypothesis, or some action or event that *would*, *could*, or *might* take place under given conditions.

　　Uscirei, ma non ho tempo. / *I would go out, but I do not have time.*

　　Comprerebbero quella macchina, ma non hanno i soldi. / *They would buy that car, but they don't*
　　　　have the money.

EXERCISE Set 15–1

A. Supply the missing conditional forms of the verbs **comprare**, **mettere**, **dormire**, and **lavarsi**, giving the English equivalents.

EXAMPLE:	lui ____	=	_____
	lui comprerebbe	=	he would buy
	lui metterebbe	=	he would put
	lui dormirebbe	=	he would sleep
	lui si laverebbe	=	he would wash himself

1. **io** _____ = _____

　　　　= _____

　　　　= _____

　　　　= _____

2. tu _____ = _____

              = _____

              = _____

              = _____

3. noi _____ = _____

              = _____

              = _____

              = _____

4. loro _____ = _____

              = _____

              = _____

              = _____

5. voi _____ = _____

              = _____

              = _____

              = _____

6. lei _____ = _____

              = _____

              = _____

              = _____

Now, supply the missing conditional forms of the verbs **baciare**, **noleggiare**, **comunicare**, and **spiegare**, giving the English equivalents.

7. io _____ = _____

              = _____

              = _____

              = _____

8. tu _____ = _____

              = _____

              = _____

              = _____

9. noi _____ = _____

              = _____

              = _____

              = _____

10. loro _____ = _____

              = _____

              = _____

              = _____

11. voi _____ = _____

= _____

= _____

= _____

12. Lei _____ = _____

= _____

= _____

= _____

B. You are given future forms. Give the corresponding conditional forms.

EXAMPLE: **io mangerò**
io mangerei

1. **io pagherò**   = _____

2. **tu risponderai**   = _____

3. **lui capirà**   = _____

4. **lei produrrà**   = _____

5. **noi baceremo**   = _____

6. **voi vi sposerete**   = _____

7. **loro scieranno**   = _____

8. **io assaggerò**   = _____

9. **tu giocherai**   = _____

C. Say the following things in Italian.

1. I would speak Italian more, but first I must study the verbs.

   _____

2. Is it true that you (fam., sing.) would study Spanish instead of Italian?

   _____

3. My friend (m.) would get up earlier each day, but he is always very tired.

   _____

4. We would gladly pay for the coffee, but we have no money.

   _____

5. Would you (fam., pl.) help me understand Italian grammar **(grammatica)**, please?

   _____

6. I know that they would understand what you are doing.

   _____

7. I would watch that TV program, but I don't have time.

_____

8. She would like those pastries for sure.

_____

9. He would like that team more, but it never wins.

_____

Illustrative Dialogue

Antonio:	**Pronto. Giorgio. *Ti piacerebbe* uscire stasera?**	Hello. Giorgio. Would you like to go out tonight?
Giorgio:	***Mi piacerebbe*, ma non posso.**	I would like to, but I can't.
Antonio:	**Perché? Devi studiare? Io non *mi preoccuperei* così tanto!**	Why? Do you have to study? I wouldn't worry so much!
Giorgio:	**Tu non *ti preoccuperesti* mai, ma io sì!**	You would never worry, but I would.
Antonio:	**Va bene. *Saresti* libero (free) domani?**	Fine. Would you be free tomorrow?
Giorgio:	**Domani sì, ma *preferirei* andare a prendere un caffè al bar. Va bene?**	Tomorrow yes, but I would prefer to go and get a coffee at the coffee bar. OK?
Antonio:	**Va bene.**	OK.

EXERCISE Set 15–2

Answer the following questions based on the dialogue. Use complete sentences.

GRAMMAR TIP

In answering some of the questions below you might need to resort to the use of indirect speech. In general, direct *speech involves talking directly to someone.* Indirect *speech involves talking about someone or something. Notice that there are differences between the two forms of speech.*

Indirect speech	**Direct speech**
Carlo chiede se loro sono italiani.	**Carlo chiede: "Siete italiani?"**
Carlo asks if they are Italian.	*Carlo asks: "Are you Italian?"*

---

1. **Che cosa chiede Antonio a Giorgio?**

_____

2. **Come risponde Giorgio?**

_____

3. **Perché non può uscire Giorgio?**

_____

4. Cosa dice Antonio allora?

_____

5. Dove preferirebbe andare Giorgio domani?

_____

Irregular Verbs

As in the case of the future, most irregular verbs in the conditional are formed by dropping the first and last vowels of the infinitive ending. Take, for example, **andare** / _to go_:

1. Drop both vowels:

   andare   →   **andr-**

2. Add the usual conditional endings:

(io)	**andrei**	I would go
(tu)	**andresti**	you (fam.) would go
(lui/lei/Lei)	**andrebbe**	he, she, you (pol.) would go
(noi)	**andremmo**	we would go
(voi)	**andreste**	you would go
(loro)	**andrebbero**	they would go

Other common verbs conjugated in this way are the same ones taken up in Chapter 13. Just the first person singular forms are given here for convenience:

avere / _to have_	→	**avrei** / _I would have_
cadere / _to fall_	→	**cadrei** / _I would fall_
dovere / _to have to_	→	**dovrei** / _I would have to_
potere / _to be able to_	→	**potrei** / _I would be able to, I could_
sapere / _to know_	→	**saprei** / _I would know_
vedere / _to see_	→	**vedrei** / _I would see_

Again, with the verbs **dare**, **dire**, **fare**, **stare**, **porre** (and verbs made up with it like **comporre**), and **trarre** (and verbs made up with it such as **attrarre**) do what you have learned to do above with regular verbs. Drop the final vowel of the infinitive and add the usual endings:

dare	→	**dar-**	→	**darei** / _I would give_
dire	→	**dir-**	→	**direi** / _I would say_
fare	→	**far-**	→	**farei** / _I would do_
stare	→	**star-**	→	**starei** / _I would stay_
porre	→	**porr-**	→	**porrei** / _I would pose_
trarre	→	**trarr-**	→	**trarrei** / _I would draw (pull)_

As in the case of the future, there are only a few verbs that are completely irregular in the conditional:

bere / _to drink_

(io)	**berrei**	I would drink
(tu)	**berresti**	you (fam.) would drink
(lui/lei/Lei)	**berrebbe**	he, she, you (pol.) would drink
(noi)	**berremmo**	we would drink
(voi)	**berreste**	you would drink
(loro)	**berrebbero**	they would drink

essere / *to be*

(io)	**sarei**	I would be
(tu)	**saresti**	you (fam.) would be
(lui/lei/Lei)	**sarebbe**	he, she, you (pol.) would be
(noi)	**saremmo**	we would be
(voi)	**sareste**	you would be
(loro)	**sarebbero**	they would be

rimanere / *to remain*

(io)	**rimarrei**	I would remain
(tu)	**rimarresti**	you (fam.) would remain
(lui/lei/Lei)	**rimarrebbe**	he, she, you (pol.) would remain
(noi)	**rimarremmo**	we would remain
(voi)	**rimarreste**	you would remain
(loro)	**rimarrebbero**	they would remain

venire / *to come*

(io)	**verrei**	I would come
(tu)	**verresti**	you (fam.) would come
(lui/lei/Lei)	**verrebbe**	he, she, you (pol.) would come
(noi)	**verremmo**	we would come
(voi)	**verreste**	you would come
(loro)	**verrebbero**	they would come

volere / *to want to*

(io)	**vorrei**	I would want to
(tu)	**vorresti**	you (fam.) would want to
(lui/lei/Lei)	**vorrebbe**	he, she, you (pol.) would want to
(noi)	**vorremmo**	we would want to
(voi)	**vorreste**	you would want to
(loro)	**vorrebbero**	they would want to

EXERCISE Set 15–3

You are given future forms. Give the corresponding conditional forms. Use each verb freely.

EXAMPLE: io andrò
io andrei / Io andrei in Italia, ma non ho soldi/Io andrei al cinema ma non ho tempo/...

1. **noi andremo**   =   _____

2. **tu avrai**   =   _____

3. **lui saprà**   =   _____

4. **lei potrà**   =   _____

5. **noi cadremo**   =   _____

6. **voi vedrete**   =   _____

7. **loro daranno**   =   _____

8. **io starò**   =   _____

9. **tu dirai**   =   _____

10. **loro comporranno** = _____

11. **tu trarrai**   =   _____

12. **noi berremo**   =   _____

13. **voi sarete**   =   _____

14. **lui rimarrà**   =   _____

15. **loro verranno**   =   _____

16. **lei vorrà**   =   _____

Prospettiva personale

Answer the following questions with complete sentences. Use the glossary at the back of this book if you do not know some word in Italian or else use a dictionary.

EXAMPLE: **Dove vorresti andare quest'estate?**
             Quest'estate vorrei andare in Italia/andare al mare/...

la grammatica	grammar
libero	free
il matrimonio	matrimony, wedding
migliore	better, best
il paese	country
l'opinione (f.)	opinion

1. **Dove andresti regolarmente in vacanza? Perché?**

   _____

2. **Ti piacerebbe studiare la grammatica francese? Perché?**

   _____

3. **Avresti un po' di tempo libero stasera per studiare i verbi?**

   _____

4. **Secondo te, quale film dovrebbe vincere l'Oscar quest'anno?**

   _____

5. **Come si dovrebbe vestire una persona per un matrimonio?**

   _____

6. **Che tempo dovrebbe fare regolarmente, secondo te?**

   _____

7. **Quale squadra potrebbe vincere il Superbowl quest'anno?**

   _____

8. **Che cosa vorresti fare più spesso?**

   _____

9. **Dove vorresti andare l'anno prossimo?**

_____

10. **Quale sarebbe, nella tua opinione, il miglior(e) paese del mondo?**

_____

Uses and Features

The conditional is used most of the time as follows:

1. To express a conditional, potential, or hypothetical action.

   **Andrei** **al cinema volentieri, ma non ho tempo.** / _I would gladly go to the movies, but I don't have time._

   Lo _**comprerei**_**, ma non ho soldi.** / _I would buy it, but I don't have any money._

2. To convey courtesy or politeness.

   Mi _**potrebbe**_ **aiutare?** / _Could you help me?_

   **Vorrei** **un caffè, grazie.** / _I would like a coffee, thanks._

3. To express an indirect quotation.

   Maria ha detto che _**verrebbe**_ **domani.** / _Mary said that she would be coming tomorrow._

4. To express probability.

   Quanto _**costerebbe**_ **quel televisore?** / _How much does that TV set probably cost?_

5. To quote someone else's opinion.

   Secondo lui, quella ragazza _**sarebbe**_ **spagnola.** / _According to him, that girl is (probably) Spanish._

   Nella loro opinione, l'Italia _**sarebbe**_ **il miglior paese del mondo.** / _In their opinion, Italy is the best country in the world._

Finally, note the meanings of **potere**, **dovere**, and **volere** in the conditional:

	Present		Conditional	
potere	**Lo posso fare.**	_I can do it._	**Lo potrei fare.**	_I could do it._
dovere	**Lo devo fare.**	_I have to do it._	**Lo dovrei fare.**	_I should do it._
volere	**Lo voglio fare.**	_I want to do it._	**Lo vorrei fare.**	_I would like to do it._

EXERCISE Set 15–4

Say the following things in Italian.

1. They would gladly go to the coffee bar, but they don't have time.

_____

2. Mrs. Smith, could you help me?

_____

3. Who would like a coffee?

_____

4. Franco said that they would be arriving tomorrow.

_____

5. How much does that new car probably cost?

_____

6. In her opinion, that boy is (likely) Italian.

_____

7. According to him, she is (likely) American.

_____

8. They could come a little later, no?

_____

9. She shouldn't be doing that.

_____

10. Mr. Smith, would you like a cappuccino?

_____

Crossword Puzzle 15

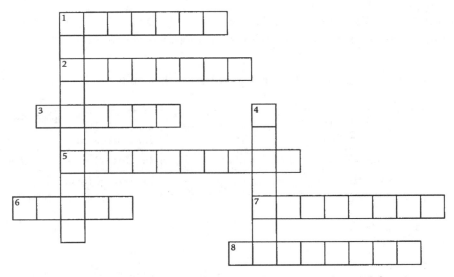

You are given the future form of the verb. Supply the corresponding conditional form.

Orizzontali

1. **avremo**
2. **dovrete**
3. **vedrò**
5. **berranno**
6. **sarò**
7. **staremo**
8. **rimarrò**

Verticali

1. **andranno**
4. **farai**

16
The Conditional Perfect

Conjugation of the Conditional Perfect

The conditional perfect, called the **condizionale passato** in Italian, is a compound tense. Therefore, it is conjugated with an auxiliary verb, either **avere** / *to have* or **essere** / *to be*, and the past participle of the verb, in that order. See Chapter 9 for the relevant details regarding past participles and the use of one or the other auxiliary verb.

In this case, the auxiliary verbs are in the conditional. Here are examples of verbs conjugated with **avere**:

First conjugation: **parlare** / *to speak*

(io)	avrei	parlato	I would have spoken
(tu)	avresti	parlato	you (fam.) would have spoken
(lui/lei/Lei)	avrebbe	parlato	he, she, you (pol.) would have spoken
(noi)	avremmo	parlato	we would have spoken
(voi)	avreste	parlato	you would have spoken
(loro)	avrebbero	parlato	they would have spoken

Second conjugation: **vendere** / *to sell*

(io)	avrei	venduto	I would have sold
(tu)	avresti	venduto	you (fam.) would have sold
(lui/lei/Lei)	avrebbe	venduto	he, she, you (pol.) would have sold
(noi)	avremmo	venduto	we would have sold
(voi)	avreste	venduto	you would have sold
(loro)	avrebbero	venduto	they would have sold

Third conjugation: **finire** / *to finish*

(io)	avrei	finito	I would have finished
(tu)	avresti	finito	you (fam.) would have finished
(lui/lei/Lei)	avrebbe	finito	he, she, you (pol.) would have finished
(noi)	avremmo	finito	we would have finished
(voi)	avreste	finito	you would have finished
(loro)	avrebbero	finito	they would have finished

Here are examples of verbs conjugated with **essere**:

First Conjugation: **arrivare** / *to arrive*

(io)	sarei	arrivato/a	I would have arrived
(tu)	saresti	arrivato/a	you (fam.) would have arrived
(lui)	sarebbe	arrivato	he would have arrived
(lei)	sarebbe	arrivata	she would have arrived
(Lei)	sarebbe	arrivato/a	you (pol.) would have arrived

(noi)	saremmo	arrivati/e	we would have arrived
(voi)	sareste	arrivati/e	you would have arrived
(loro)	sarebbero	arrivati/e	they would have arrived

Second Conjugation: **cadere** / *to fall*

(io)	sarei	caduto/a	I would have fallen
(tu)	saresti	caduto/a	you (fam.) would have fallen
(lui)	sarebbe	caduto	he would have fallen
(lei)	sarebbe	caduta	she would have fallen
(Lei)	sarebbe	caduto/a	you (pol.) would have fallen
(noi)	saremmo	caduti/e	we would have fallen
(voi)	sareste	caduti/e	you would have fallen
(loro)	sarebbero	caduti/e	they would have fallen

Third Conjugation: **uscire** / *to go out*

(io)	sarei	uscito/a	I would have gone out
(tu)	saresti	uscito/a	you (fam.) would have gone out
(lui)	sarebbe	uscito	he would have gone out
(lei)	sarebbe	uscita	she would have gone out
(Lei)	sarebbe	uscito/a	you (pol.) would have gone out
(noi)	saremmo	usciti/e	we would have gone out
(voi)	sareste	usciti/e	you would have gone out
(loro)	sarebbero	usciti/e	they would have gone out

For a list of common verbs conjugated with **essere** see Chapter 9. Again, all reflexive verbs are conjugated with **essere**:

divertirsi / *to enjoy oneself*

(io)	mi	sarei	divertito/a	I would have enjoyed myself
(tu)	ti	saresti	divertito/a	you (fam.) would have enjoyed yourself
(lui)	si	sarebbe	divertito	he would have enjoyed himself
(lei)	si	sarebbe	divertita	she would have enjoyed herself
(Lei)	si	sarebbe	divertito/a	you (pol.) would have enjoyed yourself
(noi)	ci	saremmo	divertiti/e	we would have enjoyed ourselves
(voi)	vi	sareste	divertiti/e	you would have enjoyed yourselves
(loro)	si	sarebbero	divertiti/e	they would have enjoyed themselves

---

TIP

Notice that the conditional perfect is generally translated as follows:

| **Avrei mangiato la pizza.** | = | *I would have eaten pizza.* |
| **Sarei andato.** | = | *I would have gone.* |

The main use of this tense is to indicate that something *would have, could have, should have,* or *might have* happened.

> **Io *sarei andato* al cinema, ma non avevo tempo.** / *I would have gone to the movies, but I didn't have time.*

> **Avrei dovuto farlo**, ma non avevo voglia. / *I should have done it, but I didn't feel like it.*

EXERCISE Set 16–1

A. Supply the missing conditional perfect forms of the verbs **cominciare**, **credere**, **capire**, and **fare**, giving the English equivalents.

Example: **lui** _____   =   _____
                lui avrebbe cominciato   =   he would have begun
                lui avrebbe creduto   =   he would have believed
                lui avrebbe capito   =   he would have understood
                lui avrebbe fatto   =   he would have made

1. **io** _____   =   _____

                    =   _____

                    =   _____

                    =   _____

2. **tu** _____   =   _____

                    =   _____

                    =   _____

                    =   _____

3. **noi** _____ =   _____

                    =   _____

                    =   _____

                    =   _____

4. **loro** _____ =   _____

                    =   _____

                    =   _____

                    =   _____

5. **voi** _____ =   _____

                    =   _____

                    =   _____

                    =   _____

6. **lei** _____ =   _____

                    =   _____

                    =   _____

                    =   _____

Now, supply the missing conditional perfect forms of the verbs **andare**, **venire**, **essere**, and **mettersi**, giving the English equivalents.

7. **io** _____ = _____

               = _____

               = _____

               = _____

8. **tu** _____ = _____

               = _____

               = _____

               = _____

9. **noi** _____ = _____

               = _____

               = _____

               = _____

10. **loro** _____ = _____

               = _____

               = _____

               = _____

               = _____

11. **voi** _____ = _____

               = _____

               = _____

               = _____

12. **Lei** _____ = _____

               = _____

               = _____

               = _____

B. Say the following things in Italian.

1. I would have gone to the party, but I didn't have time.

_____

2. My parents would have gone to Italy last year, but they didn't have the money.

_____

3. I would have gone out with him, but I had to study.

_____

4. Usually I would have done that myself *(io stesso/a)*, but this time she decided to do it.

_____

5. They too would have gotten up early yesterday, but they forgot.

_____

6. We would have gotten married earlier *(prima)*, but we didn't have enough *(abbastanza)* money for the wedding.

_____

7. He would have bought that car, but it cost too much.

_____

Illustrative Dialogue

abbastanza	enough	**in giro**	around
dappertutto	everywhere	**magari**	perhaps
essere d'accordo	to agree	**peccato**	too bad, a pity
fantastico	fantastic		

Tina:	**È vero Sandra che *saresti andata* in Italia, l'estate scorsa?**	Is it true Sandra that you had gone (in all likelihood) to Italy, last summer?
Sandra:	**Sì. Mi sono divertita molto. Ma sono stata solo da mia nonna tutto il tempo.**	Yes. I had lots of fun. But I stayed only at my grandmother's place for the whole time.
Tina:	**Peccato! *Saresti dovuta andare* a vedere le città più famose.**	A pity! You should have gone to see the most famous cities.
Sandra:	**È vero, ma non *avrei avuto* abbastanza tempo, perché mia nonna mi ha portato in giro dappertutto.**	It's true, but I would not have had enough time, because my grandmother took me around everywhere.
Tina:	**Magari potremmo andare insieme in futuro, va bene?**	Perhaps we could go together in the future, OK?
Sandra:	**Sarebbe una cosa fantastica.**	It would be a fantastic thing.
Tina:	**Sono d'accordo.**	I agree.

EXERCISE Set 16–2

Answer the following questions based on the dialogue. Use complete sentences.

1. **Dove sarebbe andata Sandra l'estate scorsa?**

_____

2. **Dov'è stata Sandra tutto il tempo?**

_____

3. **Dove sarebbe dovuta andare, secondo Tina?**

_____

4. **Perché Sandra non è andata?**

_____

5. **Perché?**

_____

Uses and Features

As you have seen, the conditional perfect is used primarily to refer to an action that occurred before another simple conditional action (Chapter 15):

Mi ha detto che *sarebbe venuto*. / *He told me that he would (would have) come.*

Sapeva che io *avrei capito*. / *He knew that I would have understood.*

Notice the meaning of **potere**, **volere**, and **dovere** in the present and conditional perfect tenses:

Lo *potrei* fare. / *I could do it.*

Lo *avrei potuto* fare. / *I could have done it.*

Lo *vorrei* fare. / *I would like to do it.*

Lo *avrei voluto* fare. / *I would like to have done it.*

Lo *dovrei* fare. / *I should do it.*

Lo *avrei dovuto* fare. / *I should have done it.*

EXERCISE Set 16–3

Say the following things in Italian.

1. She indicated to me that they would (would have) come to the party, but had to work.

   _____

2. He knew that she would have understood everything.

   _____

3. We could do it, but we don't feel like it.

   _____

4. He could have done it, but he didn't feel like it.

   _____

5. They would like to do it, but they don't have time.

   _____

6. They would have liked to do it, but they didn't have time.

   _____

7. You (fam., sing.) should do it, no matter (**nono stante**) what they say.

   _____

8. You (fam., sing.) should have done it, no matter what they said.

   _____

Prospettiva personale

It's time to make the conditional perfect relevant to your own life! Answer as in the example.

EXAMPLE: **What would you have done if you...had had a lot of money?**
            Sarei diventato più ricco, avrei dato soldi a persone bisognose (needy), etc.

What would you have done if you…?

1. had had a lot of money

_____

_____

2. had had the possibility to learn Italian as a child

_____

_____

3. had had the possibility to govern your country

_____

_____

Crossword Puzzle 16

Missing from each verb, which is in the conditional perfect, is the auxiliary. Supply it.

Orizzontali

1. **Tu … fatto**
3. **Voi … detto**
4. **Noi … dato**
5. **Loro … stati**
6. **lei … andata**

Verticali

1. **Io … mangiato**
2. **Loro … bevuto**
4. **Lui … letto**
5. **Io mi … alzato**

Part Four

The Subjunctive Tenses

The Subjunctive: An Overview

What Is the Subjunctive?

The *subjunctive* is a mood that allows you to express a point of view, fear, doubt, hope, possibility—in sum, anything that is not a fact. In a way, the subjunctive is a counterpart to the indicative, the mood that allows you to convey facts and information.

The main thing to note about the subjunctive is that it is used, mainly, in a subordinate clause. What is a subordinate clause, you might ask?

A complex sentence has at least one subordinate clause—a *clause*, by the way, is a group of related words that contains a subject and predicate and is part of the main sentence. The subjunctive is used, as mentioned, mainly in a subordinate clause, generally introduced by **che** / *that, which, who*. So, when expressing something that is a doubt, an opinion, etc. with a verb in the main clause (the verb to the left of **che**), then put the verb in the subordinate clause (the verb to the right of **che**) in the subjunctive:

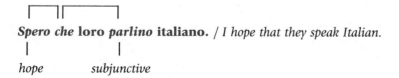

Spero che *loro parlino* **italiano.** / *I hope that they speak Italian.*

hope   *subjunctive*

Subjunctive vs. Indicative

Not all verbs in subordinate clauses (those after **che**) are necessarily to be put in the subjunctive—only those connected to a main clause verb that expresses a "nonfact" (opinion, fear, supposition, anticipation, wish, hope, doubt, etc.).

Indicative	Subjunctive
Sa che *è* la verità. He knows that it is the truth.	*Pensa* che *sia* la verità. He thinks that it is the truth.
È certo che *paga* lui. It's certain that he will pay.	*È improbabile* che *paghi* lui. It's improbable that he will pay.

17
The Present Subjunctive

Regular Verbs

To form the present subjunctive of regular verbs, called the **presente del congiuntivo** in Italian, do the following:

First Conjugation:

1. Drop the infinitive ending, **-are**:

     parlare / *to speak* → **parl-**

2. Add the following endings to the stem:

(io)	**-i**
(tu)	**-i**
(lui/lei/Lei)	**-i**
(noi)	**-iamo**
(voi)	**-iate**
(loro)	**-ino**

3. Here's the result:

...che (io)	**parli**	...that I speak, I am speaking, I may speak
...che (tu)	**parli**	...that you (fam.) speak, you are speaking, you may speak
...che (lui/lei/Lei)	**parli**	...that he, she, you (pol.) speak(s), he, she, you is/are speaking, he, she, you may speak
...che (noi)	**parliamo**	...that we speak, we are speaking, we may speak
...che (voi)	**parliate**	...that you speak, you are speaking, you may speak
...che (loro)	**parlino**	...that they speak, they are speaking, they may speak

If the first-conjugation infinitive ending is **-ciare** or **-giare**, then drop the **-are** and retain the **-i** of the ending, but do not write a "double **-i**" when adding on the present subjunctive endings:

cominciare / *to begin*	→ **cominci-**	
...che (io)	**cominci**	...that I begin, I am beginning, I may begin
...che (tu)	**cominci**	...that you (fam.) begin, you are beginning, you may begin
...che (lui/lei/Lei)	**cominci**	...that he, she, you (pol.) begin(s), he, she, you is/are beginning, he, she, you may begin
...che (noi)	**cominciamo**	...that we begin, we are beginning, we may begin
...che (voi)	**cominciate**	...that you begin, you are beginning, you may begin
...che (loro)	**comincino**	...that they begin, they are beginning, they may begin

mangiare / *to eat* →	**mangi-**	
...che (io)	**mangi**	...that I eat, I am eating, I may eat
...che (tu)	**mangi**	...that you (fam.) eat, you are eating, you may eat
...che (lui/lei/Lei)	**mangi**	...that he, she, you (pol.) eat(s), he, she, you is/are eating, he, she, you may eat
...che (noi)	**mangiamo**	...that we eat, we are eating, we may eat
...che (voi)	**mangiate**	...that you eat, you are eating, you may eat
...che (loro)	**mangino**	...that they eat, they are eating, they may eat

If the infinitive ends in **-iare**, the same pattern of "not doubling the **-i**" applies, unless the **-i** is stressed during the conjugation, in which case it is retained before the **-i** ending only (see Chapter 8).

If the first-conjugation infinitive ending is **-care** or **-gare**, drop the **-are** but add an **"h"** before the present subjunctive endings, indicating that the hard sound is to be retained:

cercare / *to look for, to search for* →	**cerch-**	
...che (io)	**cerchi**	...that I search, I am searching, I may search
...che (tu)	**cerchi**	...that you (fam.) search, you are searching, you may search
...che (lui/lei/Lei)	**cerchi**	...that he, she, you (pol.) search(es), he, she, you is/are searching, he, she, you may search
...che (noi)	**cerchiamo**	...that we search, we are searching, we may search
...che (voi)	**cerchiate**	...that you search, you are searching, you may search
...che (loro)	**cerchino**	...that they search, they are searching, they may search
pagare / *to pay* →	**pagh-**	
...che (io)	**paghi**	...that I pay, I am paying, I may pay
...che (tu)	**paghi**	...that you (fam.) pay, you are paying, you may pay
...che (lui/lei/Lei)	**paghi**	...that he, she, you (pol.) pay(s), he, she, you is/are paying, he, she, you may pay
...che (noi)	**paghiamo**	...that we pay, we are paying, we may pay
...che (voi)	**paghiate**	...that you pay, you are paying, you may pay
...che (loro)	**paghino**	...that they pay, they are paying, they may pay

Second Conjugation:

1. Drop the infinitive ending, **-ere**:

    scrivere / *to write* → **scriv-**

2. Add the following endings to the stem:

(io)	**-a**
(tu)	**-a**
(lui/lei/Lei)	**-a**
(noi)	**-iamo**
(voi)	**-iate**
(loro)	**-ano**

3. Here's the result:

...che (io)	**scriva**	...that I write, I am writing, I may write
...che (tu)	**scriva**	...that you (fam.) write, you are writing, you may write
...che (lui/lei/Lei)	**scriva**	...that he, she, you (pol.) write(s), he, she, you is/are writing, he, she, you may write

...che (noi)	scriviamo	...that we write, we are writing, we may write
...che (voi)	scriviate	...that you write, you are writing, you may write
...che (loro)	scrivano	...that they write, they are writing, they may write

Third Conjugation:

As in the case of the present indicative (Chapter 1), there are two types of conjugation patterns that apply to third-conjugation verbs.

To form the present subjunctive of *Type 1*, do the same things you have been doing so far:

1. Drop the infinitive ending, **-ire**:

   dormire / *to sleep*   →   **dorm-**

2. Add the following endings to the stem:

(io)	-a
(tu)	-a
(lui/lei/Lei)	-a
(noi)	-iamo
(voi)	-iate
(loro)	-ano

3. Here's the result:

...che (io)	dorma	...that I sleep, I am sleeping, I may sleep
...che (tu)	dorma	...that you (fam.) sleep, you are sleeping, you may sleep
...che (lui/lei/Lei)	dorma	...that he, she, you (pol.) sleep(s), he, she, you is/are sleeping, he, she, you may sleep
...che (noi)	dormiamo	...that we sleep, we are sleeping, we may sleep
...che (voi)	dormiate	...that you sleep, you are sleeping, you may sleep
...che (loro)	dormano	...that they sleep, they are sleeping, they may sleep

To form the present subjunctive of *Type 2* verbs, do the following:

1. Drop the infinitive ending, **-ire**:

   finire / *to finish*   →   **fin-**

2. Add the following endings to the stem:

(io)	-isca
(tu)	-isca
(lui/lei/Lei)	-isca
(noi)	-iamo
(voi)	-iate
(loro)	-iscano

3. Here's the result:

...che (io)	finisca	...that I finish, I am finishing, I may finish
...che (tu)	finisca	...that you (fam.) finish, you are finishing, you may finish
...che (lui/lei/Lei)	finisca	...that he, she, you (pol.) finish(es), he, she, you is/are finishing, he, she, you may finish
...che (noi)	finiamo	...that we finish, we are finishing, we may finish
...che (voi)	finiate	...that you finish, you are finishing, you may finish
...che (loro)	finiscano	...that they finish, they are finishing, they may finish

TIP

Be careful once again when you pronounce the third person plural forms! The accent is not placed on the ending, but on a syllable before the ending:

parlino / *they may speak*

|

stress

Reflexive verbs are conjugated as described above but, of course, with the addition of reflexive pronouns. Here's an example:

alzarsi / *to get up* → **alz-**

...che (io)	mi	alzi	...that I get up
...che (tu)	ti	alzi	...that you (fam.) get up
...che (lui/lei/Lei)	si	alzi	...that he, she, you (pol.) get(s) up
...che (noi)	ci	alziamo	...that we get up
...che (voi)	vi	alziate	...that you get up
...che (loro)	si	alzino	...that they get up

TIP

Because the endings are often the same, you will need to use the subject pronouns much more frequently with the subjunctive

È necessario che *tu finisca* quel lavoro. / *It is important that you finish that job.*
È necessario che *lui finisca* quel lavoro. / *It is important that he finish that job.*

As mentioned in the previous overview unit, the subjunctive is used in subordinate clauses, generally introduced by **che**. So, when expressing something that is a doubt, an opinion, etc. with a verb in the main clause (the verb to the left of **che**), put the verb in the subordinate clause (the verb to the right of **che**) in the subjunctive.

The best way to learn which main clause verbs require the subjunctive is to memorize the most commonly used ones. Here are a few of them:

credere / *to believe*	**pensare** / *to think*
desiderare / *to desire*	**sembrare** / *to seem*
dubitare / *to doubt*	**sperare** / *to hope*
immaginare / *to imagine*	**volere** / *to want*

Impersonal verbs and expressions also require that the subordinate clause verb be in the subjunctive:

È probabile che lui non ti riconosca più. / *It's probable that he may not recognize you anymore.*
Bisogna che voi studiate di più. / *It is necessary that you study more.*

Here are a few of these:

bisognare che / *to be necessary that*	**essere probabile** / *to be probable*
essere necessario / *to be necessary*	**succedere** / *to happen*
essere possibile / *to be possible*	

Superlative expressions also require the subjunctive:

Lei è la persona più intelligente che io conosca. / *She is the most intelligent person (that) I know.*

Certain conjunctions and indefinite structures also require the subjunctive:

Dovunque tu vada, io ti seguirò. / *Wherever you go, I will follow you.*
Benché piova, esco lo stesso. / *Although it is raining, I'm going out just the same.*

Here are the most common ones:

a meno che...non / *unless*   **nonostante** / *despite*
affiinché / *so that*   **perché** / *so that*
benché / *although*   **prima che** / *before*
chiunque / *whoever*   **purché** / *provided that*
dovunque / *wherever*   **qualunque** / *whichever*
nel caso che / *in the event that*   **sebbene** / *although*

Finally, the subjunctive is used in "wish" or "exhortation" expressions.

Che *scriva* **lui!** / *Let him write!*

Che *piova*, **se vuole!** / *Let it rain, if it wants to!*

EXERCISE Set 17–1

A. Supply the missing present subjunctive forms of the verbs **arrivare, baciare, noleggiare, indicare,** and **spiegare**, giving the English equivalents.

EXAMPLE: lui _____   =   _____

lui *arrivi, baci, noleggi,*   =   he arrives, kisses, rents,
indichi, spieghi   indicates, explains

È necessario che...

1. **io**   _____   =   _____

2. **tu**   _____   =   _____

3. **noi**   _____   =   _____

4. **loro**   _____   =   _____

5. **voi**   _____   =   _____

6. **lei**   _____   =   _____

Now, supply the missing present subjunctive forms of the verbs **leggere, partire, capire,** and **divertirsi**, giving the English equivalents.

7. **io**   _____   =   _____

8. **tu**   _____   =   _____

9. **noi**   _____   =   _____

10. **loro**   _____   =   _____

11. **voi**   _____   =   _____

12. **Lei**   _____   =   _____

B. How do you say the following things in Italian?

la camera   bedroom   **il fatto**   fact
cucinare   to cook   **pronto**   ready

1. He thinks (that) they are arriving tonight.

_____

2. I imagine (that) she understands everything.

_____

3. They doubt that you (fam., pl.) will finish in time.

_____

4. You (fam., sing.) are the least elegant person I know.

_____

5. Let it snow!

_____

6. She wants me to call her tonight (She wants that I call her tonight).

_____

7. It seems that you know Maria too.

_____

8. I hope that Alessandro writes that e-mail.

_____

9. Do you (fam., sing.) also believe that I speak Italian well?

_____

10. We desire that they play soccer better.

_____

11. It is necessary that he study more.

_____

12. It is possible that they speak Italian.

_____

13. It is probable that we will buy that car.

_____

14. Although it is raining outside, I am going out just the same.

_____

15. Unless she phones, we will not go to the movies.

_____

16. So that you (fam., sing.) eat pasta, I will cook it myself.

_____

17. Whoever desires to do it, I agree!

_____

18. Wherever she lives, I will go.

_____

19. In the event that he reads that e-mail, you (fam., sing.) should be ready to call him.

_____

20. Despite the fact that you (fam., sing.) never phone, I still like you.

_____

21. Before you (pl.) leave for Italy, you should ensure that you have enough money.

_____

22. I will do it, provided that you (fam., sing.) phone me first.

_____

23. Whatever language they speak, I know that he will understand them.

_____

Illustrative Dialogue

Madre:	**Giorgio, stai studiando?** _È importante_ **che tu** _studi_ **molto.**	Giorgio, are you studying? It's important that you study a lot.
Giorgio:	**Lo so. È necessario,** _affinché_ **io** _impari_ **a parlare bene la lingua italiana.**	I know. It's necessary so that I can learn to speak the Italian language well.
Madre:	**Giorgio** _spero_ **veramente che tu** _impari_ **bene a parlare, così potrai andare in Italia a conoscere i nonni.**	Giorgio, I really hope that you learn how to speak well; in this way you will be able to go to Italy to meet your grandparents.
Giorgio:	**Mi piacerebbe molto!**	I would like that a lot.
Madre:	**Quando hai finito,** _bisogna_ **che tu** _pulisca_ **la tua camera, va bene?**	When you have finished, it's necessary that you clean your room, OK?
Giorgio:	**Sì, mamma, lo farò.**	Yes, mom, I'll do it.

EXERCISE Set 17–2

Answer the following questions based on the dialogue. Use complete sentences.

1. Che cosa è importante, secondo la madre di Giorgio?

_____

2. Secondo Giorgio, perché è necessario che lui studi molto?

_____

3. Dove potrà andare Giorgio, se impara a parlare l'italiano bene?

_____

4. Che deve fare Giorgio quando ha finito di studiare?

_____

5. Lo farà?

_____

Irregular Verbs

The verbs that are irregular in the present indicative are also irregular in the present subjunctive. Here is a list of the conjugations of all such verbs introduced so far. The forms are given without English translation:

andare / *to go* — (io) vada, (tu) vada, (lui/lei/Lei) vada, (noi) andiamo, (voi) andiate, (loro) vadano

avere / *to have* — (io) abbia, (tu) abbia, (lui/lei/Lei) abbia, (noi) abbiamo, (voi) abbiate, (loro) abbiano

bere / *to drink* — (io) beva, (tu) beva, (lui/lei/Lei) beva, (noi) beviamo, (voi) beviate, (loro) bevano

dare / *to give* — (io) dia, (tu) dia, (lui/lei/Lei) dia, (noi) diamo, (voi) diate, (loro) diano

dire / *to tell, to say* — (io) dica, (tu) dica, (lui/lei/Lei) dica, (noi) diciamo, (voi) diciate, (loro) dicano

dolere / *to ache* — (io) dolga, (tu) dolga, (lui/lei/Lei) dolga, (noi) dogliamo, (voi) dogliate, (loro) dolgano

dovere / *to have to* — (io) deva (debba), (tu) deva (debba), (lui/lei/Lei) deva (debba), (noi) dobbiamo, (voi) dobbiate, (loro) devano (debbano)

essere / *to be* — (io) sia, (tu) sia, (lui/lei/Lei) sia, (noi) siamo, (voi) siate, (loro) siano

fare / *to do, to make* — (io) faccia, (tu) faccia, (lui/lei/Lei) faccia, (noi) facciamo, (voi) facciate, (loro) facciano

morire / *to die* — (io) muoia, (tu) muoia, (lui/lei/Lei) muoia, (noi) moriamo, (voi) moriate, (loro) muoiano

nascere / *to be born* — (io) nasca, (tu) nasca, (lui/lei/Lei) nasca, (noi) nasciamo, (voi) nasciate, (loro) nascano

piacere / *to like* — (io) piaccia, (tu) piaccia, (lui/lei/Lei) piaccia, (noi) piacciamo, (voi) piacciate, (loro) piacciano

porre / *to pose* — (io) ponga, (tu) ponga, (lui/lei/Lei) ponga, (noi) poniamo, (voi) poniate, (loro) pongano

potere / *to be able to* — (io) possa, (tu) possa, (lui/lei/Lei) possa, (noi) possiamo, (voi) possiate, (loro) possano

rimanere / *to remain* — (io) rimanga, (tu) rimanga, (lui/lei/Lei) rimanga, (noi) rimaniamo, (voi) rimaniate, (loro) rimangano

salire / *to climb* — (io) salga, (tu) salga, (lui/lei/Lei) salga, (noi) saliamo, (voi) saliate, (loro) salgano

sapere / *to know* — (io) sappia, (tu) sappia, (lui/lei/Lei) sappia, (noi) sappiamo, (voi) sappiate, (loro) sappiano

scegliere / *to choose* — (io) scelga, (tu) scelga, (lui/lei/Lei) scelga, (noi) scegliamo, (voi) scegliate, (loro) scelgano

stare / *to stay* — (io) stia, (tu) stia, (lui/lei/Lei) stia, (noi) stiamo, (voi) stiate, (loro) stiano

trarre / *to draw (pull)* — (io) tragga, (tu) tragga, (lui/lei/Lei) tragga, (noi) traiamo, (voi) traiate, (loro) traggano

uscire / *to go out* — (io) esca, (tu) esca, (lui/lei/Lei) esca, (noi) usciamo, (voi) usciate, (loro) escano

valere / *to be worth* — (io) valga, (tu) valga, (lui/lei/Lei) valga, (noi) valiamo, (voi) valiate, (loro) valgano

| **venire** / *to come* | (io) venga, (tu) venga, (lui/lei/Lei) venga, (noi) veniamo, (voi) veniate, (loro) vengano |
| **volere** / *to want* | (io) voglia, (tu) voglia, (lui/lei/Lei) voglia, (noi) vogliamo, (voi) vogliate, (loro) vogliano |

Recall that verbs ending in **-durre** can be rendered hypothetically "regular" as follows:

1. Change the ending in your mind to **-cere**:

   dedurre → **"deducere"**

2. Drop the **-ere** ending of the "hypothetical" verb stem:

   deducere → **deduc-**

3. Add the usual endings (previously):

   (io) *deduca*, **(tu)** *deduca*, **(lui/lei/Lei)** *deduca*, **(noi)** *deduciamo*, **(voi)** *deduciate*, **(loro)** *deducano*

Also, keep in mind what that pesky verb **piacere** means in Italian, even when it is used in the present subjunctive:

> **Dubito che gli** *piacciano* **gli spaghetti.** / *I doubt that he likes spaghetti ("spaghetti are pleasing to him").*
>
> **Penso che anche a lei** *piaccia* **andare al cinema.** / *I think that she also likes to go to the movies ("going to the movies is pleasing to her").*

EXERCISE Set 17–3

Change the verbs into subjunctive by adding the indicated expression to the given sentence. Follow the example.

EXAMPLE: **Giovanni va al cinema stasera (Dubito che...)**
             Dubito che Giovanni vada al cinema stasera.

1. **Loro vanno in Italia quest'anno (È probabile che...)**

   _____

2. **Tu hai trentatré anni (Penso che...)**

   _____

3. **Loro bevono il cappuccino (Sembra che...)**

   _____

4. **Lui dà la penna a Maria (Bisogna che...)**

   _____

5. **Voi dite la verità (Speriamo che...)**

   _____

6. **Loro devono studiare di più (Sembra che...)**

   _____

 7. C'è anche Alessandro (Immagino che...)

_____

 8. Fa bel tempo (Bisogna che...)

_____

 9. Nasce domani forse il bambino (Speriamo che...)

_____

10. Non gli piacciono le caramelle (Credo che...)

_____

11. Marco può venire alla festa (Sembra che...)

_____

12. Loro rimangono a casa domani (Penso che...)

_____

13. La sua amica sa parlare l'italiano molto bene (Dubito che...)

_____

14. Lui sceglie sempre lo stesso programma (Sembra che...)

_____

15. Alessandro sta molto bene (Penso che...)

_____

16. Loro escono insieme (Credo che...)

_____

17. Quel film vale la pena di vedere (Dubito che...)

_____

18. Loro vengono alla festa (Speriamo che...)

_____

19. Lui vuole andare in Italia (Penso che...)

_____

Progressive Forms

The present subjunctive has a progressive form as well, allowing you to zero in on an ongoing action that is to be expressed in the subjunctive mood:

> **Penso che in questo momento, mia sorella _stia mangiando_.** / _I think that at this moment, my sister is eating._
>
> **Sembra che loro _stiano guardando_ la televisione.** / _It seems that they are watching TV._

The present subjunctive progressive is formed with the present subjunctive of the verb **stare** / _to stay, to be_ and the gerund of the verb, in that order. Here are three verbs conjugated in the present progressive subjunctive:

First conjugation: **parlare** / *to speak*

...che (io)	**stia**	**parlando**	...that I am speaking
...che (tu)	**stia**	**parlando**	...that you (fam.) are speaking
...che (lui/lei/Lei)	**stia**	**parlando**	...that he, she, you (pol.) is/are speaking
...che (noi)	**stiamo**	**parlando**	...that we are speaking
...che (voi)	**stiate**	**parlando**	...that you are speaking
...che (loro)	**stiano**	**parlando**	...that they are speaking

Second conjugation: **vendere** / *to sell*

...che (io)	**stia**	**vendendo**	...that I am selling
...che (tu)	**stia**	**vendendo**	...that you (fam.) are selling
...che (lui/lei/Lei)	**stia**	**vendendo**	...that he, she, you (pol.) is/are selling
...che (noi)	**stiamo**	**vendendo**	...that we are selling
...che (voi)	**stiate**	**vendendo**	...that you are selling
...che (loro)	**stiano**	**vendendo**	...that they are selling

Third conjugation: **finire** / *to finish*

...che (io)	**stia**	**finendo**	...that I am finishing
...che (tu)	**stia**	**finendo**	...that you (fam.) are finishing
...che (lui/lei/Lei)	**stia**	**finendo**	...that he, she, you (pol.) is/are finishing
...che (noi)	**stiamo**	**finendo**	...that we are finishing
...che (voi)	**stiate**	**finendo**	...that you are finishing
...che (loro)	**stiano**	**finendo**	...that they are finishing

---

EXERCISE Set 17–4

Change the verbs into the subjunctive by adding the indicated expression to the given sentence. Follow the example.

EXAMPLE: **In questo momento...mia sorella sta leggendo (Penso che...)**
                Penso che in questo momento mia sorella stia leggendo.

In questo momento...

1. **Giorgio sta mangiando (Penso che...)**

   _____

2. **voi state guardando un programma alla televisione (Maria crede che...)**

   _____

3. **Marco sta dormendo (Sembra che...)**

   _____

4. **io sto scrivendo (Lui crede che...)**

   _____

5. **i miei amici stanno uscendo (Lei pensa che...)**

   _____

6. **noi stiamo bevendo un caffè (Loro credono che...)**

_____

7. **voi state leggendo (Dubito che...)**

_____

8. **lui sta suonando il violoncello (Sembra che...)**

_____

9. **lei sta cantando (Sembra che...)**

_____

Uses and Features

In summary, the subjunctive mood allows you to convey a point of view, fear, doubt, hope, possibility—that is, anything that is not a fact or a certainty. Specifically, the present subjunctive is used in subordinate clauses after verbs that express the following:

1. Wish, insistence, preference, suggestion, or request.
   Voglio che lo _faccia_ Maria. / _I want Mary to do it._
   Prefersico che _venga_ anche lui. / _I prefer that he come too._

2. Doubt, fear, joy, hope, or some other emotion.
   Dubito che voi _sappiate_ l'italiano. / _I doubt that you know Italian._
   Speriamo che tutto _vada_ bene. / _Let's hope that everything goes well._

3. Opinion, point of view, perspective, or some other state of mind.
   Penso che _sia_ vero. / _I think that it is true._
   Credo che _venga_ anche lei. / _I think that she is coming too._

It is also used

4. After certain impersonal expressions that indicate necessity, uncertainty, importance, possibility, or likelihood.
   È necessario che lo _faccia_ anche tu. / _It is necessary that you do it too._
   È importante che _vengano_ anche loro. / _It is important that they come too._

5. After certain conjunctions that indicate a hypothetical state, a condition, purpose, etc.
   Benché _piova_, esco lo stesso. / _Although it is raining, I'm going out just the same._
   Affinché tu _possa_ riuscire, devi studiare di più. / _In order for you to succeed, you must study more._

6. After certain conjunctions of time.
   Prima che _arrivino_, bisogna preparare la cena! / _Before they arrive, we need to prepare dinner!_

7. After certain adverbs.
   Dovunque tu _vada_, io ti seguirò. / _Wherever you go, I will follow you._

8. In wish expressions.
   Che _sia_ vero? / _Could it be true?_

EXERCISE Set 17–5

Say the following things in Italian.

1. Could he also be coming to the party?

   _____

2. Could he be telling the truth?

   _____

3. We prefer that they come to the movies as well.

   _____

4. She doubts that they know how to speak Italian.

   _____

5. Let's hope that he arrives soon.

   _____

6. I think that he is telling the truth.

   _____

7. It is necessary that they do it too.

   _____

8. Although it is snowing, I'm going shopping just the same.

   _____

9. In order for you to be able to speak Italian well, you must study more.

   _____

10. Before they leave for Italy, they need to save *(risparmiare)* money!

   _____

Crossword Puzzle 17

Change the verb into the subjunctive.

È importante che...

Orizzontali

3. **loro arrivano presto**
4. **tu puoi fare quello**
5. **tu non guardi la televisione stasera**
7. **lui va in Italia**
8. **tu non accendi il televisiore**
9. **noi dobbiamo uscire**
10. **voi siete contenti**

Verticali

1. **loro sanno dove sei**
2. **tu poni quella domanda**
6. **voi dite la verità**

18
The Past Subjunctive

Conjugation of the Past Subjunctive

The past subjunctive, called the **congiuntivo passato** in Italian, is a compound tense. Therefore, it is conjugated with an auxiliary verb, either **avere** / *to have* or **essere** / *to be*, and the past participle of the verb, in that order. See Chapter 9 for the relevant details regarding past participles and the use of one or the other auxiliary verb.

In this case, the auxiliary verbs are in the present subjunctive. Here are examples of verbs conjugated with **avere**:

First conjugation: **parlare** / *to speak*

...che (io)	**abbia**	**parlato**	...that I have spoken, I spoke
...che (tu)	**abbia**	**parlato**	...that you (fam.) have spoken, you spoke
...che (lui/lei/Lei)	**abbia**	**parlato**	...that he, she, you (pol.) has/have spoken, he, she, you spoke
...che (noi)	**abbiamo**	**parlato**	...that we have spoken, we spoke
...che (voi)	**abbiate**	**parlato**	...that you have spoken, you spoke
...che (loro)	**abbiano**	**parlato**	...that they have spoken, they spoke

Second conjugation: **vendere** / *to sell*

...che (io)	**abbia**	**venduto**	...that I have sold, I sold
...che (tu)	**abbia**	**venduto**	...that you (fam.) have sold, you sold
...che (lui/lei/Lei)	**abbia**	**venduto**	...that he, she, you (pol.) has/have sold, he, she, you sold
...che (noi)	**abbiamo**	**venduto**	...that we have sold, we sold
...che (voi)	**abbiate**	**venduto**	...that you have sold, you sold
...che (loro)	**abbiano**	**venduto**	...that they have sold, they sold

Third conjugation: **finire** / *to finish*

...che (io)	**abbia**	**finito**	...that I have finished, I finished
...che (tu)	**abbia**	**finito**	...that you (fam.) have finished, you finished
...che (lui/lei/Lei)	**abbia**	**finito**	...that he, she, you (pol.) has/have finished, he, she, you finished
...che (noi)	**abbiamo**	**finito**	...that we have finished, we finished
...che (voi)	**abbiate**	**finito**	...that you have finished, you finished
...che (loro)	**abbiano**	**finito**	...that they have finished, they finished

Here are examples of verbs conjugated with **essere**:

First Conjugation: **arrivare** / *to arrive*

...che (io)	sia	**arrivato/a**	...that I have arrived, I arrived
...che (tu)	sia	**arrivato/a**	...that you (fam.) have arrived, you arrived
...che (lui)	sia	**arrivato**	...that he has arrived, he arrived
...che (lei)	sia	**arrivata**	...that she has arrived, she arrived
...che (Lei)	sia	**arrivato/a**	...that you (pol.) have arrived, you arrived
...che (noi)	siamo	**arrivati/e**	...that we have arrived, we arrived
...che (voi)	siate	**arrivati/e**	...that you have arrived, you arrived
...che (loro)	siano	**arrivati/e**	...that they have arrived, they arrived

Second Conjugation: **cadere** / *to fall*

...che (io)	sia	**caduto/a**	...that I have fallen, I fell
...che (tu)	sia	**caduto/a**	...that you (fam.) have fallen, you fell
...che (lui)	sia	**caduto**	...that you have fallen, you fell
...che (lei)	sia	**caduta**	...that she has fallen, she fell
...che (Lei)	sia	**caduto/a**	...that you have fallen, you fell
...che (noi)	siamo	**caduti/e**	...that we have fallen, we fell
...che (voi)	siate	**caduti/e**	...that you have fallen, you fell
...che (loro)	siano	**caduti/e**	...that they have fallen, they fell

Third Conjugation: **uscire** / *to go out*

...che (io)	sia	**uscito/a**	...that I have gone out, I went out
...che (tu)	sia	**uscito/a**	...that you (fam.) have gone out, you went out
...che (lui)	sia	**uscito**	...that he has gone out, he went out
...che (lei)	sia	**uscita**	...that she has gone out, she went out
...che (Lei)	sia	**uscito/a**	...that you (pol.) have gone out, you went out
...che (noi)	siamo	**usciti/e**	...that we have gone out, we went out
...che (voi)	siate	**usciti/e**	...that you have gone out, you went out
...che (loro)	siano	**usciti/e**	...that they have gone out, they went out

For a list of common verbs conjugated with **essere** see Chapter 9 or the summary section at the back of the book in Appendix B. Again, all reflexive verbs are conjugated with **essere**. Here's one example:

divertirsi / *to enjoy oneself, to have fun*

...che (io)	mi	sia	**divertito/a**	...that I have enjoyed myself, I enjoyed myself
...che (tu)	ti	sia	**divertito/a**	...that you (fam.) have enjoyed yourself, you enjoyed yourself
...che (lui)	si	sia	**divertito**	...that he has enjoyed himself, he enjoyed himself
...che (lei)	si	sia	**divertita**	...that she has enjoyed herself, she enjoyed herself
...che (Lei)	si	sia	**divertito/a**	...that you (pol.) have enjoyed yourself, you enjoyed yourself
...che (noi)	ci	siamo	**divertiti/e**	...that we have enjoyed ourselves, we enjoyed ourselves
...che (voi)	vi	siate	**divertiti/e**	...that you have enjoyed yourselves, you enjoyed yourselves
...che (loro)	si	siano	**divertiti/e**	...that they have enjoyed themselves, they enjoyed themselves

The past subjunctive corresponds to the present perfect in temporal usage and overall features (see Chapter 9). For a list of irregular past participles, see the summary at the back. Essentially, it expresses a past action with respect to the main clause verb, which usually is in the present.

> **Non *è possibile*** che lui *abbia capito*. / *It's not possible that he understood.*
>
> ***Credo*** che loro *siano* già *partiti*. / *I think that they have already left.*
>
> ***Sebbene*** *sia venuta* anche lei, lui non *è* felice. / *Although she too has come, he is not happy.*

EXERCISE Set 18–1

A. Change the verb into the subjunctive by adding the indicated expression.

EXAMPLE: **Maria ha mangiato gli spaghetti (Penso che...)**
Penso che Maria abbia mangiato gli spaghetti.

1. **Io ho cominciato a studiare l'italiano (Loro dubitano che...)**

   _____

2. **Tu hai letto quel romanzo già (Lei crede che...)**

   _____

3. **Mio fratello ha pagato il conto (Immagino che...)**

   _____

4. **Ha fatto bel tempo ieri (Penso che...)**

   _____

5. **Noi abbiamo bevuto il caffè al bar ieri (Lui crede che...)**

   _____

6. **Voi avete già visto quel film (Immagino che...)**

   _____

7. **Loro li hanno già comprati (Spero che...)**

   _____

8. **Io sono andata in Italia l'anno scorso (I miei amici pensano che...)**

   _____

9. **Tu sei uscito poco tempo fa (Lui pensa che...)**

   _____

10. **Mia sorella è arrivata qualche minuto fa (Penso che...)**

    _____

11. **Noi siamo venuti alla festa (Lui crede...)**

    _____

12. **Voi siete tornati in Italia l'anno scorso (Mia madre crede che...)**

    _____

13. Loro si sono alzati tardi ieri (Lei pensa che…)

_____

14. Tu ti sei sposata l'anno scorso (Sembra che…)

_____

15. Lui si è divertito in Italia (Sembra che…)

_____

B. Choose either a (present subjunctive) or b (past subjunctive) according to sense.

1. Marco crede che tu … con Maria tra qualche minuto.
   a. esca
   b. sia uscito

2. Marco crede che tu … con Maria ieri sera.
   a. esca
   b. sia uscito

3. Loro pensano che voi … in Italia l'anno prossimo.
   a. andiate
   b. siate andati

4. Loro pensano che voi … in Italia l'anno scorso.
   a. andiate
   b. siate andati

5. Benché …, esco lo stesso.
   a. piova
   b. abbia piovuto

6. Benché …, sono uscita lo stesso.
   a. piova
   b. abbia piovuto

7. È probabile che lui … la prossima settimana.
   a. si sposi
   b. si sia sposato

8. È probabile che lui … la settimana scorsa.
   a. si sposi
   b. si sia sposato

Illustrative Dialogue

| la partita | game, match | segnare | to score |
| il gol | goal | | |

Luigi:	Bruno, chi ha vinto la partita ieri, il Milan o la Juventus?		Bruno, who won the game (match) yesterday, Milan or Juventus?
Bruno:	Penso che *abbia vinto* la Juventus, uno a zero.		I think that Juventus won, 1–0.
Luigi:	Chi ha segnato il gol?		Who scored the goal?
Bruno:	Non so chi *l'abbia segnato*.		I don't know who scored it.
Luigi:	Il calcio è uno sport fantastico. E penso che *sia* sempre *stato* così.		Soccer is a fantastic sport. And I think that it has always been so.
Bruno:	Sono d'accordo. Ciao.		I agree. Bye.
Luigi:	A presto!		See you soon.

EXERCISE Set 18-2

Answer the following questions based on the dialogue. Use complete sentences.

1. Che cosa chiede Luigi a Bruno?

_____

2. Che cosa pensa Bruno?

_____

3. Bruno sa chi ha segnato il gol?

_____

4. Che cosa pensa del calcio Luigi?

_____

5. È d'accordo Bruno?

_____

Uses and Features

As mentioned, the past subjunctive corresponds to the present perfect in temporal usage. As you have seen, the difference is that it comes after a verb, conjunction, adverb, or expression that requires the subjunctive mood.

Non credo che lui _abbia capito_. / _I don't believe he understood._
Non è possibile che loro _siano_ già _partiti_. / _It's not possible that they have already left._
Benché _sia venuta_ anche lei, lui non è felice. / _Although she too has come, he is not happy._
Lei è la persona più intelligente che io _abbia conosciuto_. / _She is the most intelligent person I have ever known._

EXERCISE Set 18-3

Say the following things in Italian.

1. Although it snowed yesterday, I decided to go shopping just the same.

_____

2. It's possible that they have already gone to the coffee shop.

_____

3. He doesn't know who scored the goal yesterday.

_____

4. He is the happiest person that I have ever known.

_____

5. It seems that they have already seen that movie.

_____

6. I think that my sister has already done that.

_____

7. Everyone thinks that I (f.) went to Italy last year.

_____

8. Do you (fam., sing.) really think that he understood?

_____

9. It is not true that I have eaten all the spaghetti.

_____

Crossword Puzzle 18

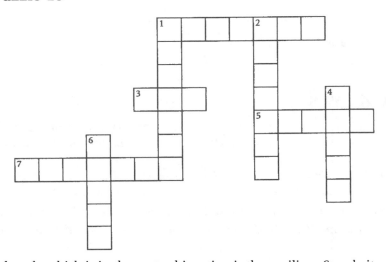

Missing from each verb, which is in the past subjunctive, is the auxiliary. Supply it.

Orizzontali

1. **Lui pensa che noi ... mangiato già.**
3. **Dubito che il signor Smith ... arrivato.**
5. **Penso che l'... già fatto lui.**
7. **Immagino che loro ... guardato la TV ieri sera.**

Verticali

1. **Io credo che loro ... già visto quel film.**
2. **Spero che voi ... già imparato i verbi.**
4. **Lui crede che noi ... usciti insieme.**
6. **Lui crede che voi vi ... sposati ieri.**

19
The Imperfect Subjunctive

Regular Verbs

To form the imperfect subjunctive of regular verbs, called the **congiuntivo imperfetto** in Italian, do the following:

1. Drop the **-re** from the infinitive endings **-are**, **-ere**, or **-ire**:

   parlare / *to speak* → **parla-**
   scrivere / *to write* → **scrive-**
   finire / *to finish* → **fini-**

2. Add the following endings to the stem according to person and number:

(io)	**-ssi**
(tu)	**-ssi**
(lui/lei/Lei)	**-sse**
(noi)	**-ssimo**
(voi)	**-ste**
(loro)	**-ssero**

3. Here's the result:

First conjugation:

...che (io)	parlassi	...that I was speaking, I used to speak
...che (tu)	parlassi	...that you (fam.) were speaking, you used to speak
...che (lui/lei/Lei)	parlasse	...that he, she, you (pol.) was/were speaking, he, she, you used to speak
...che (noi)	parlassimo	...that we were speaking, we used to speak
...che (voi)	parlaste	...that you were speaking, you used to speak
...che (loro)	parlassero	...that they were speaking, they used to speak

Second conjugation:

...che (io)	scrivessi	...that I was writing, I used to write
...che (tu)	scrivessi	...that you (fam.) were writing, you used to write
...che (lui/lei/Lei)	scrivesse	...that he, she, you (pol.) was/were writing, he, she, you used to write
...che (noi)	scrivessimo	...that we were writing, we used to write
...che (voi)	scriveste	...that you were writing, you used to write
...che (loro)	scrivessero	...that they were writing, they used to write

Third conjugation:

...che (io)	finissi	...that I was finishing, I used to finish
...che (tu)	finissi	...that you (fam.) were finishing, you used to finish

...che (lui/lei/Lei)	finisse	...that he, she, you (pol.) was/were finishing, he, she, you used to finish
...che (noi)	finissimo	...that we were finishing, we used to finish
...che (voi)	finiste	...that you were finishing, you used to finish
...che (loro)	finissero	...that they were finishing, they used to finish

---

TIP

Be careful again when you pronounce the third person plural forms! The accent is not *placed on the ending, but on the syllable before the ending:*

parlassero	**scrivessero**	**finissero**
stress	stress	stress

The imperfect subjunctive corresponds to the imperfect indicative in temporal usage and overall features (see Chapter 10). Essentially, it conveys the idea of repeated action in the past with respect to a main clause verb, which usually (although not necessarily) is in the past itself.

Non *era possibile* che lui *capisse*. / *It wasn't possible that he understood.*

Credevo che loro *partissero*. / *I thought that they were leaving.*

Mi *sembrava* che lui *dicesse* la verità. / *It seemed to me that he was telling the truth.*

Benché *piovesse* ieri, *sono uscito* lo stesso. / *Although it was raining yesterday, I went out just the same.*

The imperfect subjunctive is also used after **se** / *if* in counterfactual statements when the main clause verb is in the conditional.

*Se tu *andassi* a Roma, *vedresti* il Colosseo.* / *If you were to go to Rome, you would see the Coliseum.*

Se potessimo, andremmo in Italia subito. / *If we could, we would go to Italy right away.*

It is also used in sentences beginning with **magari** / *I wish, if only,* expressing a wish or desire.

*Magari non *piovesse*!* / *I wish it wouldn't rain!*

Magari vincessi la lotteria! / *If only I would win the lottery!*

EXERCISE Set 19–1

A. Supply the missing imperfect subjunctive forms of the verbs **arrivare**, **baciare**, and **spiegare**, giving the English equivalents.

| EXAMPLE: | lui _____ | = | _____ |
| | *lui arrivasse, baciasse, spiegasse* | = | he was arriving, kissing, explaining |

Magari...

1. io	_____	=	_____
2. tu	_____	=	_____
3. noi	_____	=	_____
4. loro	_____	=	_____
5. voi	_____	=	_____
6. lei	_____	=	_____

Now, supply the missing imperfect subjunctive forms of the verbs **potere**, **capire**, and **mettersi**, giving the English equivalents.

Magari...

7. io   _____   =   _____

8. tu   _____   =   _____

9. noi   _____   =   _____

10. loro   _____   =   _____

11. voi   _____   =   _____

12. lui   _____   =   _____

B. Change the verb into the subjunctive by adding the indicated expression.

EXAMPLE: **Maria mangiava gli spaghetti (Pensavo che...)**
              Pensavo che Maria mangiasse gli spaghetti.

    1. **Io cominciavo a studiare l'italiano (Loro dubitavano che...)**

    _____

    2. **Tu leggevi quel romanzo (Lei credeva che...)**

    _____

    3. **Mio fratello studiava a quest'ora (Io pensavo che...)**

    _____

    4. **Lei usciva con Marco (Pensavo che...)**

    _____

    5. **Noi guardavamo la televisione ogni sera da giovani (Lui credeva che...)**

    _____

    6. **Pioveva ieri (Sembra che...)**

    _____

    7. **Loro speravano di andare in Italia (Credo che...)**

    _____

    8. **Io andavo in Italia ogni estate da bambino (I miei amici pensano che...)**

    _____

    9. **Tu volevi uscire (Lui pensava che...)**

    _____

C. Choose either **a** (imperfect subjunctive) or **b** (present conditional) as the case may be.

il cellulare	cell phone	**in ritardo**	late
la chiamata	call	**telefonico**	phone (adjectival)
digitale	digital	**usare**	to use
in orario	on time		

1. Se io ..., andrei subito in Italia.
   a. **potessi**
   b. **potrei**

2. Se tu mangiassi quella pasta, ti ... di sicuro.
   a. **piacesse**
   b. **piacerebbe**

3. Se loro ... più soldi, comprerebbero un nuovo televisore digitale.
   a. **avessero**
   b. **avrebbero**

4. Se noi studiassimo di più, ... parlare l'italiano meglio.
   a. **sapessimo**
   b. **sapremmo**

5. Magari ... anche lui alla festa!
   a. **venisse**
   b. **verrebbe**

6. Magari non ...!
   a. **nevicasse**
   b. **nevicherebbe**

7. Se lui ... più presto la mattina, non sarebbe sempre in ritardo ma in orario.
   a. **si alzasse**
   b. **si alzerebbe**

8. Se potessi, ... solo il mio cellulare per le chiamate telefoniche.
   a. **usassi**
   b. **userei**

Prospettiva personale

Say what you would do if…

EXAMPLE: **Se avessi più soldi…**
                Se avessi più soldi andrei in Italia in vacanza/comprerei una Ferrari/…

1. **Se avessi più soldi…**

   _____

2. **Se vincessi la lotteria…**

   _____

3. **Se vincesse la mia squadra preferita…**

   _____

4. **Se sapessi parlare bene l'italiano…**

   _____

5. **Se avessi più tempo nella mia vita…**

   _____

Illustrative Dialogue

infatti	in fact	**la segreteria telefonica**	answering machine
il messaggio	message		

Claudia: **Tina, ti avevo chiamato ieri perché pensavo che tu *volessi* uscire. Ti ho lasciato un messaggio sulla tua segreteria telefonica.**

Tina, I had called you yesterday because I thought that you wanted to go out. I left you a message on your answering machine.

Tina:	Non stavo molto bene. Volevo chiamarti, ma pensavo che tu *avessi* molto da fare.	I wasn't well. I wanted to call you, but I thought that you had a lot to do.
Claudia:	Infatti. Ma lo stesso, volevo che tu *venissi* al cinema con me.	Quite. But just the same I wanted you to come to the movies with me.
Tina:	Oggi sto meglio. Perché non andiamo stasera?	I feel better today. Why don't we go tonight?
Claudia:	Va bene. Ti chiamo verso le sei.	OK. I'll call you around six.
Tina:	D'accordo.	Fine.

EXERCISE Set 19–2

Answer the following questions based on the dialogue. Use complete sentences.

1. **Perché Claudia aveva chiamato Tina ieri?**

   _____

2. **Dove ha lasciato un messaggio?**

   _____

3. **Come stava Tina ieri?**

   _____

4. **Che cosa pensava Tina?**

   _____

5. **Che cosa voleva Claudia?**

   _____

6. **Quando chiamerà Tina, Claudia?**

   _____

Irregular Verbs

The same verbs that are irregular in the imperfect indicative (Chapter 10) are irregular in the corresponding subjunctive mood. The following verbs can be considered to be "regular" if their infinitive form is changed as suggested in previous chapters:

bere / *to drink*	→	**"bevere"**	→	**beve-**	*(io bevessi, tu bevessi, etc.)*
dire / *to say, to tell*	→	**"dicere"**	→	**dice-**	*(io dicessi, tu dicessi, etc.)*
fare / *to do, to make*	→	**"facere"**	→	**face-**	*(io facessi, tu facessi, etc.)*
porre / *to pose*	→	**"ponere"**	→	**pone-**	*(io ponessi, tu ponessi, etc.)*
trarre / *to draw (pull)*	→	**"traere"**	→	**trae-**	*(io traessi, tu traessi, etc.)*

This applies, of course, to all verbs ending in **-durre**:

| **dedurre** / *to deduce* | → | **"deducere"** | → | **deduce-** *(io deducessi, tu deducessi, etc.)* |

This leaves only the following as irregular:

dare / *to give*

...che (io)	**dessi**	...that I was giving, I used to give
...che (tu)	**dessi**	...that you (fam.) were giving, you used to give
...che (lui/lei/Lei)	**desse**	...that he, she, you (pol.) was/were giving, he, she, you used to give
...che (noi)	**dessimo**	...that we were giving, we used to give
...che (voi)	**deste**	...that you were giving, you used to give
...che (loro)	**dessero**	...that they were giving, they used to give

essere / *to be*

...che (io)	**fossi**	...that I was, I used to be
...che (tu)	**fossi**	...that you (fam.) were, you used to be
...che (lui/lei/Lei)	**fosse**	...that he, she, you (pol.) was/were, he, she, you used to be
...che (noi)	**fossimo**	...that we were, we used to be
...che (voi)	**foste**	...that you were, you used to be
...che (loro)	**fossero**	...that they were, they used to be

stare / *to stay, to be*

...che (io)	**stessi**	...that I was staying, I used to stay
...che (tu)	**stessi**	...that you (fam.) were staying, you used to stay
...che (lui/lei/Lei)	**stesse**	...that he, she, you (pol.) was/were staying, he, she, you used to stay
...che (noi)	**stessimo**	...that we were staying, we used to stay
...che (voi)	**steste**	...that you were staying, you used to stay
...che (loro)	**stessero**	...that they were staying, they used to stay

---

EXERCISE Set 19–3

A. Supply the missing imperfect subjunctive forms of the verbs **essere**, **dare**, and **stare**, giving the English equivalents.

EXAMPLE:

lui _____	=	_____
lui fosse, desse, stesse	=	he was, he was giving, he was staying

Magari...

1. io	_____	=	_____
2. tu	_____	=	_____
3. noi	_____	=	_____
4. loro	_____	=	_____
5. voi	_____	=	_____
6. lei	_____	=	_____

B. Change the verb into the subjunctive by adding the indicated expression.

EXAMPLE: **Maria beveva il cappuccino (Pensavo che...)**
                Pensavo che Maria bevesse il cappuccino.

l'attenzione (f.)	attention	**la poesia**	poem
la classe	class		

1. **Io bevevo il latte regolarmente (Loro dubitavano che...)**

   _____

2. **Tu dicevi sempre la verità (Lei credeva che...)**

   _____

3. **Mio fratello non faceva niente (Io pensavo che...)**

   _____

4. **Lei poneva molte domande in classe (Penso che...)**

   _____

5. **Noi attraevamo molta attenzione da giovani (Lui crede che...)**

   _____

6. **Traducevo le poesie italiane da giovane (Loro pensano che...)**

   _____

7. **Tu davi del tu al professore (Credevo che...)**

   _____

Progressive Form

There is also a progressive form of the imperfect subjunctive, allowing you to zero in on an imperfect action to be expressed in the subjunctive mood:

> **Penso che ieri mia sorella *stesse mangiando*, mentre io *stavo guardando* la TV ieri.** / *I think that my sister was eating, while I was watching TV yesterday.*

The imperfect subjunctive progressive is formed with the imperfect subjunctive of the verb **stare** / *to stay, to be* and the gerund of the verb, in that order. Here are three verbs conjugated in this tense:

First conjugation: **parlare** / *to speak*

...che (io)	**stessi**	**parlando**	...that I was speaking
...che (tu)	**stessi**	**parlando**	...that you (fam.) were speaking
...che (lui/lei/Lei)	**stesse**	**parlando**	...that he, she, you (pol.) was/were speaking
...che (noi)	**stessimo**	**parlando**	...that we were speaking
...che (voi)	**steste**	**parlando**	...that you were speaking
...che (loro)	**stessero**	**parlando**	...that they were speaking

Second conjugation: **vendere** / *to sell*

...che (io)	**stessi**	**vendendo**	that I was selling
...che (tu)	**stessi**	**vendendo**	that you (fam.) were selling
...che (lui/lei/Lei)	**stesse**	**vendendo**	that he, she, you (pol.) were selling
...che (noi)	**stessimo**	**vendendo**	that we were selling
...che (voi)	**steste**	**vendendo**	that you were selling
...che (loro)	**stessero**	**vendendo**	that they were selling

Third conjugation: **finire** / *to finish*

...che (io)	**stessi**	**finendo**	that I was finishing
...che (tu)	**stessi**	**finendo**	that you (fam.) were finishing
...che (lui/lei/Lei)	**stesse**	**finendo**	that he, she, you (pol.) were finishing
...che (noi)	**stessimo**	**finendo**	that we were finishing
...che (voi)	**steste**	**finendo**	that you were finishing
...che (loro)	**stessero**	**finendo**	that they were finishing

---

EXERCISE Set 19–4

Change the verb into the subjunctive by adding the indicated expression.

EXAMPLE: **Maria stava bevendo il cappuccino (Pensavo che...)**
Pensavo che Maria stesse bevendo il cappuccino.

1. **Giorgio stava mangiando (Non sapevo che...)**

   _____

2. **voi stavate guardando un programma alla televisione (Maria credeva che...)**

   _____

3. **Marco stava dormendo (Sembra che...)**

   _____

4. **io stavo scrivendo (Lui credeva che...)**

   _____

5. **i miei amici stavano uscendo (Lei pensa che...)**

   _____

6. **noi stavamo bevendo un caffè (Loro credevano che...)**

   _____

7. **voi stavate leggendo quel romanzo (Dubito che...)**

   _____

8. **lui stava suonando il pianoforte (Sembra che...)**

   _____

9. **lei stava cantando (È probabile che...)**

   _____

Uses and Features

The imperfect subjunctive is used in subordinate clauses for the same reasons as the present or past subjunctive (Chapters 17 and 18). The main difference between the use of the present subjunctive tense and this tense is the time of the action:

1. If the verb in the main clause is in the present or future, then the present subjunctive in the dependent clause is normally called for.

   But if the main verb is in a past or conditional tense, then the imperfect subjunctive will likely be required:

   Penso che *sia* **vero.** / *I think it is true.*

   Pensavo che *fosse* **vero.** / *I thought it was true.*

   È importante che *venga* **anche lui.** / *It is important that he come too.*

   Sarebbe importante che *venisse* **anche lui.** / *It would be important that he come too.*

2. As you have seen, the imperfect subjunctive is also used after **se** / *if* in counterfactual statements when the main clause verb is in the conditional:

   Se tu *andassi* **a Firenze, vedresti il famoso Duomo.** / *If you were to go to Florence, you would see the famous Duomo.*

   Se *potessimo*, **andremmo in vacanza.** / *If we could, we would go on a holiday.*

3. And, as you have also seen, it is used in sentences beginning with **magari** / *I wish, if only* to express a wish or desire:

   Magari *venisse* **anche lui!** / *I wish he would also come!*

EXERCISE Set 19–5

Say the following things in Italian.

giusto	right, correct	**davvero**	really, truly

1. I think that what he is saying is true.

   _____

2. I thought that what he did was the right thing to do.

   _____

3. It is important that he study more.

   _____

4. It would be important that he study more.

   _____

5. If you (fam., pl.) were to go to Italy, you would really enjoy yourselves.

   _____

6. If we could, we would go to the movies.

   _____

7. I wish she would do that!

   _____

8. I wish it wouldn't be so cold!

_____

9. If that were true, then I wouldn't be here.

_____

Crossword Puzzle 19

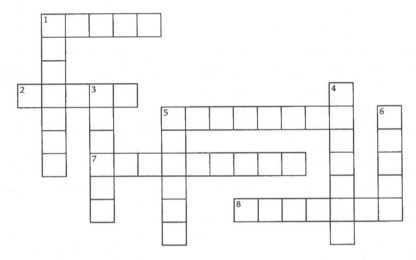

Change the verb into the imperfect subjunctive.

Pensavamo che...

Orizzontali

1. **lui era italiano**
2. **tu davi del tu al professore**
5. **loro si amavano**
7. **loro sapevano parlare l'italiano**
8. **lei diceva la verità**

Verticali

1. **faceva bel tempo**
3. **tu stavi bene**
4. **lei poteva uscire**
5. **lei aveva 40 anni**
6. **lui dava del tu al professore**

20
The Pluperfect Subjunctive

Conjugation of the Pluperfect Subjunctive

The pluperfect subjunctive, called the **trapassato congiuntivo** in Italian, is a compound tense. Therefore, it is conjugated with an auxiliary verb, either **avere** / *to have* or **essere** / *to be*, and the past participle of the verb, in that order. See Chapter 9 for the relevant details regarding past participles and the use of one or the other auxiliary verb.

In the pluperfect subjunctive, the auxiliary verbs are in the imperfect subjunctive. Here are examples of verbs conjugated with **avere**:

First conjugation: **parlare** / *to speak*

...che (io)	**avessi**	**parlato**	...that I had spoken
...che (tu)	**avessi**	**parlato**	...that you (fam.) had spoken
...che (lui/lei/Lei)	**avesse**	**parlato**	...that he, she, you (pol.) had spoken
...che (noi)	**avessimo**	**parlato**	...that we had spoken
...che (voi)	**aveste**	**parlato**	...that you had spoken
...che (loro)	**avessimo**	**parlato**	...that they had spoken

Second conjugation: **vendere** / *to sell*

...che (io)	**avessi**	**venduto**	...that I had sold
...che (tu)	**avessi**	**venduto**	...that you (fam.) had sold
...che (lui/lei/Lei)	**avesse**	**venduto**	...that he, she, you (pol.) had sold
...che (noi)	**avessimo**	**venduto**	...that we had sold
...che (voi)	**aveste**	**venduto**	...that you had sold
...che (loro)	**avessimo**	**venduto**	...that they had sold

Third conjugation: **finire** / *to finish*

...che (io)	**avessi**	**finito**	...that I had finished
...che (tu)	**avessi**	**finito**	...that you (fam.) had finished
...che (lui/lei/Lei)	**avesse**	**finito**	...that he, she, you (pol.) had finished
...che (noi)	**avessimo**	**finito**	...that we had finished
...che (voi)	**aveste**	**finito**	...that you had finished
...che (loro)	**avessimo**	**finito**	...that they had finished

Here are examples of verbs conjugated with **essere**:

First Conjugation: **arrivare** / *to arrive*

...che (io)	**fossi**	**arrivato/a**	...that I had arrived
...che (tu)	**fossi**	**arrivato/a**	...that you (fam.) had arrived
...che (lui)	**fosse**	**arrivato**	...that he had arrived
...che (lei)	**fosse**	**arrivata**	...that she had arrived
...che (Lei)	**fosse**	**arrivato/a**	...that you (pol.) had arrived

...che (noi)	fossimo	arrivati/e	...that we had arrived
...che (voi)	foste	arrivati/e	...that you had arrived
...che (loro)	fossero	arrivati/e	...that they had arrived

Second Conjugation: **cadere** / *to fall*

...che (io)	fossi	caduto/a	...that I had fallen
...che (tu)	fossi	caduto/a	...that you (fam.) had fallen
...che (lui)	fosse	caduto	...that he had fallen
...che (lei)	fosse	caduta	...that she had fallen
...che (Lei)	fosse	caduto/a	...that you (pol.) had fallen
...che (noi)	fossimo	caduti/e	...that we had fallen
...che (voi)	foste	caduti/e	...that you had fallen
...che (loro)	fossero	caduti/e	...that they had fallen

Third Conjugation: **uscire** / *to go out*

...che (io)	fossi	uscito/a	...that I had gone out
...che (tu)	fossi	uscito/a	...that you (fam.) had gone out
...che (lui)	fosse	uscito	...that he had gone out
...che (lei)	fosse	uscita	...that she had gone out
...che (Lei)	fosse	uscito/a	...that you (pol.) had gone out
...che (noi)	fossimo	usciti/e	...that we had gone out
...che (voi)	foste	usciti/e	...that you had gone out
...che (loro)	fossero	usciti/e	...that they had gone out

For a list of common verbs conjugated with **essere**, see Chapter 9 or the summaries section at the back in Appendix B. Again, all reflexive verbs are conjugated with **essere**. Here's one example:

divertirsi / *to enjoy oneself, to have fun*

...che (io)	mi	fossi	divertito/a	...that I had enjoyed myself
...che (tu)	ti	fossi	divertito/a	...that you (fam.) had enjoyed yourself
...che (lui)	si	fosse	divertito	...that he had enjoyed himself
...che (lei)	si	fosse	divertita	...that she had enjoyed herself
...che (Lei)	si	fosse	divertito/a	...that you (pol.) had enjoyed yourself
...che (noi)	ci	fossimo	divertiti/e	...that we had enjoyed ourselves
...che (voi)	vi	foste	divertiti/e	...that you had enjoyed yourselves
...che (loro)	si	fossero	divertiti/e	...that they had enjoyed themselves

This tense corresponds to the pluperfect indicative (Chapter 11) in usage and overall features. It allows you to express a past action that occurred before another past action.

> **Mi *era sembrato* che lui *avesse detto* la verità.** / *It seemed to me that he had told the truth.*
>
> **Eravamo contenti che voi *foste venuti*.** / *We were happy that you had come.*
>
> **Benché *avesse piovuto* tutto il mese, andavamo sempre fuori.** / *Although it had rained the entire month, we went out just the same.*

TIP

Essentially, if the main clause verb is in a past tense then the verb in the subordinate clause is generally in the pluperfect subjunctive.

Present   Past

| |

Spero   **che**   *abbia capito.* / *I hope that he has understood.*

Past   Pluperfect

| |

Speravo   **che**   *avesse capito.* / *I was hoping that he (had) understood.*

As was the case with the imperfect subjunctive (Chapter 19), the pluperfect subjunctive is also used after **se** / *if* in counterfactual statements. In this case, it is used when the main clause verb is in the conditional or conditional perfect, depending on sense:

Se *avessi avuto* **i soldi, la** *avrei comprata.* / *If I had had the money, I would have bought it.*

Se tu *avessi studiato* **ieri, oggi non** *ti preoccuperesti.* / *If you had studied yesterday, today you wouldn't worry.*

EXERCISE Set 20–1

Change the verb into the pluperfect subjunctive by adding the indicated expression.

EXAMPLE: **Maria ha già mangiato gli spaghetti (Pensavo che...)**
               Penso che Maria avesse già mangiato gli spaghetti.

1. **Io ho appena cominciato a studiare l'italiano (Loro dubitavano che...)**

   _____

2. **Tu hai già letto quel romanzo già (Lei pensava che...)**

   _____

3. **Mio fratello ha pagato il conto (Non era possibile che...)**

   _____

4. **Ha fatto bel tempo l'estate scorsa, ma invece no (Pensavano che...)**

   _____

5. **Noi abbiamo già bevuto il caffè (Lui credeva che...)**

   _____

6. **Voi avete già visto quel film (Immaginavo che...)**

   _____

7. **Loro li hanno già comprati (Speravo che...)**

   _____

8. **Io sono andata in Italia l'anno scorso (I miei amici credevano che...)**

_____

9. **Tu sei già uscito (Lui aveva pensato che...)**

_____

10. **Mia sorella è arrivata già (Avrei pensato che...)**

_____

11. **Noi siamo venuti alla festa (Lui credeva che...)**

_____

12. **Voi siete tornati già in Italia l'anno scorso (Mia madre credeva che...)**

_____

13. **Loro si sono alzati tardi ieri (Lei pensava che...)**

_____

14. **Tu ti sei sposata l'anno scorso (Tutti credevano che...)**

_____

15. **Lui si è divertito in Italia (Mi è sembrato che...)**

_____

Illustrative Dialogue

Maria:	**Marco, pensavo che tu _fossi_ già _andato_ via. Come mai sei ancora qui?**	Marco, I thought that you had already gone away. How come you are still here?
Marco:	**C'è molto da fare. Se _avessi lavorato_ ieri, oggi non sarei dovuto rimanere più a lungo.**	There's much to do. If I had worked yesterday, today I wouldn't have to remain a bit longer.
Maria:	**Capisco!**	I understand!
Marco:	**E se tu mi _avessi aiutato_ la settimana scorsa, oggi ci sarebbe molto meno da fare.**	And if you had helped me last week, today there would be much less to do.
Maria:	**Hai ragione. Quando hai finito verresti a prendere un caffè al bar?**	You're right. When you have finished would you come to have a coffee at the coffee shop?
Marco:	**Volentieri.**	Gladly.

| **EXERCISE Set 20–2** |

Answer the following questions based on the dialogue. Use complete sentences.

1. **Che cosa pensava Maria?**

_____

2. **Come mai Marco è ancora al lavoro?**

_____

3. **Che cosa non avrebbe dovuto fare Marco, se ieri avesse lavorato?**

_____

4. **Cosa ci sarebbe oggi se Maria avesse aiutato Marco la settimana scorsa?**

_____

5. **Cosa chiede Maria a Marco di fare quando ha finito?**

_____

Uses and Features

As mentioned, in essence, the pluperfect subjunctive corresponds to the pluperfect indicative in temporal usage. The difference is that it comes after a verb, conjunction, adverb, or expression that requires the subjunctive mood in the subordinate clause:

> **Non era possibile che loro _fossero venuti_.** / It wasn't possible that they had come.

And, as mentioned, it is also used after **se** / if in counterfactual statements:

> **Se _avessi avuto_ più tempo, lo avrei fatto.** / If I had had more time, I would have done it.

EXERCISE Set 20–3

Say the following things in Italian.

essere bene   to be good   **essere meglio**   to be better

1. I thought that he had told the truth.

_____

2. I thought that he had already done it.

_____

3. It was important that he had called.

_____

4. It would have been good for him to have come as well (that he had come too).

_____

5. If you (fam., pl.) were to have gone to Italy, you would have really enjoyed yourselves.

_____

6. If we could have, we would have gone to the movies.

_____

7. It was better that she had done it!

_____

8. I wish it wouldn't have been so hot!

_____

9. If that were to have been true, then I wouldn't have gone.

_____

Crossword Puzzle 20

Missing from each verb, which is in the pluperfect subjunctive, is the auxiliary. Supply it.

Ieri...

Orizzontali

1. **Pensavo che lui ... studiato già.**
2. **Credevo che lei ... stata già in Italia.**
3. **Dubitavo che voi ... preso il caffè insieme.**
4. **Pensavo che loro ... già andati via.**
5. **Lei credeva che noi ... scelto le caramelle.**

Verticali

1. **Credevo che loro ... già fatto quello.**
2. **Lui pensava che noi ... stati già a Milano.**
3. **Lui non sapeva se io ... telefonato.**
4. **Credevo che voi vi ... divertiti.**

Part Five

Other Tenses

Other Tenses: An Overview

What Is the Imperative?

The *imperative* is a verbal mood that allows you to express a command, request, or warning:

> **Apri la bocca!** / *Open your mouth!*
> **Dica la verità!** / *Tell the truth!*
> **Non fare quello!** / *Don't do that!*

Notice that there is no first person singular form in the imperative, for it would make no sense.

What Is the Passive?

All the sentences and exercises that have preceded this unit have been *active* in their form. The verb in such sentences expresses the action performed by the subject. But for many active sentences, there are corresponding *passive* ones in which the action is performed *on* the subject.

Active	Passive
Maria legge il libro. Mary reads the book.	**Il libro è letto da Maria.** The book is read by Mary.

What Is the Causative?

A *causative* verbal construction allows you to express the idea of getting someone or something to do something:

Gli *ho fatto lavare* i piatti. / *I had him wash the dishes (I got him to wash the dishes).*

***Farò venire* anche lui alla festa.** / *I'll have him also come to the party (I'll also get him to come to the party).*

What Is an Indefinite Tense?

A verb in an indefinite tense—such as an infinitive, a gerund, or a participle— allows you to express an action that is not specified as to time of occurrence:

Prima di *uscire*, dovrei studiare un po'. / *Before going out, I should study a bit.*

***Volendo*, lo potrei fare.** / *If I wanted to, I could do it.*

21
The Imperative

Regular Verbs

The imperative of regular verbs, called the **imperativo** in Italian, is formed as follows:

First Conjugation:

1. Drop the infinitive ending, **-are**:

   parlare / *to speak*   →   **parl-**

2. Add the following endings to the stem:

(io)	—
(tu)	**-a**
(Lei)	**-i**
(noi)	**-iamo**
(voi)	**-ate**
(Loro)	**-ino**

3. Here's the result:

(io)	—	—
(tu)	**parla**	speak (fam.)
(Lei)	**parli**	speak (pol.)
(noi)	**parliamo**	let's speak
(voi)	**parlate**	speak (fam.)
(Loro)	**parlino**	speak (pol.)

4. If the infinitive ending is **-ciare** or **-giare**, drop the **-are** and retain the **-i**, but do not write a "double -i" when adding on the endings **-i**, **-iamo**, and **-ino**:

   cominciare / *to begin*   →   **cominci-**

(io)	—	—
(tu)	**comincia**	begin (fam.)
(Lei)	**cominci**	begin (pol.)
(noi)	**cominciamo**	let's begin
(voi)	**cominciate**	begin (fam.)
(Loro)	**comincino**	begin (pol.)

   mangiare / *to eat*   →   **mangi-**

(io)	—	—
(tu)	**mangia**	eat (fam.)
(Lei)	**mangi**	eat (pol.)
(noi)	**mangiamo**	let's eat
(voi)	**mangiate**	eat (fam.)
(Loro)	**mangino**	eat (pol.)

5. If the infinitive ending is **-care** or **-gare**, drop the **-are** but add an **"h"** before the endings **-i**, **-iamo**, and **-ino**. As you know by now, this indicates that the hard sound is to be retained:

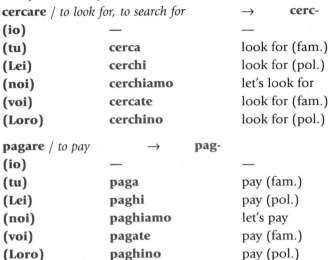

cercare / *to look for, to search for*		→	**cerc-**
(io)	—		—
(tu)	**cerca**		look for (fam.)
(Lei)	**cerchi**		look for (pol.)
(noi)	**cerchiamo**		let's look for
(voi)	**cercate**		look for (fam.)
(Loro)	**cerchino**		look for (pol.)

pagare / *to pay*		→	**pag-**
(io)	—		—
(tu)	**paga**		pay (fam.)
(Lei)	**paghi**		pay (pol.)
(noi)	**paghiamo**		let's pay
(voi)	**pagate**		pay (fam.)
(Loro)	**paghino**		pay (pol.)

Second conjugation:

1. Drop the infinitive ending, **-ere**:

   scrivere / *to write*   →   **scriv-**

2. Add the following endings to the stem:

(io)	—
(tu)	**-i**
(Lei)	**-a**
(noi)	**-iamo**
(voi)	**-ete**
(Loro)	**-ano**

3. Here's the result:

(io)	—	—
(tu)	**scrivi**	write (fam.)
(Lei)	**scriva**	write (pol.)
(noi)	**scriviamo**	let's write
(voi)	**scvrivete**	write (fam.)
(Loro)	**scrivano**	write (pol.)

For third conjugation verbs, a distinction between two types is once again applicable (see Chapter 1):

Third conjugation: Type 1

1. Drop the infinitive ending, **-ire**:

   dormire / *to sleep*   →   **dorm-**

2. Add the following endings to the stem:

(io)	—
(tu)	**-i**
(Lei)	**-a**
(noi)	**-iamo**
(voi)	**-ite**
(Loro)	**-ano**

3. Here's the result:

(io)	—	—
(tu)	**dormi**	sleep (fam.)
(Lei)	**dorma**	sleep (pol.)
(noi)	**dormiamo**	let's sleep
(voi)	**dormite**	sleep (fam.)
(Loro)	**dormano**	sleep (pol.)

Third conjugation: Type 2

1. Drop the infinitive ending, **-ire**:

finire / *to finish* → **fin-**

2. Add the following endings to the stem:

(io)	—
(tu)	**-isci**
(Lei)	**-isca**
(noi)	**-iamo**
(voi)	**-ite**
(Loro)	**-iscano**

3. Here's the result:

(io)	—	—
(tu)	**finisci**	finish (fam.)
(Lei)	**finisca**	finish (pol.)
(noi)	**finiamo**	let's finish
(voi)	**finite**	finish (fam.)
(Loro)	**finiscano**	finish (pol.)

The **voi** forms are used commonly as the plural forms of both **tu** (*familiar*) and **Lei** (*polite*) singular forms. The **Loro** (*polite*) forms are rarely used:

Tu form (sing.)
Bambina, *mangia* la mela! / *Little girl, eat the apple!*

Voi form (pl.)
Bambine, *mangiate* la mela! / *Little girls, eat the apple!*

Lei form (sing.)
Signora, *mangi* la mela! / *Madam, eat the apple!*

Loro form (pl.)
Signore, *mangino* la mela! / *Ladies, eat the apple!*

| EXERCISE Set 21–1 |

A. Supply the missing imperative forms of the verbs **guardare**, **baciare**, **parcheggiare**, and **spiegare**, giving the English equivalents.

EXAMPLE: **lui** _____   =   _____
             (tu) guarda, bacia,   watch, kiss, park, explain
             parcheggia, spiega

1. **(tu)**   _____   =   _____

2. **(noi)** _____   =   _____

3. **(Loro)** _____   =   _____

4. **(voi)** _____   =   _____

5. **(Lei)** _____   =   _____

Now, supply the missing imperative forms of the verbs **leggere**, **aprire**, **pulire**, and **indicare**, giving the English equivalents.

6. **(tu)**   _____   =   _____

7. **(noi)** _____   =   _____

8. **(Loro)** _____   =   _____

9. **(voi)** _____   =   _____

10. **(Lei)** _____   =   _____

B. Say the following things:

EXAMPLES: <u>**Command Maria:** Open your mouth!</u>
              Maria, apri la (tua) bocca!

la bocca	mouth	**la testa**	head
la minestra	soup	**la torta**	cake
gli spinaci	spinach		

Command Maria:

1. Speak Italian, please!

    _____

2. Eat the cake!

    _____

3. Close your mouth!

    _____

4. Finish the spinach!

    _____

5. Taste the soup!

    _____

6. Pay the bill!

_____

7. Sleep more!

_____

Now, give the same commands to Mr. Smith.

8. Speak Italian, please!

_____

9. Eat the cake!

_____

10. Close your mouth!

_____

11. Finish the spinach!

_____

12. Taste the soup!

_____

13. Pay the bill!

_____

14. Sleep more!

_____

Now, give the same commands to both Maria and Marco.

15. Speak Italian, please!

_____

16. Eat the cake!

_____

17. Close your mouths!

_____

18. Finish the spinach!

_____

19. Taste the soup!

_____

20. Pay the bill!

_____

21. Sleep more!

_____

Finally, give the same commands to Mr. and Mrs. Smith (use the **Loro** form).

22. Speak Italian, please!

_____

23. Eat the cake!

_____

24. Close your mouths!

_____

25. Finish the spinach!

_____

26. Taste the soup!

_____

27. Pay the bill!

_____

28. Sleep more!

_____

Illustrative Dialogue

l'acqua	water		**la pasticca**	lozenge
avere mal di	to have a sore…		**il raffreddore**	cold (illness)
la febbre	fever, temperature		**riposarsi**	to relax
la gola	throat		**il sintomo**	symptom
ovvio	obvious		**l termometro**	thermometer

Sig. Marchi:	**Dottoressa, non sto bene. Ho mal di gola e di testa e ho un po' di febbre.**	Doctor, I don't feel well. I have a sore throat and a headache, and I have a slight fever.
Dott.ssa Giusti:	_Apra_ **la bocca, per favore!** _Metta_ **questo termometro in bocca!**	Open your mouth, please! Put this thermometer into your mouth!
Sig. Marchi:	**Che cosa ho, dottoressa?**	What do I have, Doctor?
Dott.ssa Giusti:	**Non** _si preoccupi_**! Lei ha ovviamente un forte raffreddore.**	Don't worry! You have obviously a bad cold.
Sig. Marchi:	**Che cosa dovrei fare?**	What should I do?
Dott.ssa Giusti:	_Prenda_ **le pasticche che Le darò,** _beva_ **tanta acqua e** _si riposi_ **per qualche giorno!**	Take the lozenges that I will give you, drink a lot of water and relax for a few days!
Sig. Marchi:	**Grazie.**	Thank you.

```
EXERCISE Set 21–2
```

Answer the following questions based on the dialogue. Use complete sentences.

1. Chi non sta bene?

   _____

2. Che sintomi ha?

   _____

3. Che cosa gli dice di fare, la dottoressa Giusti?

   _____

4. Che cosa ha il signor Marchi?

   _____

5. Che cosa dovrebbe fare, secondo la dottoressa?

   _____

Irregular Verbs

The verbs that are irregular in the present tenses (indicative and subjunctive) are also irregular in the imperative. Here is a list of the conjugations of all such verbs introduced so far. The forms are given without English translation:

andare / to go	(io) —, (tu) va' (vai), (Lei) vada, (noi) andiamo, (voi) andate, (Loro) vadano
avere / to have	(io) —, (tu) abbi, (Lei) abbia, (noi) abbiamo, (voi) abbiate, (Loro) abbiano
bere / to drink	(io) —, (tu) bevi, (Lei) beva, (noi) beviamo, (voi) bevete, (Loro) bevano
dare / to give	(io) —, (tu) da' (dai), (Lei) dia, (noi) diamo, (voi) date, (Loro) diano
dire / to tell, to say	(io) —, (tu) di' (dici), (Lei) dica, (noi) diciamo, (voi) dite, (Loro) dicano
essere / to be	(io) —, (tu) sii, (Lei) sia, (noi) siamo, (voi) siate, (Loro) siano
fare / to do, to make	(io) —, (tu) fa' (fai), (Lei) faccia, (noi) facciamo, (voi) fate, (Loro) facciano
porre / to pose	(io) —, (tu) poni, (Lei) ponga, (noi) poniamo, (voi) ponete, (Loro) pongano
rimanere / to remain	(io) —, (tu) rimani, (Lei) rimanga, (noi) rimaniamo, (voi) rimanete, (Loro) rimangano
salire / to climb	(io) —, (tu) sali, (Lei) salga, (noi) saliamo, (voi) salite, (Loro) salgano
sapere / to know	(io) —, (tu) sappi, (Lei) sappia, (noi) sappiamo, (voi) sappiate, (Loro) sappiano
scegliere / to choose	(io) —, (tu) scegli, (Lei) scelga, (noi) scegliamo, (voi) scegliete, (Loro) scelgano
stare / to stay	(io) —, (tu) sta' (stai), (Lei) stia, (noi) stiamo, (voi) state, (Loro) stiano
trarre / to draw (pull)	(io) —, (tu) trai, (Lei) tragga, (noi) traiamo, (voi) traete, (Loro) traggano
uscire / to go out	(io) —, (tu) esci, (Lei) esca, (noi) usciamo, (voi) uscite, (Loro) escano
venire / to come	(io) —, (tu) vieni, (Lei) venga, (noi) veniamo, (voi) venite, (Loro) vengano

Recall that verbs ending in **-durre** can be rendered hypothetically "regular" as follows:

1. Change the ending in your mind to -**cere**:
   tradurre / *to translate*   →   **"traducere"**

2. Drop the **-ere** ending of the "hypothetical" verb stem:
   traducere   →   **traduc-**

3. Add the usual endings (previously):
   (io) ..., (tu) *traduci,* **(Lei)** *traduca,* **(noi)** *traduciamo,* **(voi)** *traducete,* **(Loro)** *traducano*

TIP

Notice that the polite imperative forms are the same as the corresponding present subjunctive forms.

EXERCISE Set 21–3

Say the following things.

EXAMPLES: <u>Order Claudia:</u> **Go to sleep!**
              Claudia, va' (vai) a dormire!

Order Claudia:

1. Go home!

   _____

2. Have patience!

   _____

3. Drink the milk!

   _____

4. Give Marco your pen!

   _____

5. Tell the truth!

   _____

6. Be good *(brava)*!

   _____

7. Make spaghetti!

   _____

8. Pose that question to our teacher!

   _____

9. Remain at home!

   _____

10. Choose this!

_____

11. Stay at home!

_____

12. Go out with Marco!

_____

13. Come here!

_____

14. Translate that book!

_____

Now, give the same commands to Mr. Giusti.

15. Go home!

_____

16. Have patience!

_____

17. Drink the milk!

_____

18. Give Mrs. Marchi your pen!

_____

19. Tell the truth!

_____

20. Be good!

_____

21. Make spaghetti!

_____

22. Pose that question to our teacher!

_____

23. Remain at home!

_____

24. Choose this!

_____

25. Stay at home!

_____

26. Go out with Mrs. Marchi!

_____

27. Come here!

_____

28. Translate that book!

_____

Finally, give the same commands to Claudia and Giorgio.

29. Go home!

_____

30. Have patience!

_____

31. Drink the milk!

_____

32. Give Marco your pen!

_____

33. Tell the truth!

_____

34. Be good!

_____

35. Make spaghetti!

_____

36. Pose that question to our teacher!

_____

37. Remain at home!

_____

38. Choose this!

_____

39. Stay at home!

_____

40. Go out with Marco!

_____

41. Come here!

_____

42. Translate that book!

_____

Negative Imperatives

To form the negative imperative, add **non** before the verb (as always). But you must make one adjustment: change the second person singular form to the infinitive form of the verb.

Familiar Singular Forms

Affirmative	Negative
Parla! / *Speak!*	**Non parlare!** / *Don't speak!*
Scrivi! / *Write!*	**Non scrivere!** / *Don't write!*
Finisci! / *Finish!*	**Non finire!** / *Don't finish!*

Polite Singular Forms

Affirmative	Negative
Parli! / *Speak!*	**Non parli!** / *Don't speak!*
Scriva! / *Write!*	**Non scriva!** / *Don't write!*
Finisca! / *Finish!*	**Non finisca!** / *Don't finish!*

Plural Forms

Affirmative	Negative
Parliamo! / *Let's speak!*	**Non parliamo!** / *Don't speak!*
Scrivete! / *Write (fam.)!*	**Non scrivete!** / *Don't write!*
Finiscano! / *Finish (pol.)!*	**Non finiscano!** / *Don't finish!*

EXERCISE Set 21–4

Put each command into the negative.

EXAMPLE: Maria...fa' gli spaghetti!
Maria, non fare gli spaghetti!

Maria...

1. **mangia la torta!**

   _____

2. **paga il conto!**

   _____

3. **va' a casa!**

   _____

4. **bevi il latte!**

   _____

5. **da' a Marco la tua penna!**

   _____

6. **rimani a casa!**

_____

7. **scegli questo!**

_____

8. **sta' a casa tutto il giorno!**

_____

9. **esci con Marco!**

_____

Signora Marchi...

1. **mangi la torta!**

_____

2. **paghi il conto!**

_____

3. **vada a casa!**

_____

4. **beva il latte!**

_____

5. **dia la sua penna al professore!**

_____

6. **rimanga a casa!**

_____

7. **scelga questo!**

_____

8. **stia a casa tutto il giorno!**

_____

9. **esca con il signor Giusti!**

_____

Reflexive Verbs

Reflexive verbs are conjugated in the same manner as all other verbs in the imperative. However, the position of the reflexive pronoun varies.

1. It is attached to familiar forms and to the **noi** form:
   > **Marco, _alzati!_** / _Marco, get up!_
   > **_Alziamoci!_** / _Let's get up!_
   > **Ragazzi, _alzatevi!_** / _Guys, get up!_

2. It goes before the polite forms:

Signor Smith, *si alzi!* / *Mr. Smith, get up!*
Signori, *si alzino!* / *Gentlemen, get up!*

Here is one verb conjugated completely for you:

lavarsi / *to wash oneself* → **lav-**

(io)	—	—
(tu)	**lavati**	wash yourself (fam.)
(Lei)	**si lavi**	wash yourself (pol.)
(noi)	**laviamoci**	let's wash ourselves
(voi)	**lavatevi**	wash yourselves (fam.)
(Loro)	**si lavino**	wash yourselves (pol.)

In the case of the negative forms, remember that the infinitive is used in the second person singular. The pronoun can be attached or put before the verb. Note that attaching the pronoun to the infinitive requires that you drop the final -e of the infinitive:

Affirmative	Negative
Lavati! / *Wash yourself!*	**Non lavarti!** / *Wash yourself!*
	Non ti lavare! / *Wash yourself!*
Alzati! / *Get up!*	**Non alzarti!** / *Don't get up!*
	Non ti alzare! / *Don't get up!*

EXERCISE Set 21–5

Say the following things.

EXAMPLE: <u>Order Pietro: "Don't get up!"</u>
    Non alzarti! / Non ti alzare!

Order Pietro:

1. Fall asleep!

_____

2. Get bored, if you want!

_____

3. Don't get angry!

_____

4. Don't forget to write to your aunt!

_____

5. Enjoy yourself in Italy!

_____

Make the following suggestions to Mrs. Rossi.

    6. Take a shower!

    _____

    7. Don't meet with the teacher!

    _____

    8. Don't complain!

    _____

    9. Put on the new suit!

    _____

Order Pietro and Marco:

    10. Don't worry!

    _____

    11. Get ready!

    _____

    12. Try on the new jackets!

    _____

Make the following suggestions to Mr. and Mrs. Corelli.

    13. Remember to come to the party!

    _____

    14. Excuse yourselves!

    _____

    15. Don't wake up late tomorrow!

    _____

Uses and Features

As you have seen throughout this chapter, the imperative allows you to give commands.

As a final feature, note that the reflexive pronouns and object pronouns are attached to the familiar and **noi** forms of the imperative.

Familiar Forms

    Giovanni, *paga* il conto! / *John, pay the bill!*
    Giovanni, *pagalo*! / *John, pay it!*
    Sarah, *telefonami*! / *Sarah, phone me!*
    Amici, *chiamateci*! / *Friends, call us!*

Polite Forms

      Signor Verdi, *paghi* **il conto!** / *Mr. Verdi, pay the bill!*
      Signor Verdi, *lo paghi***!** / *Mr. Verdi, pay it!*
      Signora Smith, *mi telefoni***!** / *Mrs. Smith, phone me!*

As you saw above, the second person singular imperative forms of **dare** / *to give*, **dire** / *to say*, **fare** / *to do*, **andare** / *to go*, and **stare** / *to stay* are often written with an apostrophe:

      Da' **la penna a me!** / *Give the pen to me!*
      Di' **la verità!** / *Tell the truth!*
      Fa' **qualcosa!** / *Do something!*
      Va' **via!** / *Go away!*
      Sta' **qui!** / *Stay here!*

When attaching pronouns to these forms, you must double the first letter (sound) of the pronoun:

      Dammi **la penna!** / *Give me the pen!*
      *Dilla***!** / *Tell it (la verità)!*
      *Fallo***!** / *Do it!*

There is, of course, no double "**gl**":

      Digli **la verità!** / *Tell him the truth!*

With the second person singular negative infinitive form, you can either attach the pronouns to the infinitive or else put them before it. Again, notice that the final **-e** of the infinitive is dropped when attaching pronouns.

Affirmative	Negative
Mangialo! Eat it!	**Non** *mangiarlo***!** or **Non** *lo mangiare***!** Don't eat it!

EXERCISE Set 21–6

Say the following things in Italian.

    1. Giovanni, eat the cake! Eat it!

    _____

    2. Maria, don't drink the coffee! Don't drink it!

    _____

    3. Mrs. Smith, pay the bill! Please pay it!

    _____

    4. Giorgio, phone her!

    _____

    5. Claudia, give me the spaghetti!

    _____

    6. Bruno, give us your address!

    _____

7. Pasquale, tell the truth! Tell it!

_____

8. Maria, go away!

_____

9. Do it, Maria!

_____

10. Do it, Mrs. Smith!

_____

Crossword Puzzle 21

Put the given infinitive into the appropriate form of the imperative, as indicated.

Orizzontali

4. **Alessandro e Sarah, (venire) ... alla festa!**
5. **Marco, (uscire) ... con mia sorella!**
7. **Bruno (riposarsi) ...!**
8. **Giorgio, (sapere) ... la verità!**
9. **Ehi, ragazzi, (andare) ... insieme lì!**

Verticali

1, **Loro (bere) ... il caffè!**
2. **Signora, (dire) ... la verità!**
3. **Marco, (dedurre) ... quello che voglio!**
6. **Signorina, (stare) ... calma!**
7. **Maria, (rimanere) ... qui!**

22
The Passive & Miscellaneous Topics

The Passive

Verbs can be in the active or passive voice. The active voice is used to indicate that the subject performs the action, whereas the passive voice, called the **passivo** in Italian, is used to indicate that the subject is the receiver of the action:

Active:	**Alessandro** *mangia* **la mela.** / *Alexander is eating the apple.*
Passive:	**La mela** *è mangiata* **da Alessandro.** / *The apple is eaten by Alexander.*

Passive sentences can be formed from corresponding active ones as follows:

1. Change the order of the subject and the object:

    Alessandro **mangia** *la mela.* / *Alexander is eating the apple.*

    La mela **(mangia)** *Alessandro*

2. Change the verb into the passive form by introducing the auxiliary verb **essere** / *to be* in the same tense and mood and changing the verb into its past participle form. Recall that verbs conjugated with **essere** agree with the subject in number and gender:

    La mela *è mangiata* **(Alessandro).**

3. Put **da** / *by* in front of the passive object:

    La mela è mangiata *da* **Alessandro.** / *The apple is eaten by Alexander.*

Here are a few other examples of "passivization":

Active	Passive
La ragazza *legge* **quel libro.** The girl reads that book.	**Quel libro** *è letto dalla* **ragazza.** That book is read by the girl.
Lui *comprerà* **quella macchina.** He will buy that car.	**Quella macchina** *sarà comprata* **da lui.** That car will be bought by him.

Always be sure to remember rule (2) above. Transfer the tense and mood of the active verb to the auxiliary verb **essere**:

Active Verb			Passive Auxiliary
mangia	= present indicative	→	**è (mangiato/a)**
ha mangiato	= present perfect	→	**è stato/a (mangiato/a)**
mangiava	= imperfect indicative	→	**era (mangiato/a)**
aveva mangiato	= pluperfect indicative	→	**era stato/a (mangiato/a)**
mangiò	= past absolute	→	**fu (mangiato/a)**
mangerà	= future	→	**sarà (mangiato/a)**
avrà mangiato	= future perfect	→	**sarà stato/a (mangiato/a)**
mangerebbe	= conditional	→	**sarebbe (mangiato/a)**
avrebbe mangiato	= conditional perfect	→	**sarebbe stato/a (mangiato/a)**
(che) mangi	= present subjunctive	→	**sia (mangiato/a)**
(che) abbia mangiato	= past subjunctive	→	**sia stato/a (mangiato/a)**
(che) mangiasse	= imperfect subjunctive	→	**fosse (mangiato/a)**
(che) avesse mangiato	= pluperfect subjunctive	→	**fosse stato/a (mangiato/a)**

EXERCISE Set 22–1

Make each one of the following sentences passive.

il cartone animato	cartoon	**il portatile**	portable (laptop)
il computer	computer	**l'uomo (pl.: gli uomini)**	man
il medioevo	medieval period		

1. **Marco mangia la torta.**

_____

2. **Quell'uomo ha bevuto il cappuccino.**

_____

3. **Mia sorella guardava regolarmente i cartoni animati da bambina.**

_____

4. **Quando siamo arrivati, le tue amiche avevano già fatto la spesa.**

_____

5. **Bocaccio scrisse *Il Decamerone*.**

_____

6. **La mia amica comprerà quel computer portatile.**

_____

7. **Giovanni avrà già fatto gli spaghetti.**

_____

8. Se potesse, lui comprerebbe quella Ferrari.

___

9. Se avesse potuto, lui avrebbe comprato quella Ferrari.

___

10. Penso che Marco desideri quel portatile.

___

11. Penso che loro abbiano già comprato quella casa.

___

12. Credevo che voi aveste già assaggiato i suoi spaghetti.

___

Illustrative Dialogue

Claudia:	**Marco, da chi è *stato comprato* quel portatile?**	Marco, by whom was that laptop bought?
Marco:	***È stato comprato* da mia sorella.**	It was bought by my sister.
Claudia:	**E tu quando finirai il tuo lavoro?**	And when will you be finishing your job?
Marco:	***Sarà finito* tra poco.**	It will be finished soon.
Claudia:	**Quando *sarà* veramente *finito*, usciresti con me?**	When it will be truly finished, would you come out with me?
Marco:	**Certo. Dove?**	Of course. Where?
Claudia:	**Andiamo a vedere il nuovo film di quel famoso regista, il cui nome mi sono dimenticata. *È stato visto* da tanta gente ed *è piaciuto* molto.**	Let's go see the new movie by that famous director, whose name I have forgotten. It has been seen by many people and it has been liked a lot.
Marco:	**Va bene.**	OK.

EXERCISE Set 22–2

Answer the following questions based on the dialogue. Use complete sentences.

1. **Da chi è stato comprato il portatile?**

___

2. **Quando sarà finito il lavoro di Marco?**

___

3. **Che cosa chiede Claudia a Marco?**

___

4. **Dove vuole andare Claudia?**

___

5. **Da chi è stato visto il film?**

_____

6. **È piaciuto il film?**

_____

Miscellaneous Topics

The verb **fare** / _to do, to make_ can be used in causative constructions, called the **causativo** in Italian. These allow you to express such things as _having_ or _getting_ someone to do something.

> **Maria _fa lavare_ i piatti a suo fratello.** / _Maria has her brother wash the dishes._
> _Maria gets her brother to wash the dishes._

> **Maria li _fa lavare_ a lui.** / _Maria has him wash them._
> _Maria gets him to wash them._

> **Maria _ha fatto lavare_ i piatti a suo fratello.** / _Maria had her brother wash the dishes._
> _Maria got her brother to wash the dishes._

> **Maria li _ha fatti lavare_ a lui.** / _Maria had him wash them._
> _Maria got him to wash them._

> **Maria _farà lavare_ i piatti a suo fratello.** / _Maria will have her brother wash the dishes._
> _Maria will get her brother to wash the dishes._

> **Maria li _farà lavare_ a lui.** / _Maria will have him wash them._
> _Maria will have him wash them._

The indefinite tenses, called the **tempi indefiniti** in Italian, allow you to express actions that refer to indefinite time relations.

For example, the gerund, called the **gerundio** in Italian, is used to express an action simultaneous to another one, replacing **mentre** / _while_ + imperfect when the subject of the two clauses is the same.

> _Mentre camminavo,_ **ho visto Marco.** / _While I was walking, I saw Mark._

or

> _Camminando,_ **ho visto Marco.** / _While walking, I saw Marco._

Object pronouns are attached to the gerund:

> _Vedendolo,_ **l'ho salutato.** / _Upon seeing him, I greeted him._

There is also a past gerund, consisting of an auxiliary verb, **avere** / _to have_ or **essere** / _to be_, in the gerund form, and the past participle of the verb, in that order:

avendo parlato / _having spoken_	**essendo arrivato/a** / _having arrived_
avendo venduto / _having sold_	**essendo caduto/a** / _having fallen_
avendo dormito / _having slept_	**essendo partito/a** / _having left_

> _Avendo mangiato_ **tutto, siamo usciti.** / _Having eaten everything, we went out._

> _Essendo andati_ **in Italia, visitarono tanti bei posti.** / _Having gone to Italy, they visited many nice places._

The infinitive, called the **infinito** in Italian, is used after certain constructions and it can function as a substantive, in which case it is always assigned a masculine gender.

> **Prima di _mangiare_, abbiamo guardato la TV.** / _Before eating, we watched TV._

> _Il mangiare_ **è necessario per sopravvivere.** / _Eating is necessary to survive._

When the subjects of two clauses are the same, then the infinitive is used.

Different Subjects	The Same Subjects
Lui *crede* **che io** *scriva* **bene.** He believes that I write well.	**Lui** *crede* **di** *scrivere* **bene.** He believes that he (himself) writes well.

There is also a past infinitive consisting of an auxiliary verb in the infinitive and a past participle.

aver(e) parlato / *having spoken*	**esser(e) arrivato/a** / *having arrived*
aver(e) venduto / *having sold*	**esser(e) caduto/a** / *having fallen*
aver(e) dormito / *having slept*	**esser(e) partito/a** / *having left*

Note that the final **-e** of the auxiliary may be dropped.

> **Dopo** *aver mangiato*, **uscirò.** / *After having eaten, I will go out.*
>
> **Dopo** *esser arrivati*, **sono andati al cinema.** / *After having arrived, they went to the movies.*

Object pronouns are also attached to infinitives:

> **Invece di** *mangiarlo*, **l'ho dato a lei.** / *Instead of eating it, I gave it to her.*

EXERCISE Set 22–3

Say the following things in Italian:

camminare	to walk	**il pezzo**		piece
giù	down	**il piatto**		dish
lavare	to wash	**sopravvivere** (conj. like **vivere**)		to survive

1. Maria has already gotten her brother to wash the dishes.

   _____

2. I will get her to study more.

   _____

3. They got me to go to the bar yesterday.

   _____

4. They also got me to drink a cappuccino.

   _____

5. While she was walking yesterday, she met me.

   _____

6. Seeing me, she got me to go with her.

   _____

7. Having done everything, they went out.

   _____

8. Having gone to Italy in the spring, they were able to travel around quite a bit.

   _____

9. Drinking is necessary to survive.

_____

10. He thinks that he knows everything.

_____

11. After having gone out, they decided to go back home.

_____

12. He was given a piece of cake. But instead of eating it, he put it down.

_____

Crossword Puzzle 22

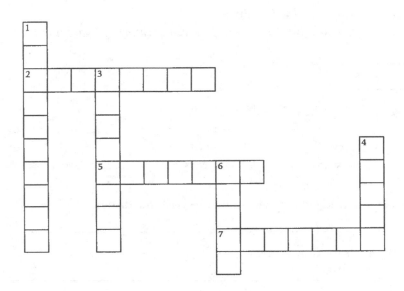

Orizzontali

2. **Prima di ..., bisogna aver appetito.**
5. **... quello, si è rivelato bugiardo** (*he revealed himself to be a liar*).
7. **Essendo ... a casa presto, hanno guardato la TV.**

Verticali

1. **... ieri, mi ha visto.**
3. **Avendo ... la TV, ha deciso di studiare.**
4. **Li ho ... fare a lui.**
6. **Avendo ... quello, si è rivelato bugiardo.**

Appendix A
Pronunciation Guide

Here are the basic facts of Italian pronunciation and spelling.

Vowels

The Italian vowels are **a, e, i, o, u.** They are pronounced as follows:

Letters	Pronunciation	As in…	Examples	Meanings
a	ah	*bah*	**cane**	*dog*
e	eh	*bet*	**bene**	*well*
i	eeh	*beet*	**vino**	*wine*
o	oh	*boat*	**oro**	*gold*
u	ooh	*boot*	**uso**	*use*

In words where the **i** and **u** come before or after another vowel (in the same syllable), they are pronounced instead as follows:

Letters	Pronunciation	As in…	Examples	Meanings
i	y	*yes*	**ieri**	*yesterday*
i	ay	*say*	**mai**	*never*
u	w	*way*	**uomo**	*man*
u	ow	*cow*	**causa**	*cause*

Single Consonants

Italian has both single and double consonants. The pronunciation of single consonants is summarized in the chart below:

Letters	Pronun.	As in...	Examples	Meaning
b	b	*bat*	**bene**	*well*
c (before a, o, u)	k	*cat*	**cane**	*dog*
ch (before e, i)	k	*ache*	**chi**	*who*
c (before e, i)	ch	*chin*	**cena**	*dinner*
ci (before a, o, u)	ch	*chew*	**ciao**	*hi/bye*
d	d	*dip*	**dopo**	*after*
f	f	*fair*	**fare**	*to do*
g (before a, o, u)	g	*gas*	**gatto**	*cat*
gh (before e, i)	g		**ghetto**	*ghetto*
g (before e, i)	j	*gym*	**gente**	*people*
gi (before a, o, u)	j	*jacket*	**giacca**	*jacket*
gli	ly	*million*	**figlio**	*son*
gn	ny	*canyon*	**bagno**	*bathroom*
l	l	*love*	**latte**	*milk*
m	m	*man*	**mano**	*hand*
n	n	*name*	**nome**	*name*
p	p	*pen*	**pane**	*bread*
q	k(w)	*quick*	**qui**	*here*
r	r	*brrrrr…*	**rosso**	*red*
s (voiceless)	s	*sip*	**sale**	*salt*
	s	*spin*	**specchio**	*mirror*
s (voiced)	z	*zip*	**casa**	*house*
	z	*zero*	**sbaglio**	*mistake*
sc (before a, o, u)	sk	*skill*	**scuola**	*school*
sch (before e, i)	sk		**schema**	*scheme*
sc (before e, i)	sh	*shave*	**scena**	*scene*
sci (before a, o, u)	sh	*shell*	**sciarpa**	*scarf*
t	t	*tent*	**tanto**	*a lot*
v	v	*vine*	**vino**	*wine*
z	ts or ds	*cats or lads*	**zio**	*uncle*

Double Consonants

Double consonants are not sounded in English, even though double letters are often used (but they represent single consonant sounds). The Italian double consonants last approximately twice as long as corresponding single ones, and are pronounced with more intensity. They occur between vowels, or between a vowel and l or r.

Examples	Meanings
arrivederci	good-bye
basso	short
bello	beautiful
camminare	to walk
formaggio	cheese
mamma	mom
nonno	grandfather
pizza	pizza

Spelling Peculiarities

In general, there is a one-to-one correspondence between a sound and the letter (or letters) used to represent it. The main exceptions are as follows.

- Words with a stressed final vowel are written with an accent mark on the vowel. The mark is usually grave. But in some words, especially those ending in -ché, the acute accent mark is often used.

Examples	Meanings
caffè	coffee
città	city
perché	why, because
poiché	since

- Words spelled with j, k, w, x, and y are words that Italians have taken from other languages, especially English.

Examples	Meanings
il jazz	jazz
il karatè	karate
il weekend	weekend

- The letter **h** is used in several present indicative tense forms of the verb **avere** / *to have*. It is always silent.

Examples	Meanings
io ho	I have
tu hai	you have (familiar)
Lei ha	you have (polite)
lui / lei ha	he / she has
loro hanno	they have

As in English, capital letters are used at the beginning of sentences and to write proper nouns (names of people, countries, etc.). However, there are a few different conventions worth noting: the pronoun **io** / I , titles, months of the year, days of the week, and adjectives and nouns referring to languages and nationalities are not capitalized.

Examples	Meanings
dottore	Dr.
professore	Professor
signora	Ms., Mrs.
cinese	Chinese
inglese	English
italiano	Italian
gennaio	January
settembre	September
ottobre	October
lunedì	Monday
martedì	Tuesday

- On the other hand, the polite pronoun **Lei** / *you,* and other corresponding polite forms, are capitalized (although this is optional).

Appendix B

Summaries

Verbs Conjugated with *Essere* in Compound Tenses

bastare	to be sufficient, to suffice, to be enough
cadere	to fall
correre	to run
costare	to cost
diventare	to become
durare	to last
esserci	to be there
essere	to be
importare	to be important, to matter
interessare	to interest, to be interested by
inventare	to invent
mancare	to lack, to miss
morire	to die
nascere	to be born
nevicare	to snow
piacere	to be pleasing to, to like
piovere	to rain
rimanere	to be left over, to remain
salire	to climb, to go up
sembrare	to seem
sopravvivere	to survive
stare	to stay, to be
succedere	to happen
tornare	to go back, to return
uscire	to go out
valere	to be worth
venire	to come
vivere	to live

Irregular Gerunds

Infinitive		Gerund
attrarre	to attract	attraendo
bere	to drink	bevendo
comporre	to compose	componendo
dare	to give	dando
dedurre	to deduce	deducendo
dire	to say, to tell, to speak	dicendo
fare	to do, to make	facendo
indurre	to induce	inducendo
introdurre	to introduce	introducendo
porre	to pose	ponendo
produrre	to produce	producendo
ridurre	to reduce	riducendo
sedurre	to seduce	seducendo
stare	to stay, to be	stando
supporre	to suppose	supponendo
tradurre	to translate	traducendo
trarre	to draw (pull)	traendo

Irregular Past Participles

Infinitive		Past Participle
accendere	to turn on	acceso
apparire	to appear	apparso
aprire	to open	aperto
attrarre	to attract	attratto
bere	to drink	bevuto
chiedere	to ask	chiesto
chiudere	to close	chiuso
comporre	to compose	composto
comprendere	to comprehend	compreso
coprire	to cover	coperto
correre	to run	corso
dare	to give	dato
decidere	to decide	deciso
dedurre	to deduce	dedotto
dipingere	to paint	dipinto

Infinitive		Past Participle
dire	to say, to tell, to speak	detto
essere	to be	stato
fare	to do, to make	fatto
indurre	to induce	indotto
introdurre	to introduce	introdotto
mettere	to put	messo
morire	to die	morto
nascere	to be born	nato
porre	to pose, to put	posto
prendere	to take	preso
produrre	to produce	prodotto
promettere	to promise	promesso
ridurre	to reduce	ridotto
rimanere	to be left over, to remain	rimasto
rispondere	to answer	risposto
rompere	to break	rotto
scegliere	to choose	scelto
scoprire	to discover	scoperto
scrivere	to write	scritto
sedurre	to seduce	sedotto
smettere	to stop, to quit	smesso
soffrire	to suffer	sofferto
sopravvivere	to survive	sopravissuto
stare	to stay, to be	stato
succedere	to happen	successo
tradurre	to translate	tradotto
trarre	to draw (pull)	tratto
valere	to be worth	valso
vedere	to see	visto/veduto
venire	to come	venuto
vincere	to win	vinto
vivere	to live	vissuto

Answers

Chapter 1

Exercise Set 1-1

A.

1. **io suono**	=	I play, I am playing, I do play
2. **tu speri**	=	you (fam., sing.) hope, you are hoping, you do hope
3. **noi prepariamo**	=	we prepare, we are preparing, we do prepare
4. **loro portano**	=	they bring, they are bringing, they do bring
5. **voi lavorate**	=	you (fam., pl.) work, you are working, you do work
6. **Lei entra**	=	you (pol., sing.) enter, you are entering, you do enter
7. **lei guarda**	=	she watches, she is watching, she does watch
8. **Loro amano**	=	you (pol., pl.) love, you are loving, you do love
9. **loro arrivano**	=	they arrive, they are arriving, they do arrive
10. **io ascolto**	=	I listen, I am listening, I do listen
11. **tu aspetti**	=	you (fam., sing.) wait, you are waiting, you do wait
12. **noi balliamo**	=	we dance, we are dancing, we do dance
13. **lei canta**	=	she sings, she is singing, she does sing
14. **noi compriamo**	=	we buy, we are buying, we do buy
15. **loro parlano**	=	they speak, they are speaking, they do speak

B.

1. **Scusi, (Lei) parla inglese?**
2. **Sì, (io) parlo inglese molto bene.**
3. **(Loro) non parlano italiano molto bene.**
4. **(Noi) parliamo italiano un po'.**
5. **Maria, anche tu parli italiano, no/non è vero?**
6. **Io invece non parlo italiano, ma mia figlia lo parla molto bene.**
7. **No, non è vero, l'autobus non arriva tra qualche minuto.**
8. **Grazie, Lei è molto gentile. (Io) amo la lingua italiana.**
9. **Alessandro suona il violoncello molto bene e Sarah suona il pianoforte e balla molto bene.**
10. **(Lei) ascolta la radio troppo.**
11. **(Noi) guardiamo la televisione molto.**
12. **Loro suonano il pianoforte bene.**
13. **(Tu) guardi sempre la televisione.**
14. **(Lei) porta una giacca nuova, no/non è vero?**
15. **(Voi) aspettate Maria, no/non è vero? (Lei) abita vicino.**

Exercise Set 1-2

A.

1. **io scrivo**	=	I write, I am writing, I do write
2. **tu comprendi**	=	you (fam., sing.) comprehend, you are comprehending, you do comprehend
3. **noi crediamo**	=	we believe, we are believing, we do believe
4. **loro mettono**	=	they put, they are putting, they do put
5. **voi godete**	=	you (fam., pl.) enjoy, you are enjoying, you do enjoy
6. **Lei legge**	=	you (pol., sing.) read, you are reading, you do read
7. **la mia amica mette**	=	my friend puts, my friend is putting, my friend does put
8. **Loro ridono**	=	you (pol., pl.) laugh, you are laughing, you do laugh
9. **loro rompono**	=	they break, they are breaking, they do break
10. **io temo**	=	I fear, I am fearing, I do fear

11. **tu vedi**	=	you (fam., sing.) see, you are seeing, you do see
12. **noi vendiamo**	=	we sell, we are selling, we do sell
13. **lui chiude**	=	he closes, he is closing, he does close
14. **noi mettiamo**	=	we put, we are putting, we do put
15. **loro prendono**	=	they take, they are taking, they do take

B.

1. **Ciao, Maria e Claudia, che leggete?**
2. **Non leggo. Scrivo un' e-mail a un'amica francese.**
3. **Scusa, ma scrivi l'e-mail in italiano?**
4. **Sì, perché la mia amica parla, legge, e scrive la lingua italiana molto bene.**
5. **Arrivederci/Ciao, a più tardi. Comprendete?**
6. **Ti scrivo un' e-mail tra/fra venti minuti, va bene?**
7. **No, non è vero, la mia amica non vende la macchina.**
8. **(La) mia nonna gode la vita! (Lei) comprende tutto!**
9. **Mio figlio e mia figlia ti credono.**
10. **Mio nonno teme sempre tutto!**
11. **Anche mio fratello vende la macchina.**
12. **Mia sorella rompe sempre qualcosa.**
13. **La mia amica francese ride sempre.**
14. **Il mio amico italiano corre sempre.**
15. **Noi godiamo la vita, perché viviamo in Italia!**

Exercise Set 1-3

A.

1. **io unisco**	=	I unite, I am uniting, I do unite
2. **tu spedisci**	=	you (fam., sing.) send, you are sending, you do send
3. **noi puniamo**	=	we punish, we are punishing, we do punish
4. **loro puliscono**	=	they clean, they are cleaning, they do clean
5. **voi preferite**	=	you (fam., pl.) prefer, you are preferring, you do prefer
6. **Lei soffre**	=	you (pol., sing.) suffer, you are suffering, you do suffer
7. **lei finisce**	=	she finishes, she is finishing, she does finish
8. **Loro capiscono**	=	you (pol., pl.) understand, you do understand
9. **i negozi aprono**	=	the stores open, the stores are opening, the stores do open
10. **io copro**	=	I cover, I am covering, I do cover
11. **tu dormi**	=	you (fam., sing.) sleep, you are sleeping, you do sleep
12. **noi partiamo**	=	we leave, we are leaving, we do leave
13. **lei scopre**	=	she discovers, she is discovering, she does discover
14. **noi sentiamo**	=	we feel/hear, we are feeling/hearing, we do feel/hear
15. **loro garantiscono**	=	they guarantee, they are guaranteeing, they do guarantee

B.

1. a   2. b   3. b   4. b   5. b   6. b   7. b   8. a   9. a   10. a   11. b   12. a   13. a   14. a   15. a

Exercise Set 1-4

A.

1. **suona**   2. **amano**   3. **viviamo**   4. **guardano**   5. **arrivano**   6. **puliamo**   7. **capisco**   8. **chiude**
9. **ascolta**

B.

1. a   2. b   3. a   4. b   5. a   6. a   7. a   8. a   9. a

Crossword Puzzle 1

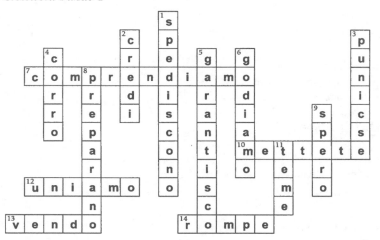

Chapter 2

Exercise Set 2-1

A.

1. **sono**	=	I am
2. **sei**	=	you (fam., sing.) are
3. **siamo**	=	we are
4. **siete**	=	you (pl.) are
5. **è**	=	you (pol., sing.) are
6. **è**	=	my friend is
7. **sono**	=	my friends are
8. **siamo**	=	you and I are
9. **siete**	=	you and he are

B.

1. **È l'una e trentatré.**
2. **Sono le tredici e trentatré.**
3. **Sono le cinque e dodici.**
4. **Sono le diciassette e dodici.**
5. **Sono le otto e cinquantacinque.**
6. **Sono le venti e cinquantacinque.**
7. **Sono le undici e diciotto.**
8. **Sono le ventitré e diciotto.**

Exercise Set 2-2

A.

1. a   2. a   3. a   4. a   5. a   6. b   7. b   8. b   9. b

B.

1. **Paolo, che ora è/che ore sono?**
2. **Sono le quattro meno venti. Ci vediamo tra/fra poco.**
3. **La lezione d'italiano è alle sette e un quarto.**
4. **È (la) mezzanotte o (il) mezzogiorno?**
5. **Le paste sono molto buone.**
6. **Maria, sei sicura?**
7. **Sì, è proprio vero, la lezione è all'una precisa.**
8. **Sono le nove e mezzo. No, sono le dieci in punto.**
9. **Siete americane?**
10. **Sono turisti americani.**

Exercise Set 2-3

A.

1. Sì, c'è (Paolo)./No, non c'è (Paolo).
2. Ecco Paolo! / Eccolo *(Here he is)*!
3. Sì, siamo italiani. / No, non siamo italiani.
4. Sì, ci sono (Marco e Mario)./No, non ci sono (Marco e Mario).
5. Ecco Marco e Maria!/Eccoli *(Here they are)*!
6. Sì, sono ricco (-a)./No, non sono ricco (-a).
7. Sì, è martedì (oggi)./No, non è martedì (oggi).
8. Ecco Maria!/Eccola *(Here she is)*!
9. Sì, c'è (Maria)./No, non c'è (Maria).
10. Sì, (loro) sono australiani. / No, (loro) non sono australiani.

B.

1. Il giorno dopo mercoledì è giovedì.
2. Gli ultimi due giorni della settimana sono sabato e domenica.
3. Il giorno prima di sabato è venerdì.
4. Il mese dopo gennaio è febbraio.
5. I mesi della primavera negli Stati Uniti sono marzo, aprile e maggio.
6. I mesi dell'inverno negli Stati Uniti sono dicembre, gennaio e febbraio.
7. I mesi dell'autunno negli Stati Uniti sono settembre, ottobre e novembre.
8. I mesi dell'estate negli Stati Uniti sono giugno, luglio e agosto.

C.

1. Il 1492 è un anno importante.
2. È il primo marzo.
3. È il quattro dicembre.
4. È il tre maggio.
5. Il mercoledì c'è sempre la lezione d'italiano.
6. Ci sono lezioni d'italiano la domenica?
7. (Io) sono di Firenze, come il mio insegnante.
8. Di dov'è (Lei), signor Sosa? È francese, spagnolo o canadese?
9. Dov'è la signora Dini?
10. (Lei) è africana, signorina Hariri? E Lei è (un) ingegnere, no/vero/non è vero?
11. Marco e Maria, siete di Milano?
12. Maria è molto intelligente. E non è una professoressa cattiva.
13. Anch'io sono molto magro (-a), come la mia dentista e il mio medico.
14. Mia sorella è molto bella. E non è grassa, come il mio avvocato o il mio meccanico.
15. I miei amici sono alti e grandi, ma poveri.
16. Lui è tedesco e lei è svizzera.
17. Le mie due amiche sono olandesi.
18. No, mio marito non è messicano; (lui) è inglese.
19. I miei due amici sono giapponesi, non cinesi.

Exercise Set 2-4

A.

1. **ho**	=	I have
2. **hai**	=	you (fam., sing.) have
3. **abbiamo**	=	Maria and I have
4. **avete**	=	You and Marco have
5. **ha**	=	you (pol., sing.) have
6. **ha**	=	Mr. Smith has
7. **hanno**	=	my friends have
8. **abbiamo**	=	we have
9. **avete**	=	you (pl.) have

B.
1. **ho**   2. **hanno**   3. **ha**   4. **hanno**   5. **hanno**   6. **ha**   7. **hanno**   8. **hanno**   9. **hanno**   10. **ho, ha**
11. **ha**   12. **Avete**   13. **abbiamo**   14. **hai**   15. **hai**

Exercise Set 2-5

A.
1. **ha**   2. **è**   3. **C'è**   4. **Sono**   5. **siamo**   6. **siete**   7. **avete**   8. **è**   9. **C'è**   10. **è**   11. **ha**   12. **avete**

B.

Cara Maria,

come va? *(Do not capitalize this opening part as you do in English).* **Quanti anni hai adesso/ora? E quanti anni hanno tuo fratello e tua sorella? Adesso/ora sono (un) medico. Sei ancora uno psicologo (una psicologa)? Che/Quale macchina hai adesso/ora? Sei sempre molto simpatica? Certo (certamente) sei intelligente!**
Ho voglia di telefonare (telefonarti). Purtroppo, ho sempre poco tempo. Sono sempre molto occupata. Forse, un giorno!
Hai ragione, sono troppo ambiziosa e ho poco tempo per i miei amici.

Ciao!
Francesca

Crossword Puzzle 2

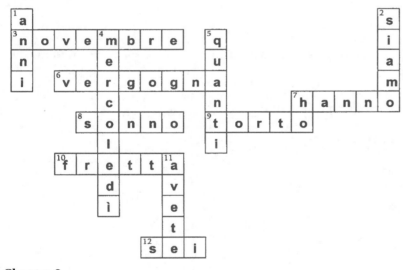

Chapter 3

Exercise Set 3-1

A. (Only the correct verb forms are given here. The reader will make up his or her own sentences in an appropriate fashion.)

1. **sappiamo**	=	we know
2. **sapete**	=	you (pl.) know
3. **so**	=	I know
4. **sai**	=	you (fam., sing.) know
5. **sa**	=	you (pol., sing.) know
6. **sa**	=	my uncle knows
7. **sanno**	=	your cousins know
8. **sappiamo**	=	you and I know
9. **sapete**	=	you and he know
10. **conosco**	=	I know, I am familiar with

11. **conosci**	=	you (fam., sing.) know, you are familiar with
12. **conosciamo**	=	we know, we are familiar with
13. **conoscete**	=	you (pl.) know, you are familiar with
14. **conosce**	=	you (pol., sing.) know, you are familiar with
15. **conosce**	=	your brother-in-law knows, your brother-in-law is familiar with
16. **conoscono**	=	your sisters know, your sisters are familiar with
17. **conoscete**	=	you and she know, you and she are familiar with
18. **conosciamo**	=	you and I know, you and I are familiar with

B.

1. a   2. b   3. a   4. b   5. a   6. a   7. b   8. b   9. b

Exercise Set 3-2

1. **Giovanni, conosci un buon ristorante in questa città?**
2. **Signor Smith, (Lei) sa il mio indirizzo e il mio numero di telefono?**
3. **(Loro) sanno molte/tante cose e conoscono anche molta/tanta gente.**
4. **Tua sorella sa parlare italiano meglio di me.**
5. **La mia insegnante d'italiano è molto brava. (Lei) sa anche parlare inglese molto bene.**
6. **Maria è una buon'amica. Tuo fratello conosce Maria?/Conosce Maria, tuo fratello?**
7. **Non conosciamo il ristorante. Ma sappiamo dov'è. È vicino a via Nazionale.**
8. **Mio fratello sa suonare il violoncello molto bene.**
9. **Tutti i miei amici conoscono tua sorella. (Lei) sa molte/tante cose.**

Exercise Set 3-3

A.

1. **conosco**   2. **sanno/conoscono**   3. **sa**   4. **sapete**   5. **sanno**   6. **so**   7. **conosci**   8. **conosce**   9. **sa**

B.

1. **Lei sa il nome di quella persona?**
2. **Loro conoscono un buon ristorante in questa città?**
3. **Anche Lei sa suonare il pianoforte, vero?**
4. **Conoscono i genitori di quella persona?**
5. **Sa il mio indirizzo?**
6. **Conosce l'insegnante d'italiano?**
7. **Sanno chi sono io?**

Crossword Puzzle 3

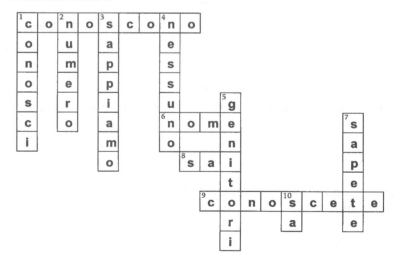

Chapter 4

Exercise Set 4-1

A.

1. **"To me is pleasing Maria"** → Mi piace Maria.
2. **"I am pleasing to Maria"** → Io piaccio a Maria.
3. **"To you are pleasing those books"** → Ti piacciono quei libri.
4. **"You are pleasing to those girls"** → Tu piaci a quelle ragazze.
5. **"To her is pleasing that boy"** → Le piace quel ragazzo.
6. **"She is pleasing to that boy"** → Lei piace a quel ragazzo.
7. **"That restaurant is pleasing to my parents"** → Quel ristorante piace ai miei genitori.
8. **"To us is pleasing the cheese"** → Ci piace il formaggio.
9. **"To them we are pleasing"** → Gli piacciamo/Noi piacciamo a loro.
10. **"To him is pleasing (the) fruit"** → Gli piace la frutta.
11. **"He is pleasing to her"** → Lui le piace/Lui piace a lei.
12. **"To you is pleasing that newspaper"** → Vi piace quel giornale.
13. **"You are pleasing to my parents"** → Voi piacete ai miei genitori.
14. **"To them are pleasing those magazines"** → Gli piacciono quelle riviste.
15. **"They are pleasing to me"** → Loro mi piacciono.

B.

1. **(1) piaci** → (2) I like you ("You are pleasing to me") → (3) Tu mi piaci.
2. **(1) piaccio** → (2) You like me ("I am pleasing to you") → (3) Io ti piaccio.
3. **(1) piace** → (2) We like her ("She is pleasing to us") → (3) Lei ci piace.
4. **(1) piacciamo** → (2) She likes us ("We are pleasing to her") → (3) Noi le piacciamo.
5. **(1) piace** → (2) We like her ("She is pleasing to us") → (3) Lei ci piace.
6. **(1) piacete** → (2) He likes you ("You are pleasing to him") → (3) Voi gli piacete.
7. **(1) piace** → (2) You like him ("He is pleasing to you") → (3) Lui vi piace.
8. **(1) piacciono** → (2) I like them ("They are pleasing to me") → (3) Loro mi piacciono.
9. **(1) piacciono** → (2) They like me ("I am pleasing to them") → (3) Io gli piaccio.

Exercise Set 4-2

1. **Mi piace la musica di Beethoven.**
2. **Mi piacciono gli spaghetti.**
3. **Ti piace quel film.**
4. **Ti piacciono quelle riviste.**
5. **Le piace il mio amico.**
6. **Le piacciono i miei amici.**
7. **Gli piace la tua macchina.**
8. **Gli piacciono quelle macchine.**
9. **Le piace quel libro.**
10. **Le piacciono quei libri.**
11. **Ci piace quel giornale.**
12. **Ci piacciono quelle persone.**
13. **Vi piace la mia amica.**
14. **Vi piacciono le mie amiche.**
15. **Gli piace quella rivista nuova.**
16. **Gli piacciono quelle riviste nuove.**

Exercise Set 4-3

1. **Non mi piace mai suonare il pianoforte./A me non piace mai suonare il pianoforte.**
2. **Non gli piace nessuno in questa città./A loro non piace nessuno in questa città.**
3. **Non mi piace quel film affatto./A me non piace quel film affatto.**
4. **Mi dispiace. Ma so che (a lei) non le dispiace.**

5. In questo momento, non mi piace nessun film nuovo./In questo momento, a me non piace nessun film nuovo.
6. Ci dispiace.
7. Non ci piace più il formaggio./A noi non piace più il formaggio.
8. Non ti piace mica quel libro nuovo, vero?/A te non piace mica quel libro nuovo, vero?
9. Non mi piace né quel libro nuovo né quel film nuovo./A me non piace né quel libro nuovo né quel film nuovo.
10. Non le piace neanche/nemmeno/neppure la mia macchina nuova./ A lei non piace neanche/nemmeno/neppure la mia macchina nuova.

Exercise Set 4-4

1. a   2. a   3. a   4. a   5. a   6. b   7. b   8. b   9. b

Exercise Set 4-5

1. Sembra buono quel ristorante?
2. L'ultima cosa che rimane è scrivere a Maria.
3. Quel film non mi interessa affatto.
4. Gli spaghetti mi bastano.
5. Mi dolgono le (mie) ossa.
6. Quelle cose importano molto.
7. Ti manco?

Crossword Puzzle 4

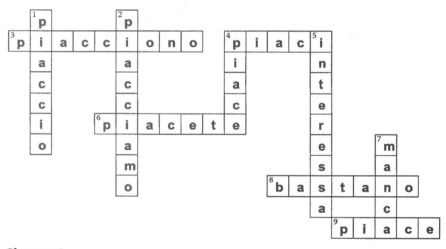

Chapter 5

Exercise Set 5-1

A.

1. **bevo**	=	I drink, I am drinking, I do drink
2. **bevi**	=	you (fam., sing.) drink, you are drinking, you do drink
3. **beviamo**	=	we drink, we are drinking, we do drink
4. **bevono**	=	they drink, they are drinking, they do drink
5. **bevete**	=	you (pl.) drink, you are drinking, you do drink
6. **beve**	=	you (pol., sing.) drink, you are drinking, you do drink
7. **do**	=	I give, I am giving, I do give
8. **dai**	=	you (fam., sing.) give, you are giving, you do give
9. **diamo**	=	you and I give, you and I are giving, you and I do give
10. **danno**	=	they give, they are giving, they do give

11. **date**	=	you and she give, you and she are giving, you and she do give	
12. **dà**	=	he gives, he is giving, he does give	
13. **dico**	=	I say, I am saying, I do say	
14. **dici**	=	you (fam., sing.) say, you are saying, you do say	
15. **diciamo**	=	we say, we are saying, we do say	
16. **dicono**	=	they say, they are saying, they do say	
17. **dite**	=	you (pl.) say, you are saying, you do say	
18. **dice**	=	you (pol., sing.) say, you are saying, you do say	
19. **faccio**	=	I make, I am making, I do make	
20. **fai**	=	you (fam., sing.) make, you are making, you do make	
21. **facciamo**	=	you and I make, you and I are making, you and I do make	
22. **fanno**	=	they make, they are making, they do make	
23. **fate**	=	you and she make, you and she are making, you and she do make	
24. **fa**	=	she makes, she is making, she does make	

B.

1. **(Noi) beviamo sempre alla salute della famiglia.**
2. **I miei amici bevono sempre forte alle feste.**
3. **Signora Marchi, perché mi dà sempre del Lei?**
4. **La signora Marchi e io ci diamo del tu d'ora in poi.**
5. **(Io) do la mano al signor Smith.**
6. **Danno quel nuovo film qui vicino?**
7. **Io dico sempre di sì e tu dici sempre di no, vero/non è vero/no?**
8. **Tu dici sempre la verità, mentre loro dicono sempre le bugie.**
9. **Mio nonno fa sempre del bene per la gente; non fa mai del male.**
10. **Mia sorella fa il medico e io faccio l'ingegnere.**

Exercise Set 5-2

A.
1. a   2. b   3. a   4. b   5. b   6. a   7. b

B.
1. **bevono**   2. **fa**   3. **dicono**   4. **dice**   5. **dite**   6. **danno**   7. **fa**   8. **fanno**   9. **fai**

Exercise Set 5-3

A.

1. **vado**	=	I go, I am going, I do go	
2. **vai**	=	you (fam., sing.) go, you are going, you do go	
3. **andiamo**	=	we go, we are going, we do go	
4. **vanno**	=	they go, they are going, they do go	
5. **andate**	=	you (pl.) go, you are going, you do go	
6. **va**	=	you (pol., sing.) go, you are going, you do go	
7. **esco**	=	I go out, I am going out, I do go out	
8. **esci**	=	you (fam., sing.) go out, you are going out, you do go out	
9. **usciamo**	=	you and I go out, you and I are going out, you and I do go out	
10. **escono**	=	they go out, they are going out, they do go out	
11. **uscite**	=	you and she go out, you and she are going out, you and she do go out	
12. **esce**	=	he goes out, he is going out, he does go out	
13. **vengo**	=	I come, I am coming	
14. **vieni**	=	you (fam., sing.) come, you are coming	
15. **veniamo**	=	we come, we are coming	
16. **vengono**	=	they come, they are coming	
17. **venite**	=	you (pl.) come, you are coming	
18. **viene**	=	she comes, she is coming	

B.

1. **Anche i nostri amici vengono alla vostra festa.**
2. **Franco, esci con Maria stasera?**
3. **Marco e Maria, dove andate?**
4. **Forse anche i loro genitori vengono alla vostra casa.**
5. **(Io) vado sempre al bar con i miei amici.**
6. **Claudia, vieni anche tu al bar?**
7. **(Io) esco sempre il sabato.**
8. **(Loro) vanno in Italia questa estate?**
9. **Vengo anch'io alla festa.**

C.

1. a   2. b   3. c   4. a   5. b   6. c

Exercise Set 5-4

A.

1. **devo**	=	I have to, I must
2. **devi**	=	you (fam., sing.) have to, you must
3. **dobbiamo**	=	we have to, we must
4. **devono**	=	they have to, they must
5. **dovete**	=	you (pl.) have to, you must
6. **deve**	=	you (pol., sing.) have to, you must
7. **posso**	=	I am able to, I can
8. **puoi**	=	you (fam., sing.) are able to, you can
9. **possiamo**	=	you and I are able to, you and I can
10. **possono**	=	they are able to, they can
11. **potete**	=	you and she are able to, you and she can
12. **può**	=	he is able to, he can
13. **voglio**	=	I want to
14. **vuoi**	=	you (fam., sing.) want to
15. **vogliamo**	=	we want to
16. **vogliono**	=	they want to
17. **volete**	=	you (pl.) want to
18. **vuole**	=	she wants to

B.

1. **Devo andare al bar.**
2. **Voglio andare in Italia quest'estate.**
3. **Posso comprare una macchina nuova adesso/ora perché ho i soldi.**
4. **Marco, perché devi sempre dire di no?**
5. **Claudia, puoi venire alla festa stasera?**
6. **Alessandro, vuoi uscire stasera?**
7. **Anche suo zio deve venire alla festa.**
8. **Lei vuole uscire, ma lui non può.**
9. **(Noi) dobbiamo sempre dire la verità.**
10. **(Noi) non possiamo andare alla sua festa perché vogliamo andare al cinema.**
11. **Alessandro e Sarah, potete uscire stasera? Volete uscire? O dovete studiare?**
12. **(Loro) vogliono sempre andare al cinema il sabato, ma oggi devono fare qualcosa importante. Allora non possono andare.**

Exercise Set 5-5

1. d   2. a   3. c   4. e   5. d   6. b

Crossword Puzzle 5

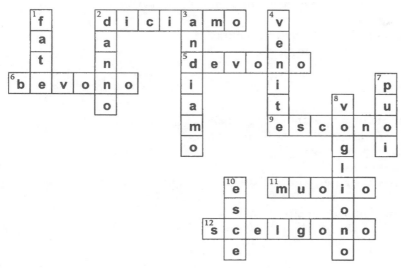

Chapter 6

Exercise Set 6-1

A.

1. **mi alzo**	=	I get up, I am getting up
2. **ti alzi**	=	you (fam., sing.) get up, you are getting up
3. **ci alziamo**	=	we get up, we are getting up
4. **si alzano**	=	they get up, they are getting up
5. **vi alzate**	=	you (pl.) get up, you are getting up
6. **si alza**	=	you (pol., sing.) get up, you are getting up
7. **mi metto**	=	I wear, I am wearing
8. **ti metti**	=	you (fam.) wear, you are wearing
9. **ci mettiamo**	=	you and I wear, you and I are wearing
10. **si mettono**	=	they wear, they are wearing
11. **vi mettete**	=	you and she wear, you and she are wearing
12. **si mette**	=	he wears, he is wearing
13. **mi sento**	=	I feel, I am feeling
14. **ti senti**	=	you (fam.) feel, you are feeling
15. **ci sentiamo**	=	we feel, we are feeling
16. **si sentono**	=	they feel, they are feeling
17. **vi sentite**	=	you (pl.) feel, you are feeling
18. **si sente**	=	you (pol., sing.) feel, you are feeling
19. **me ne vado**	=	I go away, I am going away
20. **te ne vai**	=	you (fam.) go away, you are going away
21. **ce ne andiamo**	=	we go away, we are going away
22. **se ne vanno**	=	they go away, they are going away
23. **ve ne andate**	=	you (pl.) go away, you are going away
24. **se ne va**	=	she goes away, she is going away

B.

1. a   2. c   3. b   4. a   5. a   6. a   7. c

C.

1. **Maria, perché ti vesti sempre elegantemente?**
2. **(Io) non mi vergogno di niente!**
3. **Marco, a che ora ti alzi generalmente la mattina?**
4. **Alessandro e Sarah, è vero che vi sposate quest'autunno?**

5. (Loro) si lamentano sempre di tutto.
6. Di solito mi faccio la doccia e mi faccio la barba quando mi alzo la mattina.
7. Perché si arrabbia, signorina Gentile?
8. (Loro) si annoiano sempre quando guardano la televisione.
9. (Io) mi ammalo molto facilmente se fa freddo fuori.

Exercise Set 6-2

A.

1. Una cliente si vuole provare/vuole provarsi un vestito nuovo.
2. La cliente può provarsi/si può provare tutti i vestiti che vuole.
3. La cliente non si mette mai quel tipo di vestito.
4. È un bel vestito, secondo il commesso.
5. La cliente desidera una bella camicetta per lei e poi vuole una camicia e dei bei pantaloni per suo marito.
6. Il marito della cliente si lamenta sempre dei suoi vestiti.

B.

Cliente:	Mi scusi/Scusi.
Commessa:	Desidera?
Cliente:	Posso provarmi/Mi posso provare questo bell'orologio?
Commessa:	Certo/Certamente. Forse La conosco. Come si chiama?
Cliente:	Mi chiamo Maria Marchi. E Lei, come si chiama?
Commessa:	Mi chiamo Claudia Santini. Non mi ricordo il Suo nome. Mi scusi/Scusi.
Cliente:	Non c'è problema. Anch'io mi vergogno quando mi dimentico qualcosa.

Exercise Set 6-3

1. Mi chiamo   2. ti alzi   3. ci annoiamo   4. si sposa   5. si vedono   6. ci capiamo   7. vi parlate

Crossword Puzzle 6

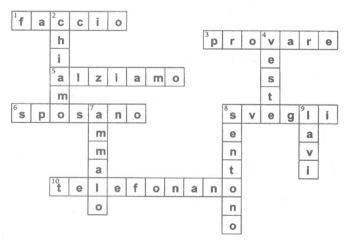

Chapter 7

Exercise Set 7-1

A.

1. **sto**	=	I am, I stay
2. **stai**	=	you (fam.) are, you stay
3. **stiamo**	=	we are, we stay
4. **stanno**	=	they are, they stay
5. **state**	=	you (pl.) are, you stay
6. **sta**	=	you (pol.) are, you stay
7. **sta**	=	her friend is, her friend stays

B.

1.

-Stai sempre attento?

-Sì, sto sempre attento.

2.

-Signora Dini, come sta?

-Sto bene, grazie.

3.

-Maria, come stai?

-Sto male/Non sto bene.

4.

-Stanno attenti i tuoi amici quando attraversano la strada?

-Sì, stanno sempre attenti.

5.

-Dobbiamo sempre stare calmi particolarmente quando abbiamo paura.

-E, per di più, dobbiamo anche stare fermi e zitti.

6.

-Marco che stai per fare?

-Sto per accendere il televisore.

Exercise Set 7-2

A.

1. sto cantando	=	I am singing
2. stai cantando	=	you (fam., sing.) are singing
3. stiamo cantando	=	we are singing
4. stanno cantando	=	they are singing
5. state cantando	=	you (pl.) are singing
6. sta cantando	=	you (pol., sing.) are singing
7. sto leggendo	=	I am reading
8. stai leggendo	=	you (fam., sing.) are reading
9. stiamo leggendo	=	you and I are reading
10. stanno leggendo	=	they are reading
11. state leggendo	=	you and she are reading
12. sta leggendo	=	he is reading
13. sto pulendo	=	I am cleaning
14. stai pulendo	=	you (fam., sing.) are cleaning
15. stiamo pulendo	=	we are cleaning
16. stanno pulendo	=	they are cleaning
17. state pulendo	=	you (pl.) are cleaning
18. sta pulendo	=	she is cleaning
19. sto andando	=	I am going
20. stai andando	=	you (fam., sing.) are going
21. stiamo andando	=	we are going
22. stanno andando	=	they are going
23. state andando	=	you (pl.) are going
24. sta andando	=	she is going

B.

1. Franco, che (cosa) stai bevendo? Stai bevendo un espresso?
2. Quale/Che film stanno dando in questo momento?
3. Signora Marchi, che sta dicendo?
4. Che (cosa) stanno facendo?
5. Marco e Maria stanno uscendo in questo momento.
6. Dov'è Alessandro? Sta dormendo.
7. Che (cosa) stanno bevendo? Stanno bevendo un cappuccino?

C.

1. **stanno andando**
2. **stanno prendendo**
3. **stanno chiacchierando**
4. **stanno bevendo**
5. **state facendo**
6. **stiamo facendo**
7. **stiamo chiacchierando**
8. **Stanno dando**

Exercise Set 7-3

A.

1. **Le due amiche si chiamano Franca e Claudia.**
2. **Stanno facendo la spesa.**
3. **Franca sta lavorando per una ditta di informatica.**
4. **Claudia sta lavorando in una banca.**
5. **Franca sta comprando delle mele, dei piselli e della carne.**
6. **Claudia sta comprando del pesce e della carne.**
7. **Le due amiche stanno programmando di uscire insieme qualche volta.**

B.

Gianni:	**Ciao, Giorgio, non ci vediamo da anni. Che stai facendo di bello?**
Giorgio:	**Ciao, Gianni. È vero. In questo momento, non sto facendo niente. E tu?**
Gianni:	**Sto lavorando in una banca. Ma sto programmando di tornare all'università.**
Giorgio:	**Sto programmando la stessa cosa.**
Gianni:	**Sai, stanno dando un nuovo film stasera. Vuoi venire con me e la mia fidanzata?**
Giorgio:	**No, grazie. In questo momento sto uscendo con Franca. Stiamo programmando di fare qualcos'altro. A presto!**
Gianni:	**Ciao!**

Exercise Set 7-4

1. a   2. a or b   3. b   4. a   5. b   6. b   7. a or b   8. b   9. a or b

Crossword Puzzle 7

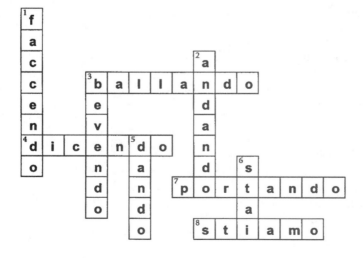

Chapter 8

Exercise Set 8-1

A.

1. **io bacio/io viaggio**	=	I kiss/I travel, etc.
2. **tu baci/tu viaggi**	=	you (fam., sing.) kiss/you travel, etc.
3. **noi baciamo/noi viaggiamo**	=	we kiss/we travel, etc.
4. **loro baciano/loro viaggiano**	=	they kiss/they travel, etc.
5. **voi baciate/voi viaggiate**	=	you (pl.) kiss/you travel, etc.
6. **Lei bacia/Lei viaggia**	=	you (pol., sing.) kiss/you travel, etc.
7. **io studio/io invio**	=	I study/I send, etc.
8. **tu studi/tu invii**	=	you study/you send, etc.
9. **io e tu studiamo/io e tu inviamo**	=	I and you study/I and you send, etc.
10. **loro studiano/loro inviano**	=	they study/they send, etc.
11. **tu e lei studiate/tu e lei inviate**	=	you and she study/you and she send, etc.
12. **lui studia/lui invia**	=	he studies/he sends, etc.
13. **io comunico/io spiego**	=	I communicate/I explain, etc.
14. **tu comunichi/tu spieghi**	=	you (fam., sing.) communicate/you explain, etc.
15. **noi comunichiamo/noi spieghiamo**	=	we communicate/we explain, etc.
16. **loro comunicano/loro spiegano**	=	they communicate/they explain, etc.
17. **voi communicate/voi spiegate**	=	you (pl.) communicate/you explain, etc.
18. **lui comunica/lui spiega**	=	he communicates/he explains, etc.

B.

1. **A che ora comincia il film?**
2. **(Io) mangio sempre (i) dolci alle feste. Che cosa mangi generalmente/di solito?**
3. **(Noi) ci abbracciamo sempre ogni volta che ci incontriamo.**
4. **Giorgio, allacci/stai allacciando la cintura di sicurezza?**
5. **Che (cosa) annunciano? / Che (cosa) stanno annuciande?**
6. **Assaggiamo/Stiamo assaggiando i dolci. Sono squisiti.**
7. **Lanciamo la palla molto bene.**
8. **Perché lasciano la scuola? È perché viaggiano molto?**
9. **Dove parcheggi la (tua) macchina generalmente/di solito?**
10. **Marco, perché cambi sempre la tua opinione?**
11. **(Io) non devio mai da studiare i verbi italiani.**
12. **Maria, che/quale e-mail invii/stai inviando alla tua amica Carla?**
13. **Franco, che (cosa) cerchi/stai cercando?**
14. **La tua opinione indica che neghi la verità.**
15. **Alessandro che fai/stai facendo? Leghi/Stai legando le (tue) scarpe?**

Exercise Set 8-2

1. **Le due persone si chiamano Carlo e Nora.**
2. **Nora cerca una matita o una penna.**
3. **Perché sta studiando e ha bisogno di scrivere qualche appunto.**
4. **Carlo ne ha alcune.**
5. **Carlo chiede a Nora: "Perché non giochi a carte con me?"**
6. **Nora non vuole giocare perché non ha tempo.**
7. **Se cambia idea, Nora chiama Carlo.**

Exercise Set 8-3

A.

1. **attraggo**	=	I attract, I am attracting
2. **attrai**	=	you (fam., sing.) attract, you are attracting
3. **attraiamo**	=	we attract, we are attracting
4. **attragono**	=	they attract, they are attracting

5. **attraete**	=	you (pl.) attract, you are attracting
6. **attrae**	=	you (pol., sing.) attract, you are attracting
7. **induco**	=	I induce, I am inducing
8. **induci**	=	you (fam., sing.) induce, you are inducing
9. **induciamo**	=	you and I induce, you and I are inducing
10. **inducono**	=	they induce, they are inducing
11. **inducete**	=	you and she induce, you and she are inducing
12. **induce**	=	he induces, he is inducing
13. **suppongo**	=	I suppose
14. **supponi**	=	you (fam., sing.) suppose
15. **supponiamo**	=	we suppose
16. **suppongono**	=	they suppose
17. **supponete**	=	you (pl.) suppose
18. **suppone**	=	she supposes

B.
1. c   2. d   3. a   4. b   5. f   6. e

Exercise Set 8-4

1. **Maria, perché ascolti quel programma radio?**
2. **Carlo aspetta la signora Smith.**
3. **Che (cosa) cerca? Cerca il suo violino.**
4. **Marco, chiedi a tua sorella di venire alla festa.**
5. **Bruno, per favore telefona al tuo professore subito.**
6. **Non so come rispondere alla Sua domanda.**
7. **Viviamo/Abitiamo in questa città da dieci anni.**
8. **Lavoro qui da lunedì.**
9. **(Lui) studia la musica da molti/tanti anni.**

Crossword Puzzle 8

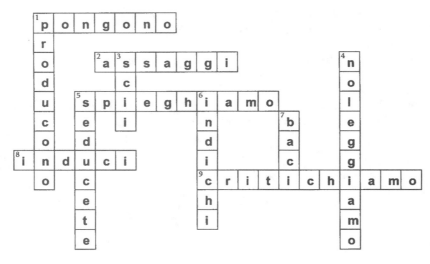

Chapter 9

Exercise Set 9-1

A.
1. **arrivato**   2. **dormito**   3. **capito**   4. **veduto/visto**   5. **creduto**   6. **lasciato**   7. **noleggiato**
8. **prodotto**   9. **supposto**   10. **apparso**   11. **bevuto**   12. **chiuso**   13. **chiesto**   14. **scelto**
15. **piaciuto**   16. **scritto**   17. **vissuto**   18. **venuto**

B.
1. **accendere**   2. **leggere**   3. **fare**   4. **essere/stare**   5. **dire**   6. **dare**   7. **correre**   8. **coprire**
9. **rispondere**   10. **morire**   11. **rompere**   12. **ridere**   13. **rimanere**   14. **prendere**   15. **scoprire**
16. **soffrire**   17. **aprire**

Exercise Set 9-2

A.
1.

ho cominciato	=	I have begun, I began
ho creduto	=	I have believed, I believed
ho dormito	=	I have slept, I slept

2.

hai cominciato	=	you (fam.) have begun, you began
hai creduto	=	you (fam.) have believed, you believed
hai dormito	=	you (fam.) have slept, you slept

3.

abbiamo cominciato	=	we have begun, we began
abbiamo creduto	=	we have believed, we believed
abbiamo dormito	=	we have slept, we slept

4.

hanno cominciato	=	they have begun, they began
hanno creduto	=	they have believed, they believed
hanno dormito	=	they have slept, they slept

5.

avete cominciato	=	you (pl.) have begun, you began
avete creduto	=	you (pl.)have believed, you believed
avete dormito	=	you (pl.)have slept, you slept

6.

ha cominciato	=	she has begun, she began
ha creduto	=	she has believed, she believed
ha dormito	=	she has slept, she slept

7.

ho messo	=	I have put, I put
ho letto	=	I have read, I read
ho scoperto	=	I have discovered, I discovered

8.

hai messo	=	you (fam.) have put, you put
hai letto	=	you (fam.) have read, you read
hai scoperto	=	you (fam.) have discovered, you discovered

9.

abbiamo messo	=	we have put, we put
abbiamo letto	=	we have read, we read
abbiamo scoperto	=	we have discovered, we discovered

10.

hanno messo	=	they have put, they put
hanno letto	=	they have read, they read
hanno scoperto	=	they have discovered, they discovered

11.

avete messo	=	you (pl.) have put, you put
avete letto	=	you (pl.) have read, you read
avete scoperto	=	you (pl.) have discovered, you discovered

12.

ha messo	=	you (pol.) have put, you put
ha letto	=	you (pol.) have read, you read
ha scoperto	=	you (pol.) have discovered, you discovered

B.

1. Maria e io non abbiamo mai guardato (abbiamo guardato mai) quel programma televisivo insieme.
2. (Loro) non hanno capito la storia che gli hai letto.
3. Paolo ha chiesto a Carla di uscire con lui, ma lei ha solo riso.
4. Il signor Dini ha noleggiato un nuovo film, ma non gli è piaciuto.
5. (Noi) abbiamo pagato il conto ieri, poiché abbiamo bevuto quasi tutto il caffè.
6. Marco, chi ti ha dato quel libro?
7. Ieri ha piovuto. Ha fatto brutto/cattivo tempo tutto il giorno/tutta la giornata.
8. (Io) ho già scritto quell'e-mail. Carla ha visto l'e-mail.
9. Franca, hai acceso il televisore? Ieri ho visto/veduto un nuovo programma.
10. Che (cosa) hanno detto (loro)? Non ho capito niente.

Exercise Set 9-3

A.

1.

sono andato/a	=	I have gone, I went
sono caduto/a	=	I have fallen, I fell
sono partito/a	=	I have left, I left

2.

sei andato/a	=	you (fam.) have gone, you went
sei caduto/a	=	you (fam.) have fallen, you fell
sei partito/a	=	you (fam.) have left, you left

3.

siamo andati/e	=	we have gone, we went
siamo caduti/e	=	we have fallen, we fell
siamo partiti/e	=	we have left, we left

4.

sono andati/e	=	they have gone, they went
sono caduti/e	=	they have fallen, they fell
sono partiti/e	=	they have left, they left

5.

siete andati/e	=	you (pl.) have gone, you went
siete caduti/e	=	you (pl.) have fallen, you fell
siete partiti/e	=	you (pl.) have left, you left

6.

è andata	=	she has gone, she went
è caduta	=	she has fallen, she fell
è partita	=	she has left, she left

7.

sono stato/a	=	I have been, I was
sono nato/a	=	I was born
sono venuto/a	=	I have come, I came

8.

sei stato/a	=	you (fam.) have been, you were
sei nato/a	=	you (fam.) were born
sei venuto/a	=	you (fam.) have come, you came

9.

siamo stati/e	=	we have been, we were
siamo nati/e	=	we were born
siamo venuti/e	=	we have come, we came

10.

sono stati/e	=	they have been, they were
sono nati/e	=	they were born
sono venuti/e	=	they have come, they came

11.

siete stati/e	=	you (pl.) have been, you were
siete nati/e	=	you (pl.) were born
siete venuti/e	=	you (pl.) have come, you came

12.

è stato/a	=	you (pol.) have been, you were
è nato/a	=	you (pol.) were born
è venuto/a	=	you (pol.) have come, you came

B.

1. I tuoi amici sono arrivati stamani, vero?
2. È vero, Maria, che tu sei stata a casa tutta la giornata ieri?
3. Loro hanno aiutato i loro amici l'intera settimana scorsa.
4. I suoi amici sono andati in Italia due anni fa. La loro vacanze è durata poco.
5. Noi siamo diventati cittadini americani qualche anno fa.
6. La sua amica ha telefonato qualche minuto fa.
7. Le sue amiche sono entrate qualche minuto fa.
8. Signora Smith, quando è stata in Italia, Lei?
9. Voi avete visto Marco?
10. A che ora siete tornati voi ieri?
11. Quei libri sono costati molto.
12. Alessandro, quanti libri hai comprato?
13. Che cosa è successo ieri a tua cugina?
14. Marco è uscito qualche minuto fa.

Exercise Set 9-4

1. Sono arrivati i nipoti di Lucia in visita.
2. I nipoti sono arrivati ieri.
3. È stata la giornata più felice della sua vita.
4. Suo nipote è diventato più alto di suo padre e sua nipote è diventata la ragazza più intelligente del mondo.
5. Il nipote è nato quasi dieci anni fa e la nipote è nata quasi sei anni fa.

Exercise Set 9-5

A.

1. mi sono divertito/a	=	I have enjoyed myself, I enjoyed myself
2. ti sei divertito/a	=	you (fam.) have enjoyed yourself, you enjoyed yourself
3. ci siamo divertiti/e	=	we have enjoyed ourselves, we enjoyed ourselves
4. si sono divertiti/e	=	they have enjoyed themselves, they enjoyed themselves
5. vi siete divertiti/e	=	you (pl.) have enjoyed yourself, you enjoyed yourself
6. si è divertita	=	she has enjoyed herself, she enjoyed herself

B.

1. Maria ti è piaciuto quel nuovo film/film nuovo? Non mi è piaciuto affatto!
2. Mi sono sempre piaciuti gli spaghetti.
3. Le è piaciuto molto Paolo, ma lei non è piaciuta a lui.
4. Io gli sono piaciuto/a, ma mia sorella non gli è piaciuta.
5. C'è stato Marco?/È stato qui Marco?
6. C'è stata Claudia?/È stata qui Claudia?
7. Ci sono stati Marco e Claudia?/Sono stati qui Marco e Claudia?
8. Ieri mi sono messo/a la giacca, i guanti, e gli stivali. Ha fatto molto freddo!
9. Mi sono vestito/a in uno stile nuovo perché mi hanno invitato alla loro festa.

Exercise Set 9-6

1. **Paolo l'ha sempre detta.**
2. **Bruno vi ha chiamato (chiamati) ieri, vero?**
3. **Mi hanno invitato/a alla festa!**
4. **Paola ti ha chiamato/a poco tempo fa.**
5. **Io l'ho comprato in quel negozio in via Nazionale.**
6. **Anche tu li hai comprati nello stesso negozio, vero?**
7. **Lui l'ha mangiata volentieri.**
8. **Lei le ha già assaggiate.**
9. **Noi l'abbiamo letta.**

Exercise Set 9-7

1. **(Noi) sappiamo che lui esce/sta uscendo con Maria.**
2. **Abbiamo saputo che lui esce/sta uscendo con Maria.**
3. **Ho conosciuto il mio/la mia insegnante d'italiano l'anno scorso.**
4. **Conosco tuo fratello molto bene. L'ho conosciuto molti anni fa.**
5. **Sono partiti/e per l'Italia stamani/questa mattina.**
6. **La tua amica ha chiamato questo pomeriggio.**
7. **(Loro) sono andati al cinema ieri sera.**
8. **L'ho già fatto/Ho già fatto quello.**
9. **Mio fratello è appena arrivato.**
10. **I miei genitori sono venuti in America qualche anno fa/alcuni anni fa.**

Crossword Puzzle 9

Chapter 10

Exercise Set 10-1

A.

1. **io andavo, mettevo, dormivo**	=	I was going, putting, sleeping, I used to go, put, sleep
2. **tu andavi, mettevi, dormivi**	=	you (fam.) were going, putting, sleeping, you used to go, put, sleep
3. **noi andavamo, mettevamo, dormivamo**	=	we were going, putting, sleeping, we used to go, put, sleep
4. **loro andavano, mettevano, dormivano**	=	they were going, putting, sleeping, they used to go, put, sleep
5. **voi andavate, mettevate, dormivate**	=	you (pl.) were going, putting, sleeping, you used to go, put, sleep

6. **Lei andava, metteva, dormiva** = you (pol.) were going, putting, sleeping, you used to go, put, sleep

7. **io baciavo, noleggiavo, mi vestivo** = I was kissing, renting, dressing myself, I used to kiss, rent, dress myself

8. **tu baciavi, noleggiavi, ti vestivi** = you (fam.) were kissing, renting, dressing yourself, you used to kiss, rent, dress yourself

9. **noi baciavamo, noleggiavamo, ci vestivamo** = we were kissing, renting, dressing ourselves, we used to kiss, rent, dress ourselves

10. **loro baciavano, noleggiavano, si vestivano** = they were kissing, renting, dressing themselves, they used to kiss, rent, dress themselves

11. **voi baciavate, noleggiavate, vi vestivate** = you (pl.) were kissing, renting, dressing yourselves, you used to kiss, rent, dress yourselves

12. **lei baciava, noleggiava, si vestiva** = she was kissing, renting, dressing herself, she used to kiss, rent, dress herself

B.
1. **io suonavo il pianoforte.**
2. **tu cantavi molto bene.**
3. **mio fratello andava al cinema spesso.**
4. **ci alzavamo tardi il sabato.**
5. **voi guardavate molto la televisione.**
6. **i suoi amici giocavano a calcio.**
7. **io mangiavo pasta spesso.**
8. **il signor Tartini andava spesso in spiaggia.**
9. **si divertivano dopo (la) scuola.**
10. **c'era sempre molto da fare.**
11. **c'erano sempre tante cose da fare.**
12. **aspettavo ansiosamente i miei programmi televisivi il sabato.**

Exercise Set 10-2

1. **Rina ha telefonato a Franca.**
2. **Franca sta non male.**
3. **Rina sta assai bene.**
4. **Ieri Rina pensava a Franca.**
5. **Nella sua famiglia parlavano di quando (le due donne) vivevano vicino di casa.**
6. **Sono passati troppi anni.**
7. **Le due donne uscivano insieme molte/tante volte.**

Exercise Set 10-3

A.
1. **io bevevo, davo, dicevo** = I was drinking, giving, saying, I used to drink, give, say

2. **tu bevevi, davi, dicevi** = you (fam.) were drinking, giving, saying, you used to drink, give, say

3. **noi bevevamo, davamo, dicevamo** = we were drinking, giving, saying, we used to drink, give, say

4. **loro bevevano, davano, dicevano** = they were drinking, giving, saying, they used to drink, give, say

5. **voi bevevate, davate, dicevate** = you (pl.) were drinking, giving, saying, you used to drink, give, say

6. **lei beveva, dava, diceva** = she was drinking, giving, saying, she used to drink, give, say

7. **io ero, facevo, stavo** = I was, I was doing, staying, I used to be, do, stay

8. **tu eri, facevi, stavi**	=	you (fam.) were, you were doing, staying, you used to be, do, stay
9. **noi eravamo, facevamo, stavamo**	=	we were, we were doing, staying, we used to be, do, stay
10. **loro erano, facevano, stavano**	=	they were, they were doing, staying, they used to be, do, stay
11. **voi eravate, facevate, stavate**	=	you (pl.) were, you were doing, staying, you used to be, do, stay
12. **lei era, faceva, stava**	=	she was, she was doing, staying, she used to be, do, stay
13. **io producevo, attraevo, supponevo**	=	I was producing, attracting, supposing, I used to produce, attract, suppose
14. **tu producevi, attraevi, supponevi**	=	you (fam.) were producing, attracting, supposing, you used to produce, attract, suppose
15. **noi producevamo, attraevamo, supponevamo**	=	we were producing, attracting, supposing, we used to produce, attract, suppose
16. **loro producevano, attraevano, supponevano**	=	they were producing, attracting, supposing, they used to produce, attract, suppose
17. **voi producevate, attraevate, supponevate**	=	you (pl.) were producing, attracting, supposing, you used to produce, attract, suppose
18. **lui produceva, attraeva, supponeva**	=	he was producing, attracting, supposing, he used to produce, attract, suppose

B.
1. **(io) bevevo il latte ogni giorno.**
2. **(tu) davi via molti giocattoli.**
3. **mio fratello diceva sempre la verità.**
4. **i miei amici ed io eravamo molto felici.**
5. **(voi) stavate a casa spesso.**
6. **faceva bel tempo quasi ogni giorno.**
7. **le mie sorelle facevano molte cose strane.**
8. **(io) ero molto studioso/a.**
9. **(tu) eri spesso triste.**

Exercise Set 10-4

1. **io stavo andando**   2. **tu stavi cominciando**   3. **noi stavamo scrivendo**   4. **loro stavano leggendo**   5. **voi stavate preferendo**   6. **lei stava dormendo**   7. **io stavo producendo**   8. **tu stavi bevendo**   9. **noi stavamo dando**   10. **loro stavano facendo**   11. **voi stavate supponendo**   12. **lui stava studiando**

Exercise Set 10-5

1. **Mentre tuo fratello suonava il violoncello, io dormivo.**
2. **Quando erano in Italia, volevano sempre andare al mare.**
3. **Da giovane, sapevo parlare (lo) spagnolo.**
4. **Mia sorella era bionda da bambina.**
5. **Quando (io) ero molto giovane, credevo a tutto quello che mi diceva mio fratello.**
6. **(Loro) preferivano sempre andare al cinema anni fa, ma io non volevo mai andare.**
7. **(Noi) mangiavamo di solito alle sei (alle diciotto) ogni sera.**
8. **Sarah non ha mai detto che voleva venire alla festa.**
9. **(Noi) ci alzavamo presto la mattina e, dunque, ci addormentavamo verso le sette (le diciannove) la sera.**

Crossword Puzzle 10

```
 1        2    3    4
 a  n  d  a  v  a  n  o
 l     o     e     o
 z     r     n  5
             l  a  v  o  r  a  v  o
 a     m     i     e
 v     l     v  6
             g  i  o  c  a  v  a
 a     v     a     g
 n     a           i        7
                            d
 o     m        8
                a  m  a  v  a     a
             v              v
          9
          p  o  r  t  a  v  a  n  o
```

Chapter 11

Exercise Set 11-1

A.

1. **io avevo mangiato, avevo creduto, avevo capito**	=	I had eaten, believed, understood
2. **tu avevi mangiato, avevi creduto, avevi capito**	=	you (fam.) had eaten, believed, understood
3. **noi avevamo mangiato, avevamo creduto, avevamo capito**	=	we had eaten, believed, understood
4. **loro avevano mangiato, avevano creduto, avevano capito**	=	they had eaten, believed, understood
5. **voi avevate mangiato, avevate creduto, avevate capito**	=	you (pl.) had eaten, believed, understood
6. **Lei aveva mangiato, aveva creduto, aveva capito**	=	you (fam.) had eaten, believed, understood
7. **io ero andato/a, ero nato/a, mi ero vestito/a**	=	I had gone, had been born, had dressed myself
8. **tu eri andato/a, eri nato/a, ti eri vestito/a**	=	you (fam.) had gone, had been born, had dressed yourself
9. **noi eravamo andati/e, eravamo nati/e, ci eravamo vestiti/e**	=	we had gone, had been born, had dressed ourselves
10. **loro erano andati/e, erano nati/e, si erano vestiti/e**	=	they had gone, had been born, had dressed themselves
11. **voi eravate andati/e, eravate nati/e, vi eravate vestiti/e**	=	you (pl.) had gone, had been born, had dressed yourselves
12. **lei era andata, era nata, si era vestita**	=	she had gone, had been born, had dressed herself

B.

1. **(Loro) avevano già mangiato, quando (lei) è arrivata.**
2. **(Io) mi ero già alzato/a, quando (tu) mi hai chiamato.**
3. **Da bambina, (lei) poteva guardare la televisione, solo dopo che aveva studiato.**
4. **Dopo che (tu) eri uscito/a, (lui) è finalmente arrivato.**
5. **Ero sicuro/a che tu lo avevi già fatto.**
6. **Bruno ha detto che aveva già visto/veduto quei film. Ed è vero. Li aveva già veduti/visti.**
7. **Nora voleva uscire solo dopo che aveva finito di guardare il suo programma preferito.**
8. **La signora Santini ha indicato che (lei) aveva appena letto quel romanzo. Ha detto che non era valso la pena.**

9. **Tutti erano contenti che tu avevi deciso di venire alla festa.**
10. **Dopo che avevano fatto delle spese, le due amiche sono andate al cinema.**

Exercise Set 11-2

1. **Sì, è vero che Maria ed Elena erano uscite insieme ieri.**
2. **Erano andate al cinema.**
3. **Tutti avevano detto che il film non valeva niente.**
4. **Elena aveva detto a Carla che voleva uscire con lei per fare delle spese.**
5. **Maria si era dimenticata di uscire con Carla.**

Exercise Set 11-3

1. a   2. a   3. a or b   4. a   5. b   6. b   7. a

Crossword Puzzle 11

```
¹a v ²e v ³a n o
 b    r    v
 b    a    e
 i    v    t
 a    a   ⁴e r ⁵a n o
 m    t        v
 o    e      ⁶s e i
                v
            ⁷h a n n o
                n
⁸e r a v a m o
```

Chapter 12

Exercise Set 12-1

A.

1. io viaggiai, credei (credetti), capii	=	I traveled, believed, understood
2. tu viaggiasti, credesti, capisti	=	you (fam., sing.) traveled, believed, understood
3. noi viaggiammo, credemmo, capimmo	=	we traveled, believed, understood
4. loro viaggiarono, crederono (credettero), capirono	=	they traveled, believed, understood
5. voi viaggiaste, credeste, capiste	=	you (pl.) traveled, believed, understood
6. Lei viaggiò, credé (credette), capì	=	you (pol., sing.) traveled, believed, understood
7. io mi vestii	=	I dressed myself
8. tu ti vestisti	=	you (fam., sing.) dressed yourself
9. noi ci vestimmo	=	we dressed ourselves
10. loro si vestirono	=	they dressed themselves
11. voi vi vestiste	=	you (pl.) dressed yourselves
12. lei si vestì	=	she dressed herself

B.

1. **i miei genitori arrivarano dall'Italia.**
2. **(io) passai un anno a Roma.**
3. **(tu) andasti in Italia.**
4. **suo figlio diventò un ingegnere.**

5. sua figlia finì di studiare (la) medicina.
6. (noi) scoprimmo l'Italia.
7. (loro) si sposarono a Firenze.
8. i nostri amici lavorarono per quella ditta.
9. (io) diventai un cittadino/una cittadina americano/a.

C.
1. Gioacchino Rossini compose *Il Barbiere di Siviglia*.
2. Guglielmo Marconi inventò la radio.
3. Cristofero Colombo scoprì il "Nuovo Mondo".
4. Scoprì il "Nuovo Mondo" nel 1492.
5. Robert E. Peary andò al Polo Nord per la prima volta.
6. Giuseppe Verdi compose *la Traviata*.

Exercise Set 12-2

1. Stasera il telequiz è all'ultima tappa.
2. Ci sono tre domande.
3. Chi indovina le tre domande vince il premio.
4. Roald Amundsen andò al Polo Sud per la prima volta.
5. Thomas Edison costruì la prima lampadina.
6. Johannes Gutenberg inventò la stampa.

Exercise Set 12-3

A.
1. ebbi   2. avesti   3. conobbe   4. conoscemmo   5. lesse   6. leggemmo   7. mi piacque
8. sapeste   9. seppero   10. scrissi   11. scrivesti   12. venne   13. venimmo   14. volle   15. voleste
16. apparvero/apparirono   17. appersero/aprirono   18. chiusi   19. comprese
20. copersero/coprirono

B.
1. Io fui in Italia due anni fa.
2. Lui decise di andare in Italia l'anno scorso.
3. Lei si mise la giacca ieri.
4. Loro nacquero in Italia.
5. Io presi una nuova decisione.
6. Lui rimase tre giorni con noi.
7. Maria ruppe il vaso.
8. Marco non rise quando dicesti quella barzelletta.
9. Loro scelsero di andare in Italia.
10. Io tenni quel bambino per mano tutto il giorno.
11. Non valse la pena di vedere quel film.
12. Quella squadra vinse lo scudetto nel 2001.
13. Lei tradusse tutto quel libro.
14. Noi bevemmo solo un caffè ciascuno.
15. Loro dissero la verità, secondo me.
16. Fece brutto tempo l'inverno scorso.
17. A chi desti quel libro?
18. Fummo in Italia molti anni fa.

Exercise Set 12-4

1. Quella squadra vinse lo scudetto nel 1948.
2. Lui disse quello tanti anni fa.
3. Loro vennero in America da bambini.
4. Scrisse un romanzo nel 1994.

5. **Loro andarono in Italia l'estate scorsa.**
6. **Bruno lesse quel libro nel 1998.**
7. **Quelle due amiche si conobbero nell'estate del 1980.**

Crossword Puzzle 12

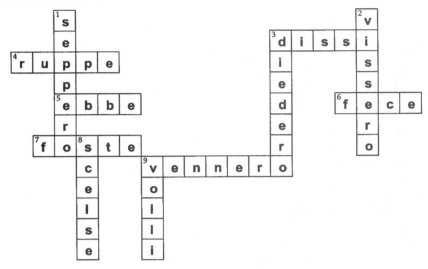

Chapter 13

Exercise Set 13-1

A.

1.

io arriverò	=	I will arrive
io crederò	=	I will believe
io dormirò	=	I will sleep

2.

tu arriverai	=	you (fam., sing.) will arrive
tu crederai	=	you (fam., sing.) will believe
tu dormirai	=	you (fam., sing.) will sleep

3.

noi arriveremo	=	we will arrive
noi crederemo	=	we will believe
noi dormiremo	=	we will sleep

4.

loro arriveranno	=	they will arrive
loro crederanno	=	they will believe
loro dormiranno	=	they will sleep

5.

voi arriverete	=	you (pl.) will arrive
voi crederete	=	you (pl.) will believe
voi dormirete	=	you (pl.) will sleep

6.

lei arriverà	=	she will arrive
lei crederà	=	she will believe
lei dormirà	=	she will sleep

7.

io bacerò	=	I will kiss
io noleggerò	=	I will rent
io comunicherò	=	I will communicate
io spiegherò	=	I will explain

8.

tu bacerai	=	you (fam., sing.) will kiss
tu noleggerai	=	you (fam., sing.) will rent
tu comunicherai	=	you (fam., sing.) will communicate
tu spiegherai	=	you (fam., sing.) will explain

9.

noi baceremo	=	we will kiss
noi noleggeremo	=	we will rent
noi comunicheremo	=	we will communicate
noi spiegheremo	=	we will explain

10.

loro baceranno	=	they will kiss
loro noleggeranno	=	they will rent
loro comunicheranno	=	they will communicate
loro spiegheranno	=	they will explain

11.

voi bacerete	=	you (pl.) will kiss
voi noleggerete	=	you (pl.) will rent
voi comunicherete	=	you (pl.) will communicate
voi spiegherete	=	you (pl.) will explain

12.

Lei bacerà	=	you (pol., sing.) will kiss
Lei noleggerà	=	you (pol., sing.) will rent
Lei comunicherà	=	you (pol., sing.) will communicate
Lei spiegherà	=	you (pol., sing.) will explain

13.

io leggerò	=	I will read
io capirò	=	I will understand
io produrrò	=	I will produce
io mi divertirò	=	I will have fun/enjoy myself

14.

tu leggerai	=	you (fam., sing.) will read
tu capirai	=	you (fam., sing.) will understand
tu produrrai	=	you (fam., sing.) will produce
tu ti divertirai	=	you (fam., sing.) will have fun/enjoy yourself

15.

noi leggeremo	=	we will read
noi capiremo	=	we will understand
noi produrremo	=	we will produce
noi ci divertiremo	=	we will have fun/enjoy ourselves

16.

loro leggeranno	=	they will read
loro capiranno	=	they will understand
loro produrranno	=	they will produce
loro si divertiranno	=	they will have fun/enjoy themselves

17.

voi leggerete	=	you (pl.) will read
voi capirete	=	you (pl.) will understand
voi produrrete	=	you (pl.) will produce
voi vi divertirete	=	you (pl.) will have fun/enjoy yourselves

18.

lui leggerà	=	he will read
lui capirà	=	he will understand
lui produrrà	=	he will produce
lui si divertirà	=	he will have fun/enjoy himself

B.

1. **Quel programma televisivo comincerà alle sei della sera (alle diciotto) e finirà alle nove della sera (alle ventuno).**
2. **Ci sarà molta gente (Ci saranno molte persone) alla festa.**
3. **(Io) so che non le piacerà quel film.**
4. **(Io) sono sicuro/a che tu gli piacerai** *(that you will be pleasing to them)*, **Alessandro.**
5. **Pagheremo noi al Bar Roma, se tu mangerai quello che diciamo noi.**
6. **(Lui) ha detto che ci sarà anche lei.**
7. **Domani Maria ed io usciremo insieme.**
8. **(Io) so di sicuro/per sicuro che voi due vi sposerete.**
9. **(Io) mi alzerò tardi domani perché è (sarà) domenica.**

Exercise Set 13-2

1. **Marco si trova dalla (da una) chiromante.**
2. **Secondo la chiromante, Marco amerà solo una donna nella sua vita.**
3. **No, la chiromante non glielo rivelerà (non rivelerà il nome della donna a Marco).**
4. **Marco amerà la donna dei suoi sogni fedelmente.**
5. **Marco la conoscerà fra qualche giorno.**
6. **Secondo Marco, conoscere il futuro costerà molto.**

Exercise Set 13-3

A.

1.

io avrò	=	I will have
io darò	=	I will give
io porrò	=	I will pose
io rimarrò	=	I will remain

2.

tu avrai	=	you (fam., sing.) will have
tu darai	=	you (fam., sing.) will give
tu porrai	=	you (fam., sing.) will pose
tu rimarrai	=	you (fam., sing.) will remain

3.

noi avremo	=	we will have
noi daremo	=	we will give
noi porremo	=	we will pose
noi rimarremo	=	we will remain

4.

loro avranno	=	they will have
loro daranno	=	they will give
loro porranno	=	they will pose
loro rimarranno	=	they will remain

5.

voi avrete	=	you (pl.) will have
voi darete	=	you (pl.) will give
voi porrete	=	you (pl.) will pose
voi rimarrete	=	you (pl.) will remain

6.

lei avrà	=	she will have
lei darà	=	she will give
lei porrà	=	she will pose
lei rimarrà	=	she will remain

7.

io vorrò	=	I will want to
io verrò	=	I will come
io sarò	=	I will be
io berrò	=	I will drink

8.

tu vorrai	=	you (fam., sing.) will want to
tu verrai	=	you (fam., sing.) will come
tu sarai	=	you (fam., sing.) will be
tu berrai	=	you (fam., sing.) will drink

9.

noi vorremo	=	we will want to
noi verremo	=	we will come
noi saremo	=	we will be
noi berremo	=	we will drink

10.

loro vorranno	=	they will want to
loro verranno	=	they will come
loro saranno	=	they will be
loro berranno	=	they will drink

11.

voi vorrete	=	you (pl.) will want to
voi verrete	=	you (pl.) will come
voi sarete	=	you (pl.) will be
voi berrete	=	you (pl.) will drink

12.

lui vorrà	=	he will want to
lui verrà	=	he will come
lui sarà	=	he will be
lui berrà	=	he will drink

B.

1. **saprò**   2. **attrarrò**   3. **comporrò**   4. **starò**   5. **farò**   6. **dirò**   7. **vedrò**   8. **potrò**   9. **dovrò**

Exercise Set 13-4

A.

1. e   2. f   3. d   4. g   5. h   6. i   7. b   8. c   9. a

B.

Carla comincerà a lavorare per una nuova ditta tra qualche settimana (alcune settimane). Le piace il suo lavoro attuale (il suo attuale lavoro), ma le piacerà ancora di più quello nuovo (il suo nuovo lavoro). Purtroppo, (lei) dovrà traslocare. Dove andrà? Traslocherà (probabilmente) vicino al suo posto di lavoro.

Nel frattempo, affitterà un appartamento vicino al lavoro. Dovrà comprare (Avrà bisogno di comprare) una nuova macchina (una nuova automobile) e non ci potrà visitare (probabilmente) molto spesso. Sappiamo, comunque, che si divertirà molto nella sua nuova vita.

Crossword Puzzle 13

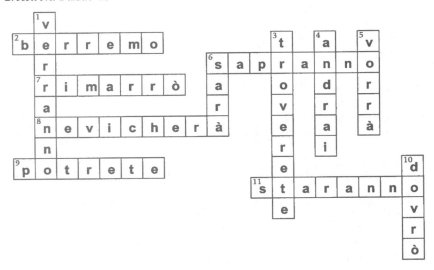

Chapter 14

Exercise Set 14-1

A.

1.

io avrò cominciato	=	I will have begun
io avrò creduto	=	I will have believed
io avrò capito	=	I will have understood
io avrò fatto	=	I will have made

2.

tu avrai cominciato	=	you (fam.) will have begun
tu avrai creduto	=	you (fam.) will have believed
tu avrai capito	=	you (fam.) will have understood
tu avrai fatto	=	you (fam.) will have made

3.

noi avremo cominciato	=	we will have begun
noi avremo creduto	=	we will have believed
noi avremo capito	=	we will have understood
noi avremo fatto	=	we will have made

4.

loro avranno cominciato	=	they will have begun
loro avranno creduto	=	they will have believed
loro avranno capito	=	they will have understood
loro avranno fatto	=	they will have made

5.

voi avrete cominciato	=	you (pl.) will have begun
voi avrete creduto	=	you (pl.) will have believed
voi avrete capito	=	you (pl.) will have understood
voi avrete fatto	=	you (pl.) will have made

6.

lei avrà cominciato	=	she will have begun
lei avrà creduto	=	she will have believed
lei avrà capito	=	she will have understood
lei avrà fatto	=	she will have made

7.

io sarò andato/a	=	I will have gone
io sarò venuto/a	=	I will have come
io sarò stato/a	=	I will have been
io mi sarò messo/a	=	I will have put on

8.

tu sarai andato/a	=	you (fam.) will have gone
tu sarai venuto/a	=	you (fam.) will have come
tu sarai stato/a	=	you (fam.) will have been
tu ti sarai messo/a	=	you (fam.) will have put on

9.

noi saremo andati/e	=	we will have gone
noi saremo venuti/e	=	we will have come
noi saremo stati/e	=	we will have been
noi ci saremo messi/e	=	we will have put on

10.

loro saranno andati/e	=	they will have gone
loro saranno venuti/e	=	they will have come
loro saranno stati/e	=	they will have been
loro si saranno messi/e	=	they will have put on

11.

voi sarete andati/e	=	you (pl.) will have gone
voi sarete venuti/e	=	you (pl.) will have come
voi sarete stati/e	=	you (pl.) will have been
voi vi sarete messi/e	=	you (pl.) will have put on

12.

Lei sarà andato/a	=	you (pol.) will have gone
Lei sarà venuto/a	=	you (pol.) will have come
Lei sarà stato/a	=	you (pol.) will have been
Lei si sarà messo/a	=	you (pol.) will have put on

B.

1. **Dopo che saranno arrivati/e, andremo al cinema insieme.**
2. **Quando si saranno sposati, andranno in Italia.**
3. **(Io) uscirò oggi, solo dopo che avrò studiato un po'.**
4. **Appena (lui) avrà finito di leggere quel libro, sono sicuro/a che ne comincerà un altro.**
5. **Dopo che quella squadra avrà vinto (probabilmente) il campionato, (io) sarò molto contento/a (felice).**
6. **Quando avrà traslocato nel suo nuovo appartamento, dove lavorerà, signor Smith?**
7. **Quella macchina/Quell'automobile sarà costata molti/tanti soldi!**
8. **(Lui) sarà già uscito.**
9. **Quando arriverà (arriva), saranno già andati/e a casa.**

Exercise Set 14-2

1. **Franca pensa che gli invitati si saranno dimenticati di venire alla festa.**
2. **Paola le risponde che (gli invitati) avranno smesso di lavorare tardi.**
3. **Secondo Paola, Franca deve imparare ad avere pazienza.**
4. **Le due amiche avranno mangiato tutto.**
5. **Dovranno controllare il loro appetito.**
6. **Perché altrimenti tutto il cibo sarà veramente finito.**

Exercise Set 14-3

1. **avrò finito**   2. **sarà uscito**   3. **arriverà**   4. **andrete**   5. **verranno**   6. **sarà andata**   7. **si saranno alzati**   8. **avranno visto/veduto**   9. **avrai assaggiato**

Crossword Puzzle 14

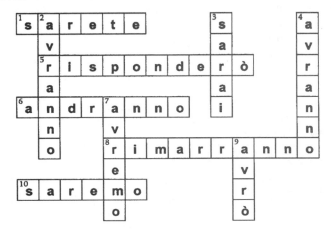

Chapter 15

Exercise Set 15-1

A.

1.

io comprerei	=	I would buy
io metterei	=	I would put
io dormirei	=	I would sleep
io mi laverei	=	I would wash myself

2.

tu compreresti	=	you (fam., sing.) would buy
tu metteresti	=	you (fam., sing.) would put
tu dormiresti	=	you (fam., sing.) would sleep
tu ti laveresti	=	you (fam., sing.) would wash yourself

3.

noi compreremmo	=	we would buy
noi metteremmo	=	we would put
noi dormiremmo	=	we would sleep
noi ci laveremmo	=	we would wash ourselves

4.

loro comprerebbero	=	they would buy
loro metterebbero	=	they would put
loro dormirebbero	=	they would sleep
loro si laverebbero	=	they would wash themselves

5.

voi comprereste	=	you (pl.) would buy
voi mettereste	=	you (pl.) would put
voi dormireste	=	you (pl.) would sleep
voi vi lavereste	=	you (pl.) would wash yourselves

6.

lei comprerebbe	=	she would buy
lei metterebbe	=	she would put
lei dormirebbe	=	she would sleep
lei si laverebbe	=	she would wash herself

7.

io bacerei	=	I would kiss
io noleggerei	=	I would rent
io comunicherei	=	I would communicate
io spiegherei	=	I would explain

8.

tu baceresti	=	you (fam., sing.) would kiss
tu noleggeresti	=	you (fam., sing.) would rent
tu comunicheresti	=	you (fam., sing.) would communicate
tu spiegheresti	=	you (fam., sing.) would explain

9.

noi baceremmo	=	we would kiss
noi noleggeremmo	=	we would rent
noi comunicheremmo	=	we would communicate
noi spiegheremmo	=	we would explain

10.

loro bacerebbero	=	they would kiss
loro noleggerebbero	=	they would rent
loro comunicherebbero	=	they would communicate
loro spiegherebbero	=	they would explain

11.

voi bacereste	=	you (pl.) would kiss
voi noleggereste	=	you (pl.) would rent
voi comunichereste	=	you (pl.) would communicate
voi spieghereste	=	you (pl.) would explain

12.

Lei bacerebbe	=	you (pol., sing.) would kiss
Lei noleggerebbe	=	you (pol., sing.) would rent
Lei comunicherebbe	=	you (pol., sing.) would communicate
Lei spiegherebbe	=	you (pol., sing.) would explain

B.

1. **io pagherei**   2. **tu risponderesti**   3. **lui capirebbe**   4. **lei produrrebbe**   5. **noi baceremmo**
6. **voi vi sposereste**   7. **loro scierebbero**   8. **io assaggerei**   9. **tu giocheresti**

C.

1. **(Io) parlerei l'italiano di più, ma prima devo/dovrò studiare i verbi.**
2. **È vero che tu studieresti lo spagnolo invece dell'italiano?**
3. **Il mio amico si alzerebbe più presto la mattina, ma è sempre molto stanco.**
4. **Noi pagheremmo volentieri per il caffè, ma non abbiamo soldi.**
5. **Mi aiutereste a capire la grammatica italiana, per favore?**
6. **(Io) so che loro capirebbero/comprenderebbero quello che stai facendo.**
7. **(Io) guarderei quel programma televisivo, ma non ho tempo.**
8. **Le piacerebbero quelle paste di sicuro.**
9. **Gli piacerebbe di più quella squadra, ma non vince mai.**

Exercise Set 15-2

1. **Antonio chiede a Giorgio: "Ti piacerebbe uscire stasera."**
   or with indirect speech:
   Antonio chiede a Giorgio se gli piacerebbe uscire.
2. **Giorgio risponde: "Mi piacerebbe ma non posso."**
   or with indirect speech:
   Giorgio risponde che gli piacerebbe uscire.
3. **Giorgio non può uscire perché deve studiare.**
4. **Allora Antonio dice: "Saresti libero domani?"**
5. **Giorgio preferirebbe andare al bar domani.**

Exercise Set 15-3

1. **noi andremmo**　2. **tu avresti**　3. **lui saprebbe**　4. **lei potrebbe**　5. **noi cadremmo**　6. **voi vedreste**　7. **loro darebbero**　8. **io starei**　9. **tu diresti**　10. **loro comporrebbero**　11. **tu trarresti**　12. **noi berremmo**　13. **voi sareste**　14. **lui rimarrebbe**　15. **loro verrebbero**　16. **lei vorrebbe**

Exercise Set 15-4

1. **(Loro) andrebbero volentieri al bar, ma non hanno tempo.**
2. **Signora Smith, mi potrebbe aiutare/potrebbe aiutarmi?**
3. **Chi vorrebbe un caffè?**
4. **Franco ha detto che (loro) arriverebbero domani.**
5. **Quanto costerebbe quella nuova macchina/automobile?**
6. **Nella sua opinione, quel ragazzo sarebbe italiano.**
7. **Secondo lui, lei sarebbe americana.**
8. **(Loro) potrebbero venire un po' più tardi, no?**
9. **(Lei) non dovrebbe fare quello.**
10. **Signor Smith, vorrebbe un cappuccino?**

Crossword Puzzle 15

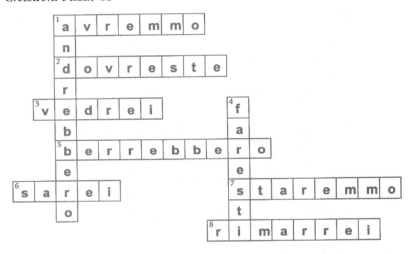

Chapter 16

Exercise Set 16-1

A.
1.

io avrei cominciato	=	I would have begun
io avrei creduto	=	I would have believed
io avrei capito	=	I would have understood
io avrei fatto	=	I would have made

2.

tu avresti cominciato	=	you (fam.) would have begun
tu avresti creduto	=	you (fam.) would have believed
tu avresti capito	=	you (fam.) would have understood
tu avresti fatto	=	you (fam.) would have made

3.

noi avremmo cominciato	=	we would have begun
noi avremmo creduto	=	we would have believed
noi avremmo capito	=	we would have understood
noi avremmo fatto	=	we would have made

4.

loro avrebbero cominciato	=	they would have begun
loro avrebbero creduto	=	they would have believed
loro avrebbero capito	=	they would have understood
loro avrebbero fatto	=	they would have made

5.

voi avreste cominciato	=	you (pl.) would have begun
voi avreste creduto	=	you (pl.) would have believed
voi avreste capito	=	you (pl.) would have understood
voi avreste fatto	=	you (pl.) would have made

6.

lei avrebbe cominciato	=	she would have begun
lei avrebbe creduto	=	she would have believed
lei avrebbe capito	=	she would have understood
lei avrebbe fatto	=	she would have made

7.

io sarei andato/a	=	I would have gone
io sarei venuto/a	=	I would have come
io sarei stato/a	=	I would have been
io mi sarei messo/a	=	I would have put on

8.

tu saresti andato/a	=	you (fam.) would have gone
tu saresti venuto/a	=	you (fam.) would have come
tu saresti stato/a	=	you (fam.) would have been
tu ti saresti messo/a	=	you (fam.) would have put on

9.

noi saremmo andati/e	=	we would have gone
noi saremmo venuti/e	=	we would have come
noi saremmo stati/e	=	we would have been
noi ci saremmo messi/e	=	we would have put on

10.

loro sarebbero andati/e	=	they would have gone
loro sarebbero venuti/e	=	they would have come
loro sarebbero stati/e	=	they would have been
loro si sarebbero messi/e	=	they would have put on

11.

voi sareste andati/e	=	you (pl.) would have gone
voi sareste venuti/e	=	you (pl.) would have come
voi sareste stati/e	=	you (pl.) would have been
voi vi sareste messi/e	=	you (pl.) would have put on

12.

Lei sarebbe andato/a	=	you (pol.) would have gone
Lei sarebbe venuto/a	=	you (pol.) would have come
Lei sarebbe stato/a	=	you (pol.) would have been
Lei si sarebbe messo/a	=	you (pol.) would have put on

B.

1. (Io) sarei andato/a alla festa, ma non avevo tempo.
2. I miei genitori sarebbero andati in Italia l'anno scorso, ma non avevano i soldi.
3. (Io) sarei uscito/a con lui, ma dovevo studiare.
4. Di solito, avrei fatto quello io stesso/a, ma questa volta ha deciso lei di farlo.
5. Anche loro si sarebbero alzati presto ieri, ma si sono dimenticati.
6. (Noi) ci saremmo sposati prima, ma non avevamo abbastanza soldi per il matrimonio.
7. (Lui) avrebbe comprato quella macchina/automobile, ma costava troppo.

Exercise Set 16-2

1. **Sandra sarebbe andata in Italia l'estate scorsa.**
2. **Sandra è stata da sua nonna tutto il tempo.**
3. **Secondo Tina, Sandra sarebbe dovuta andare a vedere le città più famose.**
4. **Sandra non è andata perché non avrebbe avuto abbastanza tempo.**
5. **Perché sua nonna l'ha portata in giro dappertutto.**

Exercise Set 16-3

1. **Lei mi ha indicato che loro sarebbero venuti alla festa, ma dovevano lavorare.**
2. **(Lui) sapeva che lei avrebbe capito tutto.**
3. **(Noi) potremmo farlo/lo potremmo fare, ma non (ne) abbiamo voglia.**
4. **(Lui) avrebbe potuto farlo/lo avrebbe potuto fare, ma non (ne) aveva voglia.**
5. **(Loro) vorrebbero farlo/lo vorrebbero fare, ma non hanno tempo.**
6. **(Loro) avrebbero voluto farlo/lo avrebbero voluto fare, ma non avevano tempo.**
7. **(Tu) dovresti farlo/lo dovresti fare, nonostante quello che dicono.**
8. **(Tu) avresti dovuto farlo/lo avresti dovuto fare, nonostante quello che dicevano.**

Crossword Puzzle 16

Chapter 17

Exercise Set 17-1

A.

1. **io arrivi, baci, noleggi, indichi, spieghi**	= I arrive, kiss, rent, indicate, explain
2. **tu arrivi, baci, noleggi, indichi, spieghi**	= you (fam., sing.) arrive, kiss, rent, indicate, explain
3. **noi arriviamo, baciamo, noleggiamo, indichiamo, spieghiamo**	= we arrive, kiss, rent, indicate, explain
4. **loro arrivino, bacino, noleggino, indichino, spieghino**	= they arrive, kiss, rent, indicate, explain
5. **voi arriviate, baciate, noleggiate, indichiate, spieghiate**	= you (pl.) arrive, kiss, rent, indicate, explain
6. **lei arrivi, baci, noleggi, indichi, spieghi**	= she arrive(s), kiss(es), rent(s), indicate(s), explain(s)
7. **io legga, parta, capisca, mi diverta**	= I read, leave, understand, have fun

8. **tu legga, parta, capisca, ti diverta**   = you (fam., sing.) read, leave, understand, have fun

9. **noi leggiamo, partiamo, capiamo, ci divertiamo**   = we read, leave, understand, have fun

10. **loro leggano, partano, capiscano, si divertano**   = they read, leave, understand, have fun

11. **voi leggiate, partiate, capiate, vi divertiate**   = you (pl.) read, leave, understand, have fun

12. **Lei legga, parta, capisca, si diverta**   = you (pol., sing.) read, leave, understand, have fun

B.

1. **(Lui) pensa che loro arrivino stasera.**
2. **(Io) immagino che lei capisca tutto.**
3. **(Loro) dubitano che tu finisca in tempo.**
4. **(Tu) sei la persona meno elegante che io conosca.**
5. **Che nevichi!**
6. **(Lei) vuole che io la chiami stasera.**
7. **Sembra che anche tu conosca Maria.**
8. **Spero che Alessandro scriva quell'e-mail.**
9. **Anche tu credi che io parli italiano bene?**
10. **(Noi) desideriamo che loro giochino meglio a calcio.**
11. **Bisogna che/È necessario che lui studi di più.**
12. **È possibile che loro parlino italiano.**
13. **È probabile che noi compriamo quella macchina/automobile.**
14. **Benché/sebbene piova fuori, esco lo stesso.**
15. **A meno che lei non telefoni, non andremo al cinema.**
16. **Affinché/Perché tu mangi la pasta, la cucinerò io stesso/a.**
17. **Chiunque desideri farlo, io sono d'accordo.**
18. **Dovunque lei abiti, io andrò.**
19. **Nel caso che lui legga quell'e-mail, tu dovresti essere pronto/a a chiamarlo.**
20. **Nonostante il fatto che tu non telefoni mai, mi piaci lo stesso.**
21. **Prima che voi partiate per l'Italia, dovreste assicurarvi che avete abbastanza soldi.**
22. **Lo farò, purché tu mi telefoni prima.**
23. **Qualunque lingua loro parlino, so che lui li capirà.**

Exercise Set 17-2

1. **Secondo la madre, è importante che Giorgio studi molto.**
2. **Secondo Giorgio, è necessario che lui studi molto affinché impari a parlare bene la lingua italiana.**
3. **Se impara a parlare l'italiano bene, Giorgio potrà andare in Italia a conoscere i nonni.**
4. **Quando ha finito di studiare, bisogna che Giorgio pulisca la sua camera/Giorgio deve pulire la sua camera.**
5. **Sì, lo farà.**

Exercise Set 17-3

1. **È probabile che loro vadano in Italia quest'anno.**
2. **Penso che tu abbia trentatré anni.**
3. **Sembra che loro bevano il cappuccino.**
4. **Bisogna che lui dia la penna a Maria.**
5. **Speriamo che voi diciate la verità.**
6. **Sembra che loro devano/debbano studiare di più.**
7. **Immagino che ci sia anche Alessandro.**
8. **Bisogna che faccia bel tempo.**

9. Speriamo che nasca domani forse il bambino.

10. Credo che non gli piacciano le caramelle.

11. Sembra che Marco possa venire alla festa.

12. Penso che loro rimangano a casa domani.

13. Dubito che la sua amica sappia parlare l'italiano molto bene.

14. Sembra che lui scelga sempre lo stesso programma.

15. Penso che Alessandro stia molto bene.

16. Credo che loro escano insieme.

17. Dubito che quel film valga la pena di vedere.

18. Speriamo che loro vengano alla festa.

19. Penso che lui voglia andare in Italia.

Exercise Set 17-4

1. Penso che Giorgio stia mangiando.

2. Maria crede che voi stiate guardando un programma alla televisione.

3. Sembra che Marco stia dormendo.

4. Lui crede che io stia scrivendo.

5. Lei pensa che i miei amici stiano uscendo.

6. Loro credono che noi stiamo bevendo un caffè.

7. Dubito che voi stiate leggendo.

8. Sembra che lui stia suonando il violoncello.

9. Sembra che lei stia cantando.

Exercise Set 17-5

1. Che venga anche lui alla festa?

2. Che dica/stia dicendo la verità?

3. Preferiamo che vengano anche loro al cinema.

4. Lei dubita che loro sappiano parlare l'italiano.

5. Speriamo che arrivi presto.

6. Penso che lui dica/stia dicendo la verità.

7. È necessario/Bisogna che lo facciano anche loro.

8. Benché/Sebbene nevichi, vado a fare delle spese lo stesso.

9. Affinché/Perché tu possa parlare l'italiano bene, devi studiare di più.

10. Prima che partano per l'Italia, devono risparmiare soldi.

Crossword Puzzle 17

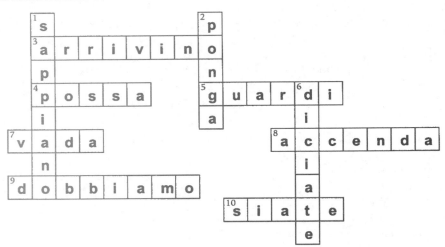

Chapter 18

Exercise Set 18-1

A.

1. Loro dubitano che io abbia cominciato a studiare l'italiano.
2. Lei crede che tu abbia letto quel romanzo già.
3. Immagino che mio fratello abbia pagato il conto.
4. Penso che abbia fatto bel tempo ieri.
5. Lui crede che noi abbiamo bevuto il caffè al bar ieri.
6. Immagino che voi abbiate già visto quel film.
7. Spero che loro li abbiano già comprati.
8. I miei amici pensano che io sia andata in Italia l'anno scorso.
9. Lui pensa che tu sia uscito poco tempo fa.
10. Penso che mia sorella sia arrivata qualche minuto fa.
11. Lui crede noi siamo venuti alla festa.
12. Mia madre crede che voi siate tornati in Italia l'anno scorso.
13. Lei pensa che loro si siano alzati tardi ieri.
14. Sembra che tu ti sia sposata l'anno scorso.
15. Sembra che lui si sia divertito in Italia.

B.

1. a   2. b   3. a   4. b   5. a   6. b   7. a   8. b

Exercise Set 18-2

1. Luigi chiede a Bruno chi ha vinto la partita ieri.
2. Bruno pensa che abbia vinto la Juventus, uno a zero.
3. No, Bruno non sa chi l'abbia segnato/abbia segnato il gol.
4. Luigi pensa che il calcio sia sempre stato uno sport fantastico.
5. Sì, Bruno è d'accordo.

Exercise Set 18-3

1. Benché/Sebbene abbia nevicato ieri, ho deciso di fare delle spese lo stesso.
2. È possibile che loro siano già andati al bar.
3. Lui non sa chi abbia segnato il gol ieri.
4. Lui è la persona più felice che io abbia mai conosciuto.
5. Sembra che loro abbiano già visto/veduto quel film.
6. (Io) penso che mia sorella abbia già fatto quello.
7. Tutti pensano che io sia andata in Italia l'anno scorso.
8. (Tu) pensi veramente che lui abbia capito?
9. Non è vero che io abbia mangiato tutti gli spaghetti.

Crossword Puzzle 18

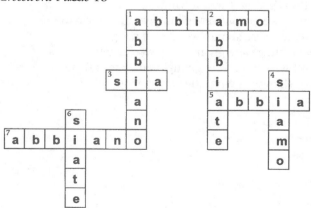

Chapter 19

Exercise Set 19-1

A.

1. io arrivassi, baciassi, spiegassi	=	I was arriving, kissing, explaining
2. tu arrivassi, baciassi, spiegassi	=	you (fam.) were arriving, kissing, explaining
3. noi arrivassimo, baciassimo, spiegassimo	=	we were arriving, kissing, explaining
4. loro arrivassero, baciassero, spiegassero	=	they were arriving, kissing, explaining
5. voi arrivaste, baciaste, spiegaste	=	you (pl.) were arriving, kissing, explaining
6. lei arrivasse, baciasse, spiegasse	=	she was arriving, kissing, explaining
7. io potessi, capissi, mi mettessi	=	I could, understood, was putting on
8. tu potessi, capissi, ti mettessi	=	you (fam.) could, understood, were putting on
9. noi potessimo, capissimo, ci mettessimo	=	we could, understood, were putting on
10. loro potessero, capissero, si mettessero	=	they could, understood, were putting on
11. voi poteste, capiste, vi metteste	=	you (pl.) could, understood, were putting on
12. lui potesse, capisse, si mettesse	=	he could, understood, was putting on

B.

1. Loro dubitavano che io cominciassi a studiare l'italiano.
2. Lei credeva che tu leggessi quel romanzo.
3. Io pensavo che mio fratello studiasse a quest'ora.
4. Pensavo che lei uscisse con Marco.
5. Lui credeva che noi guardassimo la televisione ogni sera da giovani.
6. Sembra che piovesse ieri.
7. Credo che loro sperassero di andare in Italia.
8. I miei amici pensano che io andassi in Italia ogni estate da bambino.
9. Lui pensava che tu volessi uscire.

C.

1. a   2. b   3. a   4. b   5. a   6. a   7. a   8. b

Exercise Set 19-2

1. Claudia aveva chiamato Tina ieri perché pensava che Tina volesse uscire.
2. Ha lasciato un messaggio sulla segreteria telefonica di Tina.
3. Tina non stava molto bene ieri.
4. Tina pensava che Claudia avesse molto da fare.
5. Claudia voleva che Tina venisse al cinema con lei.
6. Claudia chiamerà Tina verso le sei.

Exercise Set 19-3

A.

1. io fossi, dessi, stessi	=	I was, I was giving, I was staying
2. tu fossi, dessi, stessi	=	you (fam.) were, you were giving, you were staying
3. noi fossimo, dessimo, stessimo	=	we were, we were giving, we were staying
4. loro fossero, dessero, stessero	=	they were, they were giving, they were staying
5. voi foste, deste, steste	=	you (pl.) were, you were giving, you were staying
6. lei fosse, desse, stesse	=	she was, she was giving, she was staying

B.

1. Loro dubitavano che io bevessi il latte regolarmente.
2. Lei credeva che tu dicessi sempre la verità.
3. Io pensavo che mio fratello non facesse niente.
4. Penso che lei ponesse molte domande in classe.
5. Lui crede che noi attraessimo molta attenzione da giovani.
6. Loro pensano che traducessi le poesie italiane da giovane.
7. Credevo che tu dessi del tu al professore.

Exercise Set 19-4

1. **Non sapevo che Giorgio stesse mangiando.**
2. **Maria credeva che voi steste guardando un programma alla televisione.**
3. **Sembra che Marco stesse dormendo.**
4. **Lui credeva che io stessi scrivendo.**
5. **Lei pensa che i miei amici stessero uscendo.**
6. **Loro credevano che noi stessimo bevendo un caffè.**
7. **Dubito che voi steste leggendo quel romanzo.**
8. **Sembra che lui stesse suonando il pianoforte.**
9. **È probabile che lei stesse cantando.**

Exercise Set 19-5

1. **Penso che quello che lui dice/sta dicendo sia vero.**
2. **Pensavo che quello che ha fatto fosse la cosa giusta da fare.**
3. **È importante che lui studi di più.**
4. **Sarebbe importante che lui studiasse di più.**
5. **Se voi andaste in italia, vi divertireste davvero.**
6. **Se potessimo, andremmo al cinema.**
7. **Magari lei facesse quello/Magari lei lo facesse!**
8. **Magari non facesse così tanto freddo!**
9. **Se (quello) fosse vero, allora io non sarei qui.**

Crossword Puzzle 19

Chapter 20

Exercise Set 20-1

1. **Loro dubitavano che io avessi appena cominciato a studiare l'italiano.**
2. **Lei pensava che tu avessi già letto quel romanzo.**
3. **Non era possibile mio che fratello avesse pagato il conto.**
4. **Pensavano che avesse fatto bel tempo l'estate scorsa, ma invece no.**
5. **Lui credeva che noi avessimo già bevuto il caffè.**
6. **Immaginavo che voi aveste già visto quel film.**
7. **Speravo che loro li avessero già comprati.**
8. **I miei amici credevano che io fossi andata in Italia l'anno scorso.**
9. **Lui aveva pensato che tu fossi già uscito.**
10. **Avrei pensato che mia sorella fosse arrivata già.**
11. **Lui credeva che noi fossimo venuti alla festa.**
12. **Mia madre credeva che voi foste tornati già in Italia l'anno scorso.**
13. **Lei pensava che loro si fossero alzati tardi ieri.**

14. **Tutti credevano che tu ti fossi sposata l'anno scorso.**
15. **Mi è sembrato che lui si fosse divertito in Italia.**

Exercise Set 20-2

1. **Maria pensava che Marco fosse già andato via.**
2. **Marco è ancora al lavoro perché c'è molto da fare.**
3. **Marco non sarebbe dovuto rimanere più a lungo se avesse lavorato ieri.**
4. **Oggi ci sarebbe molto meno da fare se Maria avesse aiutato Marco la settimana scorsa.**
5. **Maria chiede a Marco di venire a prendere un caffè con lei quando ha finito di lavorare.**

Exercise Set 20-3

1. **Pensavo che avesse detto la verità.**
2. **Pensavo che lui l'avesse già fatto.**
3. **Era importante che lui avesse chiamato.**
4. **Sarebbe stato bene che fosse venuto anche lui.**
5. **Se voi foste andati in Italia, vi sareste divertiti davvero.**
6. **Se avessimo potuto, saremmo andati al cinema.**
7. **Era meglio che l'avesse fatto lei!**
8. **Magari non avesse fatto così tanto caldo!**
9. **Se (quello) fosse stato vero, allora io non (ci) sarei andato/a.**

Crossword Puzzle 20

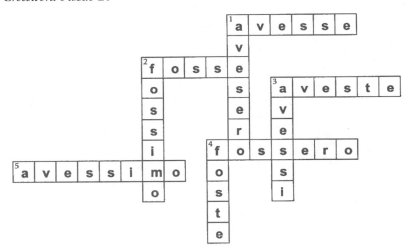

Chapter 21

Exercise Set 21-1

A.

1. (tu) guarda, bacia, parcheggia, spiega	=	*watch, kiss, park, explain*
2. (noi) guardiamo, baciamo, parcheggia, spieghiamo	=	*let's watch, kiss, park, explain*
3. (Loro) guardino, bacino, parcheggino, spieghino	=	*watch, kiss, park, explain*
4. (voi) guardate, baciate, parcheggiate, spiegate	=	*watch, kiss, park, explain*
5. (Lei) guardi, baci, parcheggi, spieghi	=	*watch, kiss, park, explain*
6. (tu) leggi, apri, pulisci, indica	=	*read, open, clean, indicate*
7. (noi) leggiamo, apriamo, puliamo, indichiamo	=	*let's read, open, clean, indicate*
8. (Loro) leggano, aprano, puliscano, indichino	=	*read, open, clean, indicate*
9. (voi) leggete, aprite, pulite, indicate	=	*read, open, clean, indicate*
10. (Lei) legga, apra, pulisca, indichi	=	*read, open, clean, indicate*

B.

Maria…

1. **parla italiano, per favore!**
2. **mangia la torta!**
3. **chiudi la (tua) bocca!**
4. **finisci gli spinaci!**
5. **assaggia la minestra!**
6. **paga il conto!**
7. **dormi di più!**

Signor Smith…

8. **parli italiano, per favore!**
9. **mangi la torta!**
10. **chiuda la (sua) bocca!**
11. **finisca gli spinaci!**
12. **assaggi la minestra!**
13. **paghi il conto!**
14. **dorma di più!**

Maria e Marco…

15. **parlate italiano, per favore!**
16. **mangiate la torta!**
17. **chiudete la (vostra) bocca!**
18. **finite gli spinaci!**
19. **assaggiate la minestra!**
20. **pagate il conto!**
21. **dormite di più!**

Signore e signora Smith…

22. **parlino italiano, per favore!**
23. **mangino la torta!**
24. **chiudano la (loro) bocca!**
25. **finiscano gli spinaci!**
26. **assaggino la minestra!**
27. **paghino il conto!**
28. **dormano di più!**

Exercise Set 21-2

1. **Il signor Marchi non sta bene.**
2. **Lui ha mal di gola e di testa e ha un po' di febbre.**
3. **La dottoress Giusti gli dice di aprire la bocca e di mettere un termometro in bocca.**
4. **Il signor Marchi ha un forte raffreddore.**
5. **Secondo la dottoressa Giusti, il signor Marchi dovrebbe prendere le pasticche che gli darà, bere tanta acqua e riposarsi per qualche giorno.**

Exercise Set 21-3

Claudia…

1. **va' (vai) a casa!**
2. **abbi pazienza!**
3. **bevi il latte!**
4. **da' (dai) a Marco la tua penna!**
5. **di' la verità!**
6. **sii brava!**
7. **fa' (fai) gli spaghetti!**
8. **poni quella domanda al nostro/alla nostra insegnante!**

9. rimani a casa!
10. scegli questo!
11. sta' (stai) a casa!
12. esci con Marco!
13. vieni qui!
14. traduci quel libro!

Signor Giusti …
15. vada a casa!
16. abbia pazienza!
17. beva il latte!
18. dia alla Signora Marchi la sua penna!
19. dica la verità!
20. sia bravo!
21. faccia gli spaghetti!
22. ponga quella domanda al nostro/alla nostra insegnante!
23. rimanga a casa!
24. scelga questo!
25. stia a casa!
26. esca con la Signora Marchi!
27. venga qui!
28. traduca quel libro!

Claudia e Giorgio…
29. andate a casa!
30. abbiate pazienza!
31. bevete il latte!
32. date a Marco la vostra penna!
33. dite la verità!
34. siate bravi!
35. fate gli spaghetti!
36. ponete quella domanda al nostro/alla nostra insegnante!
37. rimanete a casa!
38. scegliete questo!
39. state a casa!
40. uscite con Marco!
41. venite qui!
42. traducete quel libro!

Exercise Set 21-4

Maria…
1. non mangiare la torta!
2. non pagare il conto!
3. non andare a casa!
4. non bere il latte!
5. non dare a Marco la tua penna!
6. non rimanere a casa!
7. non scegliere questo!
8. non stare a casa tutto il giorno!
9. non uscire con Marco!

Signora Marchi…
1. non mangi la torta!
2. non paghi il conto!
3. non vada a casa!

4. non beva il latte!
5. non dia la sua penna al professore!
6. non rimanga a casa!
7. non scelga questo!
8. non stia a casa tutto il giorno!
9. non esca con il signor Giusti!

Exercise Set 21-5

1. Addormentati!
2. Annoiati, se vuoi!
3. Non arrabbiarti! / Non ti arrabbiare!
4. Non dimenticarti / non ti dimenticare di scrivere alla (tua) zia!
5. Divertiti in Italia!
6. Si faccia la doccia!
7. Non si incontri con l'insegnante!
8. Non si lamenti!
9. Si metta il nuovo vestito!
10. Non vi preoccupate!
11. Preparatevi!
12. Provatevi le nuove giacche!
13. Si ricordino di venire alla festa!
14. Si scusino!
15. Non si sveglino tardi domani!

Exercise Set 21-6

1. Giovanni, mangia la torta! Mangiala!
2. Maria, non bere il caffè! Non berlo! / Non lo bere!
3. Signora Smith, paghi il conto! Lo paghi, per favore!
4. Giorgio, telefonale!
5. Claudia, dammi gli spaghetti!
6. Bruno, dacci il tuo indirizzo!
7. Pasquale, di' la verità! Dilla!
8. Maria, va' via!
9. Fallo, Maria!
10. Lo faccia, Signora Smith!

Crossword Puzzle 21

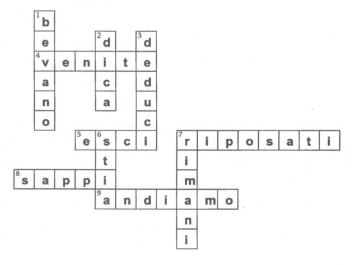

Chapter 22

Exercise Set 22-1

1. La torta è mangiata da Marco.
2. Il cappuccino è stato bevuto da quell'uomo.
3. Da bambina, i cartoni animati erano guardati regolarmente da mia sorella.
4. Quando siamo arrivati, la spesa era già stata fatta dalle tue amiche.
5. *Il Decamerone* fu scritto da Boccaccio.
6. Quel computer portatile sarà comprato dalla mia amica.
7. Gli spaghetti saranno già stati fatti da Giovanni.
8. Se potesse, quella Ferrari sarebbe comprata da lui.
9. Se avesse potuto, quella Ferrari sarebbe stata comprata da lui.
10. Penso che quel portatile sia desiderato da Marco.
11. Penso che quella casa sia stata già comprata da loro.
12. Credevo che i suoi spaghetti fossero stati già assaggiati da voi.

Exercise Set 22-2

1. Il portatile è stato comprato da sua sorella.
2. Il lavoro di Marco sarà finito tra poco.
3. Claudia chiede a Marco di uscire con lei quando il suo lavoro sarà veramente finito.
4. Claudia vuole andare a vedere il nuovo film di un famoso regista.
5. Il film è stato visto da tanta gente.
6. Sì, il film è piaciuto molto.

Exercise Set 22-3

1. Maria ha fatto già lavare i piatti a suo fratello.
2. (Io) la farò studiare di più.
3. (Loro) mi hanno fatto andare al bar ieri.
4. (Loro) mi hanno anche fatto bere un cappuccino.
5. Mentre camminava/Camminando ieri, mi ha incontrato.
6. Vedendomi, mi ha fatto andare con lei.
7. Avendo fatto tutto, sono usciti.
8. Essendo andati/e in Italia, hanno potuti viaggiare in giro assai.
9. Il bere è necessario per sopravvivere.
10. Lui pensa di sapere tutto.
11. Dopo essere usciti/e, hanno deciso di tornare a casa.
12. Gli è stato dato un pezzo di torta. Ma invece di mangiarlo, lo ha messo giù.

Crossword Puzzle 22

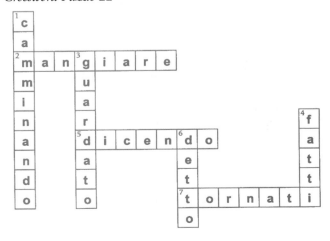

Italian-English Glossary

A

a	at
a che ora	at what time
a meno che	unless
a otto	a week from
a più tardi	later
a presto	see you soon
abbastanza	enough
abbracciare	to hug
abitare	to live
accendere	to turn on
l'acqua	water
addormentarsi	to fall asleep
adesso	now
affascinare	to fascinate, to be fascinating to
affinché	so that
affittare	to rent (a place)
africano	African
agosto	August
aiutare	to help
alcuni (-e)	some
gli alimentari	food (store)
allacciare	to fasten
allora	then, therefore, thus, so
alto	tall
altrimenti	otherwise
altro	other
alzarsi	to get up, to stand up
amare	to love
ambizioso	ambitious
americano	American
l'amica (l'amico)	friend
ammalarsi	to get sick
anche	also, too
ancora	yet, still
andare	to go
andarsene	to go away
l'anno	year
annoiarsi	to become bored
annunciare	to announce
l'annunciatore (m.), l'annunciatrice (f.)	TV announcer, host
ansioso	anxious
apparire	to appear
l'appartamento	apartment
appena	just (barely), as soon as
l'appetito	appetite

l'appuntamento	appointment, date
l'appunto	note
aprile	April
aprire	to open
arrabbiarsi	to become angry
arrivare	to arrive
arrivederci	good-bye (fam.)
arrivederLa	good-bye (pol.)
ascoltare	to listen to
aspettare	to wait for
assaggiare	to taste
assai	quite, rather
assicurare	to ensure
attento	careful
l'attenzione (f.)	attention
attrarre	to attract
attraversare	to cross
attuale	current
australiano	Australian
l'autobus (m.)	bus
l'automobile (f.)	automobile
l'autunno	autumn, fall
avere	to have
avere bisogno (di)	to need
avere caldo	to be hot
avere fame	to be hungry
avere freddo	to be cold
avere fretta	to be in a hurry
avere mal (di)	to have a sore…
avere paura	to be afraid
avere ragione	to be right
avere sete	to be thirsty
avere sonno	to be sleepy
avere torto	to be wrong
avere vergogna	to be ashamed
avere voglia (di)	to feel like
avere…anni	to be…years old
l'avvocato	lawyer

B

baciare	to kiss
ballare	to dance
il bambino (la bambina)	child
la banca	bank
il bar	espresso bar
la barzelletta	joke
basso	short
bastare	to be sufficient, to suffice, to be enough
il bel tempo	beautiful/nice weather
bello	beautiful, handsome
benché	although
bene	well, good

bere	to drink
bere alla salute	to drink to health
bere forte	to drink heavily
biondo	blond
bisogna che	it is necessary that
la bocca	mouth
bravo	good
il brutto tempo	bad weather
la bugia	lie
buon divertimento	have fun
buongiorno	good day, good morning
buono	good

C

cadere	to fall
il caffè	coffee
il calcio	soccer
caldo	hot, warm
calmo	calm
cambiare	to change
cambiare idea	to change one's mind
la camera	bedroom
la camicetta	blouse
la camicia	shirt
camminare	to walk
il campionato	championship
canadese	Canadian
cantare	to sing
i capelli	hair (head)
capire	to understand
il capolavoro	masterwork
il cappuccino	cappuccino coffee
la caramella	candy
la carne	meat
caro	dear
la carta	card
il cartone animato	cartoon
la casa	house
cattivo	bad
il cattivo tempo	bad weather
il cellulare	cell phone
la cena	dinner
cercare	to look for, to search for
certo	certainly, of course
che	that, which, who
che, cosa, che cosa	what
chi	who
chiacchierare	to chat
chiamare	to call
chiamarsi	to call oneself, to be named
la chiamata	call
chiedere	to ask

la chiromante	fortune-teller
chissà	who knows, I wonder
la chitarra	guitar
chiudere	to close
chiunque	whoever
ci vediamo	see you later
ciao	bye, hi (fam.)
ciascuno	each one
il cibo	food
il cinema	cinema, movies
cinese	Chinese
la cintura di sicurezza	seat belt
la città	city
il cittadino (la cittadina)	citizen
la classe	class
il/la cliente (m./f.)	customer
la cognata	sister-in-law
il cognato	brother-in-law
la colazione	breakfast
come	how, like, as
come va?	how's it going?
cominciare	to begin
la commessa, il commesso	store clerk
comporre	to compose
comprare	to buy
comprendere	to comprehend
il computer	computer
comunicare	to communicate
comunque	however
con	with
conoscere	to know someone, to be familiar with
contento	happy
il conto	bill
controllare	to control
copiare	to copy
coprire	to cover
correre	to run
cortese	courteous
cosa	thing
così, così	so, so
costare	to cost
costruire	to build, to make
credere	to believe
criticare	to criticize
cucinare	to cook
il cugino (la cugina)	cousin

D

d'ora in poi	from now on
da	from
dappertutto	everywhere
dare	to give

dare del Lei	to be on polite terms
dare del tu	to be on familiar terms
dare la mano	to shake hands
dare un film	to show a movie
dare via	to give away
davvero	really, truly
decidere	to decide
decisione	decision
dedurre	to deduce
il/la dentista (m./f.)	dentist
desiderare	to want, to help out, to desire
deviare	to deviate
di	of
di me	than I/me
di nuovo	again
di più	more, most
di solito	usually
dicembre	December
digitale	digital
dimenticarsi	to forget
dipingere	to paint
dire	to say, to tell, to speak
dire di no	to say no
dire di sì	to say yes
dire la verità	to tell the truth
dire una bugia/la bugia	to tell a lie, to lie
dispiacere	to feel sorry
la ditta	company, firm
diventare	to become
divertimento	enjoyment, fun
divertirsi	to enjoy oneself, to have fun
dolce	sweet
dolere	to be painful, to ache
la domanda	question
domani	tomorrow
domenica	Sunday
la donna	woman
dopo	after
dopo che	after (conjunction)
dormire	to sleep
dove	where
dovere	to have to
dovunque	wherever
dubitare	to doubt
dunque	thus, therefore
durante	during
durare	to last

E

e	and
ecco	here is, here are

elegante	elegant
entrare	to enter
l'espresso	espresso coffee
esserci	to be there
essere	to be
essere d'accordo	to agree
l'estate (f.)	summer

F

fa	ago
la faccenda	house chore
facile	easy
il fagiolo	bean
la famiglia	family
famoso	famous
la fantascienza	science fiction
fantastico	fantastic
fare	to do, to make
fare del bene	to do good (things)
fare del male	to do bad (things)
fare delle spese	to shop (in general)
fare il medico/l'avvocato/...	to be a doctor/a lawyer/...
farsi il bagno	to take a bath
farsi la barba	to shave
farsi la doccia	to take a shower
il fatto	fact
febbraio	February
la febbre	fever, temperature
felice	happy
fermo	still, motionless
la festa	holiday, feast, party
la fidanzata, il fidanzato	fiancée, fiancé
la figlia, il figlio	daughter, son
il film	film, movie
finalmente	finally
la fine	end
finire	to finish
fino a	until
il formaggio	cheese
forse	maybe
forte	strong, heavily
fortunato	fortunate, lucky
fra	within (equivalent to **tra**)
francese	French
il fratello	brother
frattempo	meanwhile
il freddo	cold
fresco	cool
la frutta	fruit
i fumetti	comic books
fuori	outside
il futuro	future

G

garantire	to guarantee
il generale	general
il genitore	parent
gennaio	January
la gente	people
gentile	kind
già	already
la giacca	jacket
giapponese	Japanese
giocare	to play
il giocattolo	toy
il giornale	newspaper
la giornata	day (all day)
il giorno	day
giovane	young
giovedì	Thursday
giù	down
giugno	June
giusto	right, correct
lo gnocco	dumpling
godere	to enjoy
il gol	goal
la gola	throat
la grammatica	grammar
grande	great, big
grasso	fat
grazie	thank you
il guanto	glove
guardare	to look at, to watch
la guerra	war

I

l'idea	idea
ieri	yesterday
ieri sera	last night
immaginare	to imagine
imparare	to learn
importante	important
importare	to be important, to matter
in	in
in giro	around
in orario	on time
in punto	on the dot
in ritardo	late
incontrarsi	to encounter
indicare	to indicate
indipendente	independent
indirizzo	address
indovinare	to guess
indurre	to induce

infatti	in fact
l'informatica	computer science
l'ingegnere (m./f.)	engineer
ingenuo	naïve, ingenuous
inglese (m.)	English
l'insegnante (m./f.)	teacher
insieme	together
intelligente	intelligent
interessante	interesting
interessare	to interest, to be interested by
introdurre	to introduce
invece	instead
inventare	to invent
l'inverno	winter
inviare	to send
invitare	to invite
l'invitato	guest
l'Italia	Italy
italiano	Italian

L

lamentarsi	to complain
la lampadina	lightbulb
lanciare	to throw
lasciare	to let, to leave (behind)
il latte	milk
lavare	to wash
lavarsi	to wash oneself
lavorare	to work
il lavoro	work, job
legare	to tie
leggere	to read
la lezione	class, lesson
lì	there
libero	free
il libro	book
la lingua	language
lo stesso	the same
luglio	July
la luna	moon
lunedì	Monday

M

ma	but
la macchina	car
la madre	mother
magari	perhaps
maggio	May
magro	skinny
male	bad, evil

Mamma mia!	Egad! (lit.: My mother!)
mancare	to lack, to miss
mangiare	to eat
la mano (le mani)	hand (hands)
il mare	sea, ocean
il marito	husband
martedì	Tuesday
marzo	March
la matita	pencil, crayon
il matrimonio	matrimony, wedding
la mattina	morning
il meccanico (la meccanica)	mechanic
il medico	doctor
il medioevo	medieval period
meglio	better
la mela	apple
il membro	member
meno	less, minus
mentre	while
mercoledì	Wednesday
il mese	month
il messaggio	message
messicano	Mexican
mettere	to put
mettersi	to put on, to wear
la mezzanotte	midnight
mezzo	half
il mezzogiorno	noon
migliore	better, best
la minestra	soup
il minuto	minute
mio	my
la moda	fashion
il modo	manner, way
la moglie	wife
molto	very, much, a lot
il mondo	world
morire	to die
la musica	music

N

nascere	to be born
la nazione	nation
necessario	necessary
negare	to deny
il negozio	store
nel caso che	in the event that
nessuno	no one, nobody
la neve	snow
nevicare	to snow
niente	nothing
il/la nipote (m./f.)	nephew, grandchild

noleggiare	to rent (car, movie, etc.)
il nome	name
non c'è di che	don't mention it
non c'è male	not bad
la nonna	grandmother
il nonno	grandfather
nonostante	despite
normale	normal
novembre	November
il numero	number
nuovo	new

O

o	or
occupato	busy
oggi	today
oggi come oggi	nowadays, these days
ogni	every
olandese	Dutch
l'opera	opera
opinione (f.)	opinion
l'ora	hour, time
ora	now
l'orologio	watch
l'osso (le ossa)	bone (bones)
ottobre	October
ovvio	obvious

P

il padre	father
il paese	country
pagare	to pay (for)
la palla	ball
il panino	bun sandwich
i pantaloni	pants
parcheggiare	to park
il/la parente	relative
parlare	to speak
la parola	word
partire	to leave, to depart
la partita	game, match
passare	to pass, to go by
il passato	past
la passeggiata	stroll, walk
la pasta	pasta, pastry
la pasticca	lozenge
la pazienza	patience
il peccato	sin, too bad, a pity
la penna	pen
pensare	to think

per	for
per favore	please
perché	why, because, so that
il pericolo	danger
però	unfortunately
la persona	person
il pesce	fish
il pezzo	piece
piacere	to be pleasing to, to like
il pianoforte	piano
il piatto	plate, dish
piccolo	small
la pioggia	rain
piovere	to rain
il pisello	pea
più	more, plus
la poesia	poem
poi	then
poiché	since
il Polo Nord	North Pole
il Polo Sud	South Pole
il pomeriggio	afternoon
porre	to pose, to put
il portafoglio	wallet
portare	to wear, to carry
portatile	portable (laptop)
possibile	possible
il posto	place
potere	to be able to
povero	poor
il pranzo	lunch
preciso	exactly, precisely
preferire	to prefer
preferito	favorite
pregare	to pray
prego	you're welcome
il premio	prize
prendere	to take
preoccuparsi	to worry
preparare	to prepare
prepararsi	to prepare oneself
presto	early
prima	before
la primavera	spring
probabile	probable
produrre	to produce
il professore (la professoressa)	professor
il programma	program
programmare	to plan
promettere	to promise
pronto	hello (answering the phone), ready
pronunciare	to pronounce
proprio	really
prossimo	next (week, year, etc.)

provarsi	to try on
lo psicologo	psychologist
pulire	to clean
punire	to punish
purché	provided that
purtroppo	unfortunately

Q

qualche	a few, some
qualcosa	something
qualcuno	someone
quale	which
qualunque	whatever, whichever
quando	when
quanto	how, how much
il quarto	quarter
quasi	almost
quello	that
questo	this
qui	here

R

la radio	radio
il raffreddore	cold (illness)
la ragazza	girl, young female
il ragazzo	boy, young male
rapido	rapid
il/la regista	director
regolare	regular
ricco	rich
ricordarsi	to remember
ridere	to laugh
ridurre	to reduce
rimanere	to be left over, to remain
rispondere	to answer
risposarsi	to relax
la risposta	answer
ristorante	restaurant
rivelare	to reveal
la rivista	magazine
il romanzo	novel
rompere	to break

S

sabato	Saturday
salire	to climb, to go up
salutarsi	to greet (one another)
la salute	health

sapere	to know something, how to do something
la scala, le scale	stair, staircase
la scarpa	shoe
scegliere	to choose
sciare	to ski
la sciarpa	scarf
scoprire	to discover
scorso	last (week, month, etc.)
scrivere	to write
lo scudetto	sports cup, prize
lo scuola	school
scusa, scusi	excuse me (fam.), excuse me (pol.)
scusarsi	to excuse oneself
se	if
sebbene	although
il secondo	second
secondo	according to
sedurre	to seduce
segnare	to score
la segreteria telefonica	answering machine
sembrare	to seem
semplice	simple
sempre	always
sentire	to feel, to hear
sentirsi	to feel
senza	without
la sera	evening
sette	seven
settembre	September
la settimana	week
sicuro	sure
la signora	Mrs., Ms.
il signore	Mr., Sir
la signorina	Ms., Miss
simile	similar
simpatico	nice, pleasant
il sintomo	symptom
smettere	to stop, to quit
il soffitto	ceiling
soffrire	to suffer
il sogno	dream
i soldi	money
solo	only
sopravvivere	to survive
la sorella	sister
gli spaghetti	spaghetti
spagnolo	Spanish
specialmente	especially
spedire	to send, to mail
sperare	to hope
la spesa	food shopping
spesso	often
la spiaggia	beach
spiegare	to explain

gli spinaci	spinach
lo sport	sport
sposarsi	to marry, to get married
la squadra	team
squisito	delicious
stamani	this morning
la stampa	printing, printing press
stanco	tired
stare	to stay, to be
stare per	to be about to
stasera	tonight
gli Stati Uniti	United States
lo stile	style
lo stivale	boot
la storia	story
la strada	road
strano	strange
lo studente, la studentessa	student
studiare	to study
studioso	studious
su	on
subito	right away
succedere	to happen
suonare	to play an instrument
svedese	Swedish
svegliarsi	to wake up
svizzero	Swiss

T

tanto	much, a lot
la tappa	stage
tardi	late
tardo	late (adjective)
la tasca	pocket
tedesco	German
telefonare	to phone
telefonico	phone (adjectival)
il telefono	phone
il telequiz	TV quiz show
il telescopio	telescope
il telespettatore	TV viewer
la televisione	television
televisivo	(of) television
il televisore	television set
temere	to fear
il tempo	time, weather
tenere	to keep, to hold
il termometro	thermometer
la testa	head
il tipo	type
tirare vento	to be windy
tornare	to go back, to return

la torta	cake
tra	in, within
tra poco	in a little while
tra qualche minuto	in a few minutes
tradurre	to translate
trarre	to draw (pull)
traslocare	to move (house)
triste	sad
troppo	too much
trovare (trovarsi)	to find (to find oneself)
tuo	your (fam., sing.)
il/la turista (m./f.)	tourist
tutti (tutte)	everyone
tutto	everything, entire, whole

U

ultimo	last
un po'	a bit
unire	to unite
l'università (f.)	university
l'uomo (gli uomini)	man (men)
usare	to use
uscire	to go out

V

va bene	OK
la vacanza	vacation
valere	to be worth
valere la pena	to be worthwhile
vaso	vase
vecchio	old
vedere	to see
veloce	fast, quick
vendere	to sell
venerdì	Friday
venire	to come
venti	twenty
il vento	wind
veramente	truly
il verbo	verb
la verdura	vegetables, greens
vergognarsi	to be ashamed
la verità	truth
vero	true
verso	around, toward
vestirsi	to get dressed
il vestito	dress, suit
via	street
viaggiare	to travel
vicino a	near

vincere	to win
il vino	wine
il violino	violin
il violoncello	cello
la visita	visit
visitare	to visit
la vita	life
vivace	lively, active
vivere	to live
la voglia	desire, urge
volentieri	gladly
volere	to want to
la volta	time, occasion

Z

la zia	aunt
lo zio	uncle
zitto	quiet

English-Italian Glossary

A

a bit	un po'
a few	qualche
according to	secondo
ache	dolere
address	l'indirizzo
African	africano
after	dopo
after (conjunction)	dopo che
afternoon	il pomeriggio
again	di nuovo
ago	fa
agree	essere d'accordo
almost	quasi
already	già
also	anche
although	benché, sebbene
always	sempre
ambitious	ambizioso
American	americano
and	e
(to) announce	annunciare
(to) answer	rispondere
answer	la risposta
answering machine	la segreteria telefonica
anxious	ansioso
apartment	l'appartamento
appear	apparire
appetite	l'appetito
apple	la mela
appointment	l'appuntamento
April	aprile
around	verso, in giro
(to) arrive	arrivare
as soon as	appena
(to) ask	chiedere
at	a
at what time	a che ora
attention	l'attenzione (f.)
(to) attract	attrarre
August	agosto
aunt	la zia
Australian	australiano
automobile	l'automobile (f.)
autumn	l'autunno

B

bad	cattivo, male
bad weather	il brutto tempo, il cattivo tempo
ball	la palla
bank	la banca
(to) be	essere
(to) be a doctor/a lawyer/...	fare il medico/l'avvocato/...
(to) be able to	potere
(to) be about to	stare per
(to) be afraid	avere paura
be ashamed	avere vergogna
(to) be ashamed	vergognarsi
(to) be born	nascere
(to) be cold	avere freddo
(to) be enough	bastare
(to) be familiar with	conoscere
(to) be fascinated by	affascinare
(to) be hot	avere caldo
(to) be hungry	avere fame
(to) be important	importare
(to) be in a hurry	avere fretta
(to) be interested by	interessare
(to) be left over	rimanere
(to) be named	chiamarsi
(to) be on familiar terms	dare del tu
(to) be on polite terms	dare del Lei
(to) be painful	dolere
(to) be pleasing to	piacere
(to) be right	avere ragione
(to) be sleepy	avere sonno
(to) be sufficient	bastare
(to) be there	esserci
(to) be thirsty	avere sete
(to) be windy	tirare vento
(to) be worth	valere
(to) be worthwhile	valere la pena
(to) be wrong	avere torto
(to) be...years old	avere...anni
beach	la spiaggia
bean	il fagiolo
beautiful	bello
beautiful/nice weather	il bel tempo
because	perché
(to) become	diventare
(to) become angry	arrabbiarsi
(to) become bored	annoiarsi
bedroom	la camera
before	prima
(to) begin	cominciare
(to) believe	credere
better, best	migliore, meglio
big	grande
bill	il conto

blond	biondo
blouse	la camicetta
bone (bones)	l'osso (le ossa)
book	il libro
boot	lo stivale
boy	il ragazzo
(to) break	rompere
breakfast	la colazione
brother	il fratello
brother-in-law	il cognato
(to) build	costruire
bun sandwich	il panino
bus	l'autobus (m.)
busy	occupato
but	ma
(to) buy	comprare
bye	ciao

C

cake	la torta
(to) call	chiamare
call	la chiamata
(to) call oneself	chiamarsi
calm	calmo
Canadian	canadese
candy	la caramella
cappuccino coffee	il cappuccino
car	la macchina
card	la carta
careful	attento
(to) carry	portare
cartoon	il cartone animato
ceiling	il soffitto
cell phone	il cellulare
cello	il violoncello
certainly	certo, certamente
championship	il campionato
(to) change	cambiare
(to) change one's mind	cambiare idea
(to) chat	chiacchierare
cheese	il formaggio
child	il bambino (la bambina)
Chinese	cinese
(to) choose	scegliere
cinema	il cinema
citizen	il cittadino (la cittadina)
city	la città
class (at school)	la lezione
class	la classe
(to) clean	pulire
(to) climb	salire
(to) close	chiudere

coffee	il caffè
cold	il freddo
cold (illness)	il raffreddore
(to) come	venire
comic books	i fumetti
(to) communicate	comunicare
company	la ditta
(to) complain	lamentarsi
(to) compose	comporre
(to) comprehend	comprendere
computer	il computer
computer science	informatica
(to) control	controllare
(to) cook	cucinare
cool	fresco
(to) copy	copiare
(to) cost	costare
country	il paese
courteous	cortese
cousin	il cugino (la cugina)
(to) cover	coprire
crayon	la matita
(to) criticize	criticare
(to) cross	attraversare
current	attuale
customer	il/la cliente (m./f.)

D

(to) dance	ballare
danger	il pericolo
date	l'appuntamento
daughter	la figlia
day	il giorno
day (all day)	la giornata
dear	caro
December	dicembre
(to) decide	decidere
decision	la decisione
(to) deduce	dedurre
delicious	squisito
dentist	il/la dentista (m./f.)
(to) deny	negare
desire	la voglia
(to) desire	desiderare
despite	nonostante
(to) deviate	deviare
(to) die	morire
digital	digitale
dinner	la cena
director	il/la regista
(to) discover	scoprire
dish	il piatto

(to) do	fare
(to) do bad (things)	fare del male
(to) do good (things)	fare del bene
doctor	medico
don't mention it	non c'è di che
(to) doubt	dubitare
down	giù
(to) draw (pull)	trarre
dream	il sogno
dress	il vestito
(to) drink	bere
(to) drink heavily	bere forte
(to) drink to health	bere alla salute
dumpling	lo gnocco
during	durante
Dutch	olandese

E

each one	ciascuno
early	presto
easy	facile
(to) eat	mangiare
Egad!	Mamma mia! (lit.: My mother!)
elegant	elegante
(to) encounter	incontrarsi
end	la fine
engineer	l'ingegnere (m./f.)
English	inglese (m.)
(to) enjoy	godere
(to) enjoy oneself	divertirsi
enjoyment	il divertimento
enough	abbastanza
(to) ensure	assicurare
(to) enter	entrare
entire	tutto
especially	specialmente
espresso bar	il bar
espresso coffee	l'espresso
evening	la sera
every	ogni
everyone	tutti (tutte)
everything	tutto
everywhere	dappertutto
evil	il male
exactly	preciso
excuse me	scusa (fam.), scusi (pol.)
(to) excuse oneself	scusarsi
(to) explain	spiegare

F

fact	il fatto
(to) fall	cadere
(to) fall asleep	addormentarsi
family	la famiglia
famous	famoso
fantastic	fantastico
(to) fascinate	affascinare
fashion	la moda
fast, quick	veloce
(to) fasten	allacciare
fat	grasso
father	il padre
favorite	preferito
(to) fear	temere
feast	la festa
February	febbraio
(to) feel	sentire, sentirsi
(to) feel like	avere voglia (di)
(to) feel sorry	dispiacere
female friend	l'amica
fever (temperature)	la febbre
fiancé, fiancée	il fidanzato, la fidanzata
film	il film
finally	finalmente
(to) find (to find oneself)	trovare (trovarsi)
(to) finish	finire
firm	la ditta
first (firstly)	prima
fish	il pesce
food	il cibo
food shopping	la spesa
foods (foodstore)	gli alimentari
for	per
(to) forget	dimenticarsi
fortunate	fortunato
fortune-teller	la chiromante
free	libero
French	francese
Friday	venerdì
from	da
from now on	d'ora in poi
fruit	la frutta
fun	il divertimento
future	il futuro

G

game	la partita
general	generale
generally	generalmente
German	tedesco

(to) get dressed	vestirsi
(to) get married	sposarsi
(to) get sick	ammalarsi
(to) get up	alzarsi
girl, young female	la ragazza
(to) give	dare
(to) give away	dare via
gladly	volentieri
glove	il guanto
(to) go	andare
(to) go away	andarsene
(to) go back	tornare
(to) go by	passare
(to) go out	uscire
(to) go up	salire
goal (score)	il gol
good	buono, bravo, bene
good day, good morning	buongiorno
good-bye	arrivederci (fam.), arrivederLa (pol.)
grammar	la grammatica
grandchild	il/la nipote (m./f.)
grandfather	il nonno
grandmother	la nonna
great, big	grande
greens	la verdura
(to) greet (one another)	salutarsi
(to) guarantee	garantire
(to) guess	indovinare
guest	l'invitato
guitar	la chitarra

H

hair (head)	i capelli
half	mezzo
hand (hands)	la mano (le mani)
handsome	bello
(to) happen	succedere
happy	felice, contento
(to) have	avere
(to) have a sore...	avere mal di
(to) have fun	divertirsi
have fun	buon divertimento
(to) have to	dovere
head	la testa
health	la salute
(to) hear	sentire
hello (answering the phone)	pronto
(to) help	aiutare
here	qui
here is, here are	ecco
hi	ciao
(to) hold	tenere

holiday	la festa
(to) hope	sperare
hot	caldo
hour, time	l'ora
house	la casa
house chore	la faccenda
how	come, quanto
how much	quanto
how's it going?	come va?
however	comunque
(to) hug	abbracciare
husband	il marito

I

idea	l'idea
if	se
(to) imagine	immaginare
important	importante
in	in
in a few minutes	tra qualche minuto
in a little while	tra poco
in fact	infatti
in the event that	nel caso che
in (within)	tra
independent	indipendente
(to) indicate	indicare
(to) induce	indurre
ingenuous	ingenuo
instead	invece
intelligent	intelligente
(to) interest	interessare
interesting	interessante
(to) introduce	introdurre
(to) invent	inventare
(to) invite	invitare
it is necessary that	bisogna che
Italian	italiano
Italy	l'Italia

J

jacket	la giacca
January	gennaio
Japanese	giapponese
job	il lavoro
joke	la barzelletta
July	luglio
June	giugno
just (barely)	appena

K

(to) keep	tenere
kind	gentile
(to) kiss	baciare
(to) know someone	conoscere
(to) know something, how to do something	sapere

L

(to) lack	mancare
language	la lingua
last	ultimo
(to) last	durare
last (week, month, etc.)	scorso
last night	ieri sera
late	tardi, in ritardo
late (adjective)	tardo
later	a più tardi
(to) laugh	ridere
lawyer	l'avvocato
(to) learn	imparare
(to) leave (behind)	lasciare
(to) leave, depart	partire
less, minus	meno
lesson	la lezione
(to) let	lasciare
lie	bugia
(to) lie	dire la bugia/le bugie
life	la vita
lightbulb	la lampadina
(to) like	piacere
like, as	come
(to) listen to	ascoltare
(to) live	abitare, vivere
lively, active	vivace
(to) look at	guardare
(to) look for	cercare
(to) love	amare
lozenge	la pasticca
lucky	fortunato
lunch	il pranzo

M

magazine	la rivista
(to) mail	spedire
(to) make	fare
male friend	l'amico
man (men)	l'uomo (gli uomini)
manner	il modo
March	marzo

(to) marry	sposarsi
masterwork	il capolavoro
matrimony	il matrimonio
(to) matter	importare
May	maggio
maybe	forse
meanwhile	frattempo
meat	la carne
mechanic	il meccanico (la meccanica)
medieval period	il medioevo
member	il membro
message	il messaggio
Mexican	messicano
midnight	la mezzanotte
milk	il latte
minute	il minuto
(to) miss	mancare
Monday	lunedì
money	i soldi
month	il mese
moon	la luna
more	più
more, most	di più
morning	la mattina
mother	la madre
mouth	la bocca
(to) move (house)	traslocare
movie	il film
movies	il cinema
Mr., Sir	signore
Mrs., Ms.	signora
Ms., Miss	signorina
much, a lot	molto, tanto
music	la musica
my	mio

N

naïve	ingenuo
name	il nome
nation	la nazione
near	vicino a
necessary	necessario
(to) need	avere bisogno (di)
nephew	il/la nipote (m./f.)
new	nuovo
newspaper	il giornale
next (week, year, etc.)	prossimo
nice	simpatico
no one, nobody	nessuno
noon	il mezzogiorno
normal	normale
North Pole	il Polo Nord

not bad	non c'è male
note	l'appunto
nothing	niente
novel	il romanzo
November	novembre
now	adesso, ora
nowadays, these days	oggi come oggi
number	il numero

O

obvious	ovvio
ocean	il mare
October	ottobre
of	di
of course	certo, certamente
often	spesso
OK	va bene
old	vecchio
on	su
on the dot	in punto
on time	in orario
only	solo
(to) open	aprire
opera	l'opera
opinion	l'opinione (f.)
or	o
other	altro
otherwise	altrimenti
outside	fuori

P

(to) paint	dipingere
pants	i pantaloni
parent	il genitore (la genitrice)
(to) park	parcheggiare
party	la festa
(to) pass	passare
past	il passato
pasta	la pasta
pastry	la pasta
patience	la pazienza
(to) pay (for)	pagare
pea	il pisello
pen	la penna
pencil	la matita
people	la gente
perhaps	magari
person	la persona
(to) phone	telefonare
phone	telefono

phone (adjectival)	telefonico
piano	il piano(forte)
piece	il pezzo
place	il posto
(to) plan	programmare
plate	il piatto
(to) play	giocare
(to) play an instrument	suonare
pleasant	simpatico
please	per favore
pocket	la tasca
poem	la poesia
poor	povero
portable (laptop)	portatile
(to) pose	porre
possible	possibile
(to) pray	pregare
precisely	preciso
(to) prefer	preferire
(to) prepare	preparare
(to) prepare oneself	prepararsi
printing, printing press	la stampa
prize	il premio
probable	probabile
(to) produce	produrre
professor	il professore, la professoressa
program	il programma (m.)
(to) promise	promettere
(to) pronounce	pronunciare
provided that	purché
psychologist	lo psicologo
(to) punish	punire
(to) put	mettere
(to) put on	mettersi

Q

quarter	il quarto
question	la domanda
quiet	zitto
(to) quit	smettere
quite	assai

R

radio	la radio
rain	la pioggia
(to) rain	piovere
rapid	rapido
rather	assai
(to) read	leggere
ready	pronto

really	proprio
really (truly)	davvero
(to) reduce	ridurre
regular	regolare
relative	il/la parente
(to) relax	risposarsi
(to) remain	rimanere
(to) remember	ricordarsi
(to) rent (a car, a movie, etc.)	noleggiare
(to) rent (a place)	affittare
restaurant	il ristorante
(to) return	tornare
(to) reveal	rivelare
rich	ricco
right (correct)	giusto
right away	subito
road	la strada
(to) run	correre

S

sad	triste
same	lo stesso
Saturday	sabato
(to) say	dire
(to) say no	dire di no
(to) say yes	dire di sì
scarf	la sciarpa
school	la scuola
science fiction	la fantascienza
(to) score	segnare
sea	il mare
(to) search for	cercare
seat belt	la cintura di sicurezza
second	il secondo
(to) seduce	sedurre
(to) see	vedere
see you later	ci vediamo
see you soon	a presto
(to) seem	sembrare
(to) sell	vendere
(to) send	spedire, inviare
September	settembre
seven	sette
(to) shake hands	dare la mano
(to) shave	farsi la barba
shirt	la camicia
shoe	la scarpa
(to) shop (in general)	fare delle spese
short	basso
(to) show a movie	dare un film
similar	simile
simple	semplice

since	poiché
(to) sing	cantare
sister	la sorella
sister-in-law	la cognata
(to) ski	sciare
skinny	magro
(to) sleep	dormire
small	piccolo
snow	la neve
(to) snow	nevicare
so	allora
so that	affinché, perché
so, so	così, così
soccer	il calcio
some	qualche, alcuni (alcune)
someone	qualcuno
something	qualcosa
son	il figlio
soup	la minestra
South Pole	il Polo Sud
spaghetti	gli spaghetti
Spanish	spagnolo
(to) speak	parlare
spinach	gli spinaci
sport	lo sport
sports cup	lo scudetto
spring	la primavera
stage	la tappa
stair	la scala
staircase	le scale
(to) stand up	alzarsi
(to) stay	stare
still	ancora
still, motionless	fermo
(to) stop	smettere
store	il negozio
store clerk	il commesso, la commessa
story	la storia
strange	strano
street	la via
stroll, walk	la passeggiata
strong	forte
student	lo studente (m.), la studentessa (f.)
studious	studioso
(to) study	studiare
style	lo stile
(to) suffer	soffrire
(to) suffice	bastare
suit	il vestito
summer	l'estate (f.)
Sunday	domenica
sure	sicuro (-a)
(to) survive	sopravvivere
Swedish	svedese

sweet	dolce
Swiss	svizzero
symptom	il sintomo

T

(to) take	prendere
(to) take a bath	farsi il bagno
(to) take a shower	farsi la doccia
tall	alto
(to) taste	assaggiare
teacher	l'insegnante (m./f.)
team	la squadra
telescope	il telescopio
television	la televisione
television (of)	televisivo
television set	il televisore
(to) tell	dire
(to) tell a lie	dire una bugia
(to) tell the truth	dire la verità
thank you	grazie
that	quello
that (which)	che
then	allora, poi
there	lì
therefore	allora
thermometer	il termometro
thing	la cosa
(to) think	pensare
this	questo
this morning	stamani
throat	la gola
(to) throw	lanciare
Thursday	giovedì
thus, therefore	allora, dunque
(to) tie	legare
time	il tempo
time, occasion	la volta
tired	stanco
today	oggi
together	insieme
tomorrow	domani
tonight	stasera
too	anche
too bad, a pity	peccato
too much	troppo
tourist	il/la turista (m./f.)
toward	verso
toy	il giocattolo
(to) translate	tradurre
(to) travel	viaggiare
true	vero
truly	veramente

truth	la verità
(to) try on	provarsi
Tuesday	martedì
(to) turn on	accendere
TV announcer, host	l'annunciatore (m.), l'annunciatrice (f.)
TV quiz show	il telequiz
TV viewer	il telespettatore
type	il tipo

U

uncle	lo zio
(to) understand	capire
unfortunately	purtroppo
(to) unite	unire
United States	gli Stati Uniti
university	l'università (f.)
unless	a meno che
until	fino a
urge	la voglia
(to) use	usare
usually	di solito

V

vacation	la vacanza
vase	il vaso
vegetables	la verdura
verb	il verbo
very	molto
violin	il violino
visit	la visita
(to) visit	visitare

W

(to) wait for	aspettare
(to) wake up	svegliarsi
(to) walk	camminare
wallet	il portafoglio
(to) want to	volere, desiderare
war	la guerra
warm	caldo
(to) wash	lavare
(to) wash oneself	lavarsi
(to) watch	guardare
watch	l'orologio
water	l'acqua
way	il modo
(to) wear	portare
weather	il tempo

wedding	il matrimonio
Wednesday	mercoledì
week	la settimana
week from	a otto
well	bene
what	che, cosa, che cosa
whatever, whichever	qualunque
when	quando
where	dove
wherever	dovunque
which	che, quale
while	mentre
who	chi, che
who knows, I wonder	chissà
whoever	chiunque
whole	tutto
why	perché
wife	la moglie
(to) win	vincere
wind	il vento
wine	il vino
winter	l'inverno
with	con
within	tra, fra
without	senza
woman	la donna
word	la parola
(to) work	lavorare
work	il lavoro
world	il mondo
(to) worry	preoccuparsi
(to) write	scrivere

Y

year	l'anno
yesterday	ieri
yet	ancora
you're welcome	prego
young	giovane
your (fam., sing.)	tuo

Helpful Guides for Mastering a Foreign Language

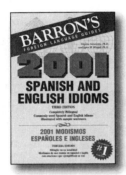

2001 Idiom Series

Indispensable resources, these completely bilingual dictionaries present the most frequently used idiomatic words and phrases to help students avoid stilted expression when writing in their newly acquired language. Each book includes illustrative sentences. Each feature is easy to locate and designed with clarity in mind.

2001 French and English Idioms, 3rd
978-0-7641-3750-1

2001 German and English Idioms, 2nd
978-0-7641-4224-6

2001 Italian and English Idioms, 2nd
978-0-8120-9030-7

2001 Russian and English Idioms
978-0-8120-9532-6

2001 Spanish and English Idioms, 3rd
978-0-7641-3744-0

Barron's Bilingual Dictionaries

These dictionaries each present 100,000 entries with translations into English and headwords in color for easy reference. Added features include full-color atlas-style maps, a concise grammar guide, verb conjugation lists, example phrases, pronunciation guides, and much more. Of special value to students and travelers, each book comes with an electronic bilingual dictionary that can be downloaded to all PCs and nearly all PDAs and smartphones!

Barron's French-English Dictionary
978-0-7641-3330-5

Barron's German-English Dictionary
978-0-7641-3763-1

Barron's Italian-English Dictionary
978-0-7641-3764-8

Barron's Spanish-English Dictionary
978-0-7641-3329-9

501 Verb Series

Here is a series to help the foreign language student successfully approach verbs and all their details. Complete conjugations of the verbs are arranged one verb to a page in alphabetical order. Verb forms are printed in boldface type in two columns, and common idioms using the applicable verbs are listed at the bottom of the page in each volume.

Some titles include a CD-ROM.

501 Arabic Verbs
978-0-7641-3622-1

501 English Verbs, 2nd, with CD-ROM
978-0-7641-7985-3

501 French Verbs, 6th, with CD-ROM
978-0-7641-7983-9

501 German Verbs, 4th, with CD-ROM
978-0-7641-9393-4

501 Hebrew Verbs, 2nd
978-0-7641-3748-8

501 Italian Verbs, 3rd, with CD-ROM
978-0-7641-7982-2

501 Japanese Verbs, 3rd
978-0-7641-3749-5

501 Latin Verbs, 2nd
978-0-7641-3742-6

501 Portuguese Verbs, 2nd
978-0-7641-2916-2

501 Russian Verbs, 3rd
978-0-7641-3743-3

501 Spanish Verbs, 6th, with CD-ROM
978-0-7641-7984-6

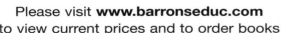

Barron's Educational Series, Inc.
250 Wireless Boulevard, Hauppauge, NY 11788
In Canada: Georgetown Book Warehouse
34 Armstrong Avenue, Georgetown, Ont. L7G 4R9

Please visit **www.barronseduc.com**
to view current prices and to order books

(#33) R1/10